ADVANCED INDUSTRIAL PSYCHOLOGY

VOLUME – II

RAM NATH SHARMA
S.S. CHANDRA

ATLANTIC
PUBLISHERS & DISTRIBUTORS

Published by
ATLANTIC PUBLISHERS AND DISTRIBUTORS
B-2, Vishal Enclave, Opp. Rajouri Garden, New Delhi-110027
Phones : 25413460, 25429987, 25466842

Sales Office
7/22, Ansari Road, Darya Ganj, New Delhi-110002
Phones : 23273880, 23275880, 23280451
Fax : 91-11-23285873
web : www.atlanticbooks.com
e-mail : info@atlanticbooks.com

Printed in India at
Nice Printing Press, Delhi

Preface

Advanced Industrial Psychology is that branch of Psychology which examines human behaviour under modern industrial circumstances. The study of human behaviour covers both external behaviour and inner feelings in which research is carried out on the concerned behavioural problems that arise in an industrial environment. The Advanced Industrial Psychology plays an important role in industry in increasing production, promoting harmonious relationship among workers and in creating better understanding between labour and management.

This book covers the undergraduate and postgraduate syllabi of all the Indian Universities. Its subject matter has been planned and treated according to the weightage given to different topics in the University syllabi. Based upon standard books, it studies industrial psychology in the setting of Indian conditions. While data have been gathered from standard books and reputed research journals published in the West, an attempt has been made to give the reader an insight into the problems of Indian industrial conditions and Indian labourers. Causes of their problems have been explored and suggestions advanced for amelioration of their conditions. Thus, the book is equally useful for all those concerned with industry and labour. It includes a discussion of the problems of industrial management and their solutions, and illustrates psychological tests and methods of measurement along with vocational guidance to the reader so that he may develop an understanding for the choice of a career and achievement of job satisfaction.

The method of presentation in this landmark publication is lucidly analytic with central headings, side headings and sub-headings given in different types to facilitate understanding. Each point has been discussed in a separate paragraph. Illustrations have been given wherever required.

The book will be an indispensable source for all professionals, researchers and students in the field of Psychology and for anyone working in the related areas for acquiring an up-to-date overviews.

Although we have done our best to make this book an ideal textbook, yet suggestions are invited for improvement of the book in its next edition.

RAM NATH SHARMA
S.S. CHANDRA

CONTENTS

VOLUME II

19

MORALE IN INDUSTRY

WHAT IS MORALE?

Whatever the industry, production does not depend exclusively upon the machines. Machines are driven by labourers. In addition to labourers, the factory has clerks, managers and other workers. If the factory is to be run efficiently and profitably, it is essential that all the human elements in the factory should co-operate and work in co-ordination. It should be in an organised affair. And this can be achieved only when all the workers are in a position to be enthusiastic and happy about their work. The attitude that the workers have towards their work in the factory makes a very great difference. It is this individual approach or viewpoint that constitutes their morale.

High Morale and Low Morale

Morale can be high as well as low. The successful industrialists make constant endeavours to maintain a high morale among their working staff because only if this is done, can the work in factory proceed smoothly and efficiently. Production is maintained at a high level and the quality of work done is admirable. On the other hand, once the morale of the factory workers has fallen, the organisation as a whole is constantly faced with problems of all kinds. Sometimes production falls while at others it is the accident rate that goes up alarmingly. Sometimes the workers do not see eye to eye and strikes are the result. Today, the importance of human relationships has come to be recognised in all industries. A high morale is evidence for the desirable condition of human relations.

Aspects of Morale

It is evident that morale has a very potent influence upon the social behaviour and conduct. It has, therefore, the two aspects — the psychological and the social. In its psychological aspect, morale is constituted by the organisation of industry, and the behaviour or mental tendency of workers towards those in authority above them. In its social aspect, morale is evidenced in the social behaviour of the workers. Accordingly, then if morale among the workers is high, they exhibit discipline, obedience and communal unity. The lower the tone of this feeling of unity, the lower will be the level of morale.

Influence of Morale upon Attitude towards the Authority

Hence, morale has a very explicit influence upon the worker's attitude towards authority. In this connection, Jenkens conducted a very interesting experiment. In it, he took up two groups in one of which the morale was very high and in other very low. In each group, besides one commander and one officiating officer, there were 17 workers. In order to measure their attitude towards those in authority, each worker was individually and secretly asked to name the officer with whom he would prefer to undertake air travel, and also the name of the officer with whom he would prefer not to undertake any such project. The results of this experiment led to the conclusion that in the case of high morale, the attitude towards authority was positive and favourable, while in the case of low morale it was negative and unfavourable. In the group which had a high morale, eight workers or soldiers chose the commander as a travelling companion while six of them selected the officiating person as more suitable. On the other hand, in the group with the low morale, no soldier chose to undertake or even prefer an air journey in the company of the commander. Contrary to this, nine soldiers gave evidence of a positive distaste for flying with the officiating individual.

Morale and Mental Condition

One characteristic of a high morale, in addition to the favourable attitude towards those in authority, is that it shuns disappointment or negation. In other words, when the morale is high, disappointment or hopelessness do not exist, and a high level of enthusiasm is maintained. If any problem does rear its head, immediate efforts are made to arrive at the solution. On the other hand, if morale in a particular group of individuals is low, frustration and disappointments increase. People lose faith in future. They are prone to find darkness all around them in which they find themselves groping, to no apparent advantage. Solutions of problems is a far cry, people being more prone to shutting their eyes and looking in the other direction. They exhibit such tendencies as fear.

Morale and Adjustment

In this manner, in conditions of high morale, organisation of the workers is strong, and they can easily adjust to changing circumstances. Usually, they are not conscious of any differences and distinctions among themselves. On the other hand, in the case of low morale, adjustability decreases.

Difference in the Morale of Individual Workers

Here, it should be kept in mind that if due to some reason, the circumstances in a factory deteriorate temporarily, there is no necessity for the morale of every worker falling. On the other hand, while the general level of morale is high in a unit, it is possible that certain individuals are influenced differently by changes and variations. On the other hand, even among the workers working in the same factory, positions and situations are different. For example, a particular worker may be in the good books of his boss, and this may give him a high morale, while other people may be suffering from low morale as they may not be in the good books of authority. Similarly, the same single occurrence or situation may have the result of improving morale of some people while it may depress others completely. For example, if, in a factory, special benefits are being made available to the individuals of a particular group, caste, tribe, or religion, this may positively affect their morale while it may have a negative influence on their less fortunate

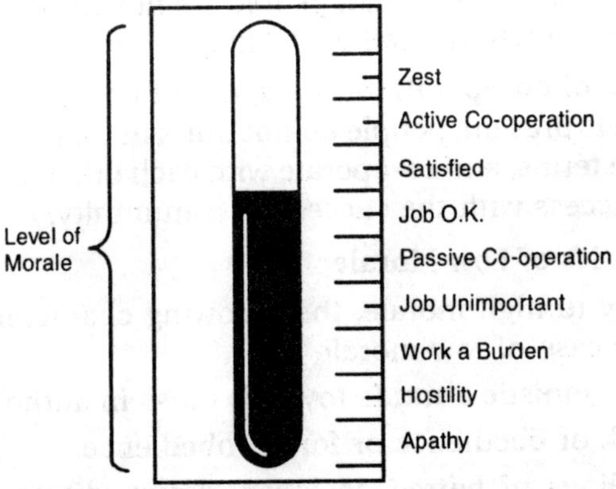

Fig. 19.1. Groups may be Compared on the Basis of Level of Morale

On the basis of scores made on questionnaires, values could be assigned to groups. The descriptive words used suggest meanings that different scale values might communicate. If these values are carefully studied, it is often possible to predict certain group behaviours, such as strikes, riots, demonstrations, formations of cliques and internal revolts.

colleagues. It may even be so deep-rooted that they may turn antagonistic towards those in authority and this may cause a further fall in their morale.

Characteristics of a High Morale

From the above description it becomes evident that the following characteristics are evident in the case of a high morale :

1. Positive or favourable attitude towards those in authority.
2. Self-induced obedience.
3. Positive feeling of respect and confidence for authorities.
4. Collective administration, unity and adjustability.
5. Rejection of frustrations and a sense of enthusiasm.
6. Mental peace and satisfaction.
7. Productivity and system in work.

Requirement for a High Level of Morale

Norman Meyer has laid much stress on team spirit in morale. Morale is maintained intact if there is a team spirit, and following things are required for maintaining a high level of team spirit :

1. Application to work. This assimilates the essence of enthusiasm and powerful motives, as a result of which the person moves consistently in the direction of pre-determined objectives.

2. Avoid diversion from work. This is a quality of existent morale. In a state of this kind, people are not easily diverted from their tasks even when faced with failure.

3. Sense of co-operation. If a sense of co-operation within a community is present, people do not think in individual terms but in collective terms, and co-operate with each other as they identify personal success with the success of community.

Characteristics of Low Morale

Contrary to high morale, the following characteristics are in evidence in case of low morale :

1. Antagonistic attitude towards those in authority.
2. Lack of obedience or forced obedience.
3. Feelings of hatred, jealousy, doubt, disrespect, lack of confidence towards those in authority.
4. Disappointment, unenthusiastic insipidity.
5. Lack of collective administration and unity, belief in lone effort.

6. Mental turmoil and unhappiness.
7. Lack of system and productivity in work.
8. Tendency to circulate all kinds of rumours.
9. Poisoning minds of others towards authority behind its back.
10. Lack of application to work.
11. Mutual conflicts and non-co-operation.

Methods of Measuring Morale

In order to discover the level of morale in a worker in any industry, it is necessary to observe the above-mentioned characteristics in him. Nowadays, morale is measured by the use of many scientific methods that reveal not only the level of morale that exists, but also the causes whereby it has come into existence. They can then be remedied and a high morale restored. The main methods are following :

1. Common worker's opinion analysis. One very popularly used method of measuring the morale is the common worker's opinion analysis method in which the opinions of the average worker are collected and analysed. For this, certain scientific questionnaires are prepared that reveal the workers' opinions regarding the various aspects of industry as well as towards the authorities. The worker does not have to reveal his name in answering these questionnaires. This has the initial advantage of assuring the worker of secrecy regarding his views. When questioned by the workers, it becomes possible to see the various scores on which the workers have complained. If some particular object or subject is a matter of complaint in a large majority of cases, efforts can be made to rectify it. Success in this method depends upon the degree to which the questionnaire is scientific, and upon the degree of truth in the workers' responses.

2. Interview of departed workers. In this method, those individuals are directly interviewed who have departed from the unit in question for various reasons. One main advantage of this method is that it reveals the reasons whereby the workers feel compelled to seek jobs elsewhere, so that future desertion on the part of present employees can be discouraged. Another feature of this method is that having left the employment of a particular concern or unit he feels free to give expression to his frank views on any and every aspect of the business. Another advantage of this method is that the views of departed employees cannot result in any harm to the administration or to those in authority. There can be no doubt that some workers may have grievances against the administration or their job that has no relation whatsoever with actual and real conditions. But if many workers leave their jobs on the same pretext, then, evidently, it is necessary to put an end to the source of complaint in order to maintain a high level of morale. In this manner, this method has proved extraordinarily useful in measuring the existing level of morale, and suggesting methods for improvements. It also locates the causes of falling morale. If, however, most of the departed employees speak well and favourably of the work and the administration of the factory or business house, then there is every reason to believe that morale is at a high level.

3. Attitude measurement. As has been pointed out earlier, morale is an expression of the workers' attitude towards their work, the authorities and general administration or organisation. Hence, the workers' attitudes can be known in order to evaluate their morale. For example, if the answers to the following queries were supplied by the workers, their attitudes in these respects could be known :

1. I work in the company under compulsion.
2. The authorities in the company believe in the policy of paying as little wages as can practicably be paid.
3. If I can get the same salary in a different company, I am prepared to resign from my present position.
4. I have no respect for or faith in those in authority above me.
5. The conditions under which I work cannot be said to be good by any standards.
6. I find no freedom, pleasure or satisfaction in my work.

The worker's attitudes can be discovered by requiring him to mark the above queries right or wrong.

If most of the workers mark the above observations as correct, then obviously, the level of morale is notoriously low. Other statements of a similar nature can be distributed among the workers in the form of a printed form or brochure and they can be required to mark them right or wrong according to their own inclination, so that the level of morale can be discovered as well as their attitudes towards various aspects of their occupation. Much importance in this method is attached to the choice of statements, which should be selected scientifically, as this makes the whole process much easier. The statements should be precise and exact so that the workers should be able to express their opinions clearly and categorically; vagueness must be avoided on both sides. This method is especially efficacious in the case of workers of clerical class. Even uneducated and illiterate workers can make a mark on the statements. As this method also does not require the worker to reveal his name, he can fearlessly and without fear of bias or prejudice give expression to his frank opinion. Various statements are evaluated previously, and the scoring can be done accordingly. This gives the whole method a certain air of validity and accuracy. Once the answers have been received, the median of the various scores can be taken to gauge the attitude of the individual worker. If most of the answers are adverse, it is concluded that morale is low, following which efforts are made to discover the causes that made it to be low, and remedies are suggested and in some cases actually applied. Generally speaking, every industry can formulate its own list of statements, but among the most important of the kind is that prepared by Arbauk and Bergon. Thurston and Kiev have made a detailed analysis of these statements.

4. Sociological method. Nowadays, particularly in the case of group studies, the sociological method is very prevalent. Moreover, a method for measuring the morale can be used to discover the characteristics of a workers' group organisation whereby the level of morale can be discovered. In the Jenkens' experiment he described characteristics of the workers' group organisation. Accordingly, the worker is given a questionnaire containing certain questions intended to throw light on the characteristics of group organisation. For example, the workers are asked to name and enumerate the individuals with whom they would like to work, or under whom they would prefer to work, in which sort of company they would prefer to work, or have anything to do. If the answers of many individuals to these questions seem to speak favourably of any one individual, and the answers seem to show respect, love and confidence for the individual, it is fairly evident that he is capable of becoming a good administrator. If he is already in the administrative cadre, then it evidences a high level of morale in the workers, for respect and confidence in authority is a sign of high morale. But if he is not so situated, then the answers seem to show lack of confidence in the existing administration a lack of confidence that can be rectified by promoting the desired individual into the administrative, block, or otherwise by advising the existing administrative group to mend its ways and adopt others, more calculated to win the confidence and respect of their subordinates. In this manner, it is evident that Moreno method can help in realising the conditions of morale in any unit, and in discovering the means of improving the existing morale.

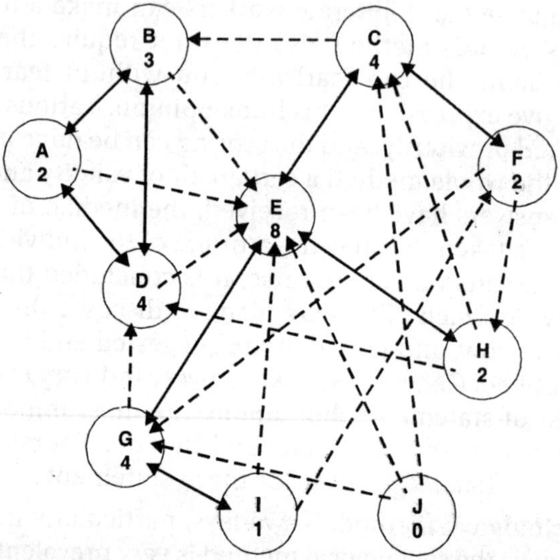

Fig. 19.2. Sociogram of a Group of Ten Workmen

Each workman is represented by a circle, the letters of the alphabet being substituted by names. Each member of the group was asked to vote for three men most desired as working companions. The numerals in the circles show the number of votes that each man received. The arrows indicate the direction of choices, whereas solid and broken lines designate mutual choices and one-way preferences, respectively. Individuals A, B and D form a triangle, E is a star, and J is an isolate.

ESSENTIAL REQUIREMENTS FOR HIGH MORALE

Having studied the methods by which morale can be measured and evaluated, it is better to make a study of the elements that determine it. These elements are roughly divided into the following three classes :

1. Physical requirements. This classification includes those physical conditions that influence morale, such as conditions of work, post, pay increase, methods of salary payment, conduct of inspector or authority, etc.

2. Mental requirements. These include such elements as praise, knowledge of success, fulfilment of co-operative needs, patience, forbearance, freedom, unity, feeling of equality, motivation, self-confidence and other psychological elements.

Physical Requirements for High Morale

1. Conditions of work. As has been evident from the account of morale all through, the conditions of work have an important influence upon it. If the conditions of work favour the worker and create interest in the work, morale is likely to be high. On the contrary, if the conditions of work are not favourable and serve to distract the interest of the worker, morale is likely to fall. 'Conditions of work' being a comprehensive term, it includes both physical and mental or psychological conditions. These will be described under 'Mental and Physical Requirements'. A fairly extensive description of them has already been given in previous chapter on 'Psychology in Industry'. Various researches have led to the belief that physical conditions of work have an important influence upon the morale in workers, as Tindall and Car have proved on the basis of their experimentation. Cair has pointed out the influence of music on the mental condition of workers. Culier's experiments seem to indicate that in bad conditions of work, morale tends to fall because the worker evinces signs of worry, distaste, irritability, anxiety, sleeplessness, laxness, lethargy, etc.

2. Position and promotion. Studying the morale of various individuals in various positions of different companies, Arbrock came to the conclusion that the attitude of foremen is better than that of clerks while that of clerks is more favourable than is the case with other classes of workers. This study reveals that the morale of individuals is also susceptible to such influences as the post that one is holding. The main psychological fact at the root of this phenomenon is that if the individual in question does not get a position that concurs with his psychological bent of mind, his enthusiasm begins to wane, and he loses confidence in those who are in authority above him. Hence if morale is to be kept high in any industry, it is essential that posts be allotted in accordance with the ability and labour of the individuals, and that these posts be improved from time to time. Much the same phenomenon came to light in a study of promotion in a previous chapter.

3. Increase in salary. It is a psychological fact that workers are primarily concerned with their salary or wages. Sheppard has stressed the fact that if the worker's wages are reassessed from time to time and appropriate changes are made, the morale tends to occupy a high level. On the contrary, if the wages remain stationary for a long time, and there is no advancement, the workers' enthusiasm is dampened, and they tend to heap blame on their officers. Increase in pay should be made dependent upon hard work and other qualities. If increase in pay depends upon the personal idiosyncrasy of the individual in power, most people become cynical as they do not like to cringe before such a person. Secondly, even the ingratiating types who win increase in pay and promotions through subservience rarely have a high morale. Hence, for pay increase to have a favourable influence upon morale, it is essential that the basis of increase be proper, and the same for everyone.

4. Method of distributing salaries. Morale is also influenced by the method of distributing salary no less than by increase in it. All studies to date on the subject have not led to any conclusive idea as to which method is definitely the best. Some methods are of course, better than certain others. Various methods will be examined briefly here :

(a) ***Share of profits*** : Under this method, the workers in companies and factories are given bonuses and share of profits from time to time. The following facts need to be mentioned in connection with this method :

(i) This method engenders dissatisfaction in the better and more efficient workers because they find that others less efficient and skilful than themselves are deriving the same benefits without actually deserving them.

(ii) In this method, the worker is never sure of his actual income in the near future because neither the quantity of profit is shared nor the time of its distribution is certain.

Despite the above clear difficulties and drawbacks, this method has been found to meet with the approval of approximately one-third of the workers. Besides, this method is also rather simple, as a consequence of which it is one of the most widely used today.

(b) ***Remuneration according to work*** : In this method, the worker is reimbursed according to the quantity of material he produces. The research made by Mathewson on this subject has made it abundantly clear that the method can succeed only if the worker is confident that the range of payment will not fall, because he usually expects that if he works more he will earn more but also thereby create a reason for the company reducing the rate of payment. Fear of this kind guides them to reduce their rate of working.

It is evident that if the worker can be convinced of the stability of payment rates, the piece wages method is superior to the bonus method, but it requires that the following facts be kept in mind :

(i) Attention should be concentrated not only on quantity but also on quality.

(ii) In paying the worker, it should be made abundantly clear to him that he is being paid according to a certain definite rate for a specific kind of work so that no doubt lingers in his mind that compels him to work slower.

(iii) In connection with remuneration, the rate should be constant and there should be no fear of the rate of payment being reduced.

If the above facts are kept in mind, and the appropriate arrangements made, the morale of the worker can be kept high through the piece wages method, because it is by this method that the worker is constantly inspired to work more and to produce better results. It is also very good from the point of view of creating good incentives.

5. Ability to profit. Among the physical requirements, other is the possibility and opportunity of progress in any concern. If the workers in a company are being paid dividends out of its profits, then it should be equally distributed. In other words, all workers should be given the opportunity to progress and earn high wages, without any discrimination. If this is not done, most of them tend to turn against the authorities in their company, while at the same time a feeling of jealousy for those who have progressed is engendered in the unfortunate ones. This destroys not only collective organisation and administrative efficiency, but also faith and belief in the authorities. Hence, the rules governing promotion and increase in salary should be equally applicable to all, and they should be clearly understood by all of them. No one should be given a chance to complain on these grounds.

Psychological Requirement for High Morale

Having completed a cursory study of the physical requirements of the morale, a detailed study of its psychological requirements will now be made :

1. Praise. It is a matter of general psychological knowledge that praise of good work and effort helps to infuse further enthusiasm and energy in the worker.

Studies conducted by such eminent psychologists as Thorndike and Hurlock, evinced that praise of a worker's effort helps to increase his motivation. In fact, the influence of the reward and punishment scheme on work is fairly evident and widely known.

Any work that derives punishment for the perpetrator is shunned by reward. Praise is a psychological reward. Praise by individuals for whom we have respect and in whose judgement we have faith, matters a lot to us. If the authorities in the factory or office praise all good effort, then morale becomes high among the workers. On the other hand, if good work and hard labour go unpraised or unnoticed, enthusiasm wanes in the worker, as he feels that he is not being valued according to his merits. This fact is one of the important reasons why work in an impersonal psychological organisation like government office is rarely of a high order of efficiency. Direct praise or blame is rarely forth-coming, except from very conscientious individuals in authority.

2. Knowledge of success. Some other experiments have brought to light the fact that if the worker is aware of the degree of success he is achieving in his work, his interest and enthusiasm in it are maintained, and so is the high level of morale. In very big factories where the individual work does no more than make only a very small cog in a very big wheel, and is not aware of the effect of his own effort towards the completed wheel, boredom and disinterest are likely to set in very early. Result of work can be bad as well as good. Knowledge of failure can only serve to lower the morale, but if the worker is again encouraged to think in terms of success, morale can be regained. As a general rule, success ensures a high morale. Success is the reward of effort. And reward is a favourable element in the creation and maintenance of morale. Colstaad's studies showed that the morale of workers in shops that have a very big turnover with large profits is much higher and better than that of workers employed in smaller organisations with a smaller turnover and lesser profits. This evidence is rooted in the psychological fact that success increases an individual's confidence in himself, and he comes to realise the need to maintain all these privileges intact. He is driven to work with even greater energy and resolve.

3. Fulfilment of collective needs. Man works not only to meet the needs of his body, such needs as food and clothing, but also to satisfy certain other collective psychological requirements. He is also desirous of meeting others, giving vent to his feelings and emotions, thoughts and beliefs, exhibiting himself, knowing himself, and winning social prestige and recognition. Any kind of work that affords all these advantages to the worker is almost certain to create a very high morale in him, but if all these things are not made available to him, morale is likely to fall, if it was ever high. Hence, for maintaining the morale of their workers, the organisers and authorities should keep in mind the fact that the worker's collective needs be also fulfilled and satisfied.

4. Forbearance and good behaviour of authorities. Workers attach much importance to the behaviour of inspectors, managers and other in authority, towards them. If their conduct towards them is not all that can be desired, general morale is likely to suffer. If the worker is constantly interrupted and scolded over his work, he loses all respect for the officer. Actually, the only course of keeping workers contented that is open to the officers and authorities is that of good and considerate behaviour towards them. In such circumstances, the workers are inclined to pay little attention to other conditions around them, and are enthusiastic enough to do anything that is likely to benefit their factory or organisation. This is due to an identify of interests that is felt by the worker. A sense of possession invades him. On the contrary, the worker's self-respect is injured if the authority above him behaves in an irresponsible manner towards him. In fact, a position of authority does not require occupational skill so much as it requires the qualities of leadership and organisation, a skill in diplomacy. A leader plays an important part in maintaining the morale of a group of people. In company offices and factories, it is good for them to have a fair knowledge of human psychology. Their behaviour towards the workers should be such that it should easily adjust in the collective organisation. Tolerance is an important quality for leaders. Tolerance not only adds to the respect that is forthcoming, it does not detract from it. But tolerance does not imply that the officer or leader should calmly overlook the mistakes of his subordinates. What is important is that due importance be given to all things brought to notice. It is hardly proper to be constantly wrangling over small and inconsequential matters. But to overlook a thing of great magnitude is again a serious fault that should be avoided. Studies conducted in the Iowa University of the United States of America have revealed that a group working under a democratic leader is more organised. In such a group, the workers continue with their duties even during the leader's absence. They have favourable mental attitudes towards the leader and other fellow-workers. Contrary to this, morale in the group and work under an authoritarian or autocratic leader is usually low, work being continued in his presence because of fear but suspended in his absence. They entertain feelings of jealousy and hatred for such a leader. In this manner, it is evident that for maintaining a high level of morale among workers, there is a great importance attached to tolerant and considerate behaviour on the part of officers.

5. Freedom of workers. In whichever company or factory a worker loses his identity to the extent of being reduced to the level of a small cog in the huge wheel, he is dissatisfied with his work because it appears heavy and insipid to him. Hence, in order to maintain the worker's morale at a high level, it is essential that he be given the maximum degree of freedom that his function and position allow. He should also not be prevented from meeting other fellow-workers, in particular those individuals who are in authority. It helps in creating a more intimate and knowledgeable atmosphere, in which he can tell his troubles to the proverbial daddy. But giving freedom does not imply that discipline should be done away with. Freedom within the framework of laws is the most desirable state of affairs.

6. Sense of organization and identity or equality. It has been pointed out earlier that collective or group organisation is indicative of high morale. Hence, it is essential that a sense of organisation and unity should circulate freely among the workers. Psychologists, May and Wright, concluded from their examinations and study that in order to maintain a high morale among the workers in industries, it is essential that the workers must have in themselves a feeling of being organised and united or equal. The workers should be able to identify themselves with their factory or office or organisation, and think of its interests as if they were their own. If this is achieved, even the most difficult times can be successfully seen through by making a collective effort by many things such as a definite name of the company or organisation, a definite dress and a common badge. Besides these, certain group objectives can be set up, the achievement of which involves organised and collective effort on the part of workers. Exerting oneself along with many others, straining for the same objectives serves to lessen tension, increase mutual goodwill and help the organisation. Workers should be made to realise that they are an important and responsible part of industry. They should also be equipped with knowledge of various parts of industry, so that they can come to look upon it as their own industry. Some millowners are under the impression that their interest lies in keeping the workers quarrelling among themselves. As a policy, this may have some immediate benefits but in the long run this is a very harmful policy because lack of collective organisation in workers lowers their morale, and this finally has an adverse influence upon the quality and quantity of work done by the workers.

Other Requirements

Apart from the above-mentioned physical and psychological determinants of morale, there are some other factors that influence it. For example, through his experiments and research, Super has established a relationship between age and morale. Similarly, the research of Arbrock has shown that the level of morale is higher in case of women workers than in the case of male workers. Actually, maintaining a very high level of morale requires careful attention to all aspects of the worker's personality and to all aspects of his work. In this connection research work is continuing that is expected to yield harvest of interesting facts.

QUESTIONS FOR EXERCISE

1. What do you mean by Industrial morale? What are its determinants?
2. What is morale? Explain the value of morale in increasing production.
3. What is industrial morale? State the main factors of the declination.
4. Write short note on industrial morale.
5. How will you define industrial morale? What are its indicators of good morale?
6. Explain the concept and the importance of industrial morale and discuss its main determinants.
7. What do you mean by dimension of morale? Discuss the various factors which are conducive to industrial morale. Cite some important studies conducted in this field.
8. What psychological factors are basic to good morale among workers?
9. What is worker's morale? How is it measured? State the determinants of morale in industry.
10. What is worker morale? How is it measured? Evaluate the methods of its measurement.
11. How is industrial morale measured?

20

Job Satisfaction

WHAT IS JOB SATISFACTION?

The term job relates to the total relationship between an individual and the employer for which he is paid. Satisfaction means the simple feeling-stage accompanying the attainment of any goal. It is feeling accompanying the attainment by an impulse of its objectives. Thus, job satisfaction refers to a person's feeling of satisfaction on the job, which acts as a motivation to work. It is not the self-satisfaction, happiness or self-contentment but the satisfaction on the job. Job dissatisfaction means absence of motivation at work.

Human resource is sum-total of inherent abilities, acquired knowledge and skills represented by the talents and aptitudes of the employed persons comprising executives, supervisors, and the rank and file employees. Human resources should be utilised to the maximum possible extent, in order to achieve individual and organisational goals. The employee's performance ultimately decides the attainment of goals. The employee performance in its turn is influenced by motivation and job satisfaction.

Definition of Job Satisfaction

1. R. Hoppoch. "Any combination of psychological, physiological and environmental circumstances that cause a person truthfully to say I am satisfied with my job."

2. E.A. Locke. Job satisfaction is defined as the "pleasurable emotional state resulting from the appraisal of one's job as achieving or facilitating the achievement of one's job values". In contrast, job dissatisfaction is defined as "the unpleasurable emotional state resulting from the appraisal of one's job as frustrating or blocking the attainment of one's job values or as entailing disvalues." Satisfaction and dissatisfaction were seen as, "a function of the perceived relationship between what one perceives it as offering or entailing".

THEORIES OF JOB SATISFACTION

Basically, there are five approaches/theories of job satisfaction. They are : (1) Fulfilment theory, (2) Discrepancy theory, (3) Equity theory, (4) Two-factor theory and (5) Social Reference Group theory.

1. Fulfilment theory. The advocates of this theory measure satisfaction in terms of rewards which a person receives or the extent to which his needs are satisfied. There is a direct/positive relationship between job satisfaction and the actual satisfaction of the expected needs.

(i) ***Limitations :*** Job satisfaction' as observed by willing, is not only a function of what a person receives but also what he feels he should receive as there would be considerable difference in the actuals and expectations of persons. Thus job satisfaction cannot be regarded as merely a function of how much a person receives from his job.

(ii) The strength of the individual's desire of his level of aspiration in a particular area should be included to predict job satisfaction accurately. This led to the development of the discrepancy theory of job satisfaction.

2. Discrepancy theory. The proponents of this theory argue that satisfaction is the function of what a person actually receives from his job situation and what he thinks he should receive or what he expects to receive. When the actual satisfaction derived is less than expected satisfaction, it results in dissatisfaction. As E.A. Loche puts it, "Job satisfaction and dissatisfaction are functions of the perceived relationship between what one wants from one's job and what one perceives it is offering."

Limitations. This approach does not make it clear whether or not over satisfaction is a part of dissatisfaction and if so, how does it differ from dissatisfaction. This led to the development of equity theory of job satisfaction.

3. Equity theory. The proponents of this theory are of the view that a person's satisfaction is determined by his perceived equity, which in turn is determined by his input-output balance compared to his comparison of others' input-output balance. Input-output balance is the perceived ratio of what a person receives from his job relative to what he contributes to the job. Equity theory is of the view that both under-and over-rewards lead to dissatisfaction. While the under-reward causes feelings of unfair treatment, over-reward leads to feelings of guilt and discomfort.

4. Two-factor theory. This theory was developed by Herzberg, Mausner, Peterson and Capwell who identified certain factors as satisfies and dissatisfied. Factors such as achievement, recognition, responsibility, etc. are satisfied. Their presence causes satisfaction but their absence does not result in dissatisfaction. Factors such as supervision, salary, working conditions, etc., are dissatisfiers, the absence of which causes dissatisfaction. Their presence, however, does not result in job satisfaction. As the studies designed to test this theory failed to give any support to it, it seems that a person can get both satisfaction and dissatisfaction at the same time, which is not valid.

5. Social reference-group theory. The social reference-group theory is similar to need-fulfilment theory except that it takes into account not the desires, needs and interests of the individual, but rather the point of view and opinions of the group to whom the individual looks for guidance. The "reference-group" defines the way in which the individual should look at the world and evaluate various phenomena in the environment including himself. According to this theory, if a job meets the interests, desires and requirements of a person's reference group, he will like it and if it does not, he will not like it. A good example of this theory has been given by C.L. Hulin who measured the effects of community characteristics on job satisfaction of female clerical workers employed in 300 different catalogue order offices. He found that with job conditions held constant job satisfaction was less among persons living in a well-to-do neighbourhood than among those whose neighbourhood was poor. Hulin provided strong evidence that frames of reference for evaluation may be provided by one's social groups and general social environment. However this theory gives an incomplete explanation since while some people may go along with group opinions and group evaluation of organisational phenomena, many people are independent of these pressures.

FACTORS OF JOB SATISFACTION

Job satisfaction refers to a general attitude which an employee retains on account of many specific attitudes in the following areas : (1) Job satisfaction, (2) Individual characteristics and (3) Relationships outside the job. Job satisfaction depends on the following different factors :

1. Personal factors. These include workers' sex, education, age, marital status and their personal characteristics, family background, socio-economic background and the like.

2. Factors inherent in the job. These factors include die work itself, conditions, influence of internal and external environment on the job which are uncontrolled by the management, etc. These factors have been found to be important in the selection of employees. Instead of being guided by their co-workers and supervisors, the skilled workers would rather like to be guided by their own inclination to choose jobs in consideration of 'what they have to do'.

3. Factors controlled by the management. These include the nature of supervision, job security, kind of work group, wage rate, promotional opportunities, transfer policy, duration of work and sense of responsibilities. All these factors greatly influence the workers. Their presence in the organisation motivates the workers and provides a sense of job satisfaction.

DETERMINANTS OF JOB SATISFACTION

According to Abraham A. Korman, two types of variables determine the job satisfaction of an individual : (1) Organisational variables and (2) Personal variables.

[A] Organisational Variables

(1) Occupational level. The higher the level of the job, the greater the satisfaction of the individual, because higher level jobs carry greater prestige and self-control. Relationship between occupational level and job satisfaction stems from social reference group theory in that our society values some jobs more than others. Hence people in valued jobs will like them more than those who are in non-valued jobs. The relationship may also stem from the need-fulfilment theory. People in higher level jobs find most of their needs satisfied than when they are in lower level ones.

(2) Job content. As job content in terms of variety and nature of tasks called for is a function of occupational level, the theoretical arguments given above apply here also. Greater the variation in job content and the less the repetitiveness with which the tasks must be performed, the greater the satisfaction of the individuals involved.

(3) Considerate leadership. As people like to be treated with consideration, considerate leadership results in higher job satisfaction than inconsiderate leadership.

(4) Pay and promotional opportunities. Other things being equal, these two variables are positively related to job satisfaction.

(5) Interaction in the work group. Interaction is most satisfying when it results :

(i) in the cognition that other person's attitudes are similar to one's own, since this permits the ready calculability of the other's behaviour and constitutes a validation of one's self;

(ii) in being accepted by others and

(iii) it facilitates the achievement of goals.

[B] Personal Variables

For some people, most jobs are dissatisfying irrespective of the organisational conditions involved, whereas for others, most jobs are satisfying. Personal variables like age, educational level, sex, etc., are responsible for this difference.

DETERMINANTS OF JOB SATISFACTION

Author	Name of the study	Determinants of job satisfaction
1. Stagner, Flebbe and Wood (1952)	Working on the rail-road; a study of job satisfaction (*Personnel Psychology*, 1952, 5, 293-306). This is a study of 715 male unionised rail-road workers.	1. General working conditions 2. Union-management relations 3. General quality of supervision 4. Grievance handling procedures.
2. Gadel (1953)	Productivity and satisfaction of full and part-time female employees (*Personnel Psychology*, 1953, 6, 327-42). This is a study of 301 women doing typing and routine clerical work. Sixty per cent of this number were at least 40 years old and more were married.	For younger group : 1. Type of work 2. Working conditions 3. Pay 4. Co-workers 5. Ease of commuting to workplace 6. Advancement opportunities For older group : 1. Security 2. Supervision 3. Company prestige 4. Working hours
3. Ross and Zander (1957)	Need satisfaction and employee turnover (*Personnel Psychology*, 1957, 10, 327-38). This is a study of skilled women in a large company.	1. Recognition 2. Autonomy 3. Doing important work 4. Fair evaluation of work done.
4. Durganand Sinha (1958)	Job satisfaction in office and manual workers (*Indian Journal of Social Work*, 1958, 19, 39-46).	1. Job status 2. Type of work 3. Supervisory 4. Work group.

(1) Age. Holding such factors as occupational level constant, most of the evidence on the relation between age and job satisfaction, seems to indicate that there is a positive relationship between the two variables up to the pre-retirement years and then there is a sharp decrease in satisfaction. An individual aspires for better and more prestigious jobs in later years of his life. Finding his channels for advancement blocked, his satisfaction declines.

(2) Educational level. With occupational level held constant, there is a negative relationship between the educational level and job satisfaction. The higher the education, the higher the reference group which the individual looks to for guidance to evaluate his job rewards.

(3) Role perception. Different individuals hold different perceptions about their role, *i.e.*, the kind of activities and behaviours they should engage in, to perform their job successfully. Job satisfaction is determined by this factor. The more accurate the role perception of an individual, the greater his satisfaction.

(4) Sex. Holding such factors as job and occupational level constant there is as no consistent evidence as to whether women are more satisfied with their jobs than men. Considering the generally lower occupational aspiration of women, one might predict this to be the case.

CREATING JOB SATISFACTION

The importance of job satisfaction is fairly evident from a description of the importance of maintaining morale in any industry. If a worker is not satisfied with his work, then both the quantity and quality of his output will suffer. If his job satisfaction increases then there is an improvement in both the quality and quantity of production. Factories in which the workers are satisfied with their work are also characterised by a high morale. The following things are generally important for creating the job satisfaction :

1. Attending to and solving problems. It is desirable that the complaints of the workers be heard patiently and the problems solved as far as possible. Factories in which the worker' demands are not heeded, suffer because the workers lose confidence in the management and become frustrated.

2. Satisfactory future. Every worker is definitely concerned about his future prospects. If the factory rules clearly lay down the conditions of promotions and advancement, and if the worker gets the expected promotion and improvement in pay scales at the right time, he feels satisfied and becomes confident of his future.

If, on the other hand, the worker feels that even good work will not be rewarded, he becomes frustrated and slack in his work.

3. Testing the worker's ability and progress. Every worker, whether in a factory or an office, desires that he should be paid according to his ability. If he has undergone some new training or has increased his ability to work in some way, he should be compensated for his better ability through a raise in salary. Organisations in which the management keeps an eye on the ability and progress of its workers normally have a high degree of job satisfaction among their workers. It is necessary that the management should give the worker some opportunity of progressing higher and higher. If, on the other hand, the organisation does not pay any attention to the abilities and increased efficiency of its staff, it suffers in the long run because the workers lose interest in their job and do not often try to improve their level of efficiency. This happens because they feel that an increase in qualifications or efficiency is not related to progress or promotion.

4. Respect for creative suggestions. Generally speaking, the worker working under a particular set of conditions is best qualified to say how and where improvements can be made. If workers are encouraged to suggest ways and means of improving the conditions of work, they often come up with very valuable ideas. This helps in increasing the job satisfaction because when the worker is praised for giving a good practical idea, he tends to pay more attention to his work in order to win more praise. If such suggestions are neglected then the worker feels dissatisfied since apparently there can be no improvement in the conditions in which he works.

5. Cordial analysis or evaluation of the work. In every organisation, the manager or the supervisor has to offer criticism of the work performed by the worker because he must point out the worker's mistakes and try to eliminate them. If this criticism is offered in a cordial and friendly way more as suggestion than as criticism, then the worker feels gratified and pays attention to it. His job satisfaction is also thereby maintained. But if the worker is abused or bitterly criticised for his mistakes, he loses his peace of mind.

***6.* Increase in wages.** Rules governing increase in salary should be clear and explicit and should be acted upon impartially and regularly. If the worker gets the anticipated increase in salary at the right time, he feels satisfied with his job. If this does not happen, dissatisfaction is the result. Increase in wages is, in fact, the most important factor in job satisfaction.

7. Praise for good performance. If workers are not praised for exceptional performances in their work, they lose interest in it and as a result, the organisation suffers. Even if they do good work, they still remain dissatisfied and disgruntled. Generally, the worker prefers to work well and remain occupied than merely to pass the time allotted to him. If he is also encouraged in his work by an occasional word of praise and respect, he is further motivated to maintain a high level of efficiency and in fact to improve it. If he is not praised for his work, his enthusiasm and zeal immediately fall.

8. Promotion according to ability. In every organisation some people are always being retired after completion of their tenure while younger people are promoted to take their places. If promotion is based upon the ability of the worker then the worker's mental satisfaction is maintained. If, on the other hand, promotion depends upon other factors such as casteism, personal favour, etc., then the worker's interest in his work declines.

9. Proper quantum of work. If job satisfaction is to be maintained, it is essential that the quantity of work does not exceed the individual's ability to complete it. If he has to work more than he comfortably can or for a long time, the worker is bound to become disgusted, depressed and tired.

10. Equal Wages for Equal Work. Labour unions in almost every industry are now demanding that there should be equal pay for equal work. In any factory or office, a worker must be paid as much as other workers are being paid in other organisations for similar work. The worker feels satisfied if this equality is maintained. If it is not, then the worker loses his satisfaction.

11. Freedom to seek help in solving problems. Very often the worker is faced by problems in his work that he cannot solve alone. In such a case he should be free to seek help and guidance from other workers or even from the managers.

12. Absence of unnecessary intervention and criticism. No individual wants to sacrifice his self-respect. If the worker is unnecessarily shown disrespect or abused, he quickly becomes dissatisfied. Hence he should be protected from useless interruptions and criticism.

13. Satisfactory hours of work. The hours of work in any factory or office should be convenient and so arranged as to offer the least possible inconvenience to the largest number of employees. If this is not looked into, the workers become dissatisfied.

14. Availability of leave and rest. In every industrial organisation, the workers should be given the proper amount of rest and holidays on festivals and other occasions of social celebrations. Nowadays it is thought necessary to give a half holiday every fifteen days in addition to the weekly holiday. Rest given on festivals and on occasions of general celebration is in addition to this. Besides, the worker is also permitted to take leave for medical or other private reasons. Female workers are allowed fairly long leave during pregnancy. It is generally seen that workers feel satisfied if the management in any organisation follows a liberal policy towards leave for workers.

It is evident from the above description of factors influencing job satisfaction that it necessitates the creation of certain conditions of work. Different factors may be of importance in different situations. Increase in wages is a common factor which is important everywhere. Promotion is another factor which plays an important role in maintaining or destroying the job satisfaction. Apart from this, the other factors may be more or less important, depending upon the situation. For example, an organisation in which the worker's educational degrees have great importance should also see to it that the worker is promoted when he adds to his qualifications. On the other hand, in an organisation in which training or academic qualifications have no value, this question will not arise at all. Finally, it can be said that job satisfaction depends on all those factors which influence morale.

QUESTIONS FOR EXERCISE

1. What is job satisfaction? Describe the various facts affecting job satisfaction.
2. Discuss the importance of job satisfaction for job performance.
3. What are the main factors leading to satisfaction in work? How do measures of labour welfare affect satisfaction of labour?
4. Write a short note on job satisfaction.
5. What do you understand by job satisfaction? Discuss the factors that influence it.
6. Explain what you understand by job satisfaction, and discuss the factors that operate as its determinants in industrial setting.
7. What do you understand by Vocational Fitness? Explain in detail.

21

The Work Curve

WORK AND PLAY

Some people say that play should be treated as work and work as play. What they mean is that one should play with the same interest with which one works and work should be made to yield the same pleasure that play does. Play as you work, and work as you play, certainly, but do not forget that the two are distinct. Such proverbs are characteristically misleading as they seem to suggest that work and play are the same. Such a notion is psychologically wrong and indefensible. Work and play differ mainly in the following respects :

1. **Difference of objectives.** When you see a child playing, you may be inclined to enquire of him as to what he is doing and why, and normally the answer would be that he is playing, and that he is playing for the sake of playing. In this way, play is a normal and common tendency, an objective and aim in itself. Play is indulged in, of its own accord, rather than from any external motivation. Usually it is seen as the contradiction of work, with the result that all children more interested in games are considered lazy. Many young students run away from the school and spend their entire time in playing and roaming about. If one enquires the reason of things from a card player, the almost inevitable response is that one may play and see for oneself. The pleasure resulting from it constitutes the reason why it is played. Now to take up the cudgels on behalf of work, one immediately perceives that no work is done without any motive and definite objective. All the hundreds and thousands of vocations peculiar to the human animal, including study and labour, are pursued with some objective in view. The actual aim may be accumulation of wealth or the achievement of fame, or any other conceivable aim, but no work can be aimless. Work is not its own objective; one does not work for the sake of working. It is the thought that it is a fruit to come in the future that infuses courage and enthusiasm in the worker labouring in the

present. But while playing a game, every movement brings its own fresh pleasures and amusements; there are no future fruits to be considered. Its pleasure is in the moment. Of course, one may astutely object that one ever present motive in the play is the desire to defeat and overcome the opponent. Then how can objective or aim be used to distinguish between the games and work? But if in answer to this question, one were asked what the winner gains in defeating his adversary and what the latter loses in being defeated, then it would have to be admitted that there is nothing concrete involved. In fact, as Drever has pointed out, the objectives and aims of play belong to the world of imagination while the aim in working belongs to the essential reality and concreteness of the world and everyday life. One often finds that work carries with it the fetters of compulsion while no such feeling accompanies the play.

2. The meaning of play is within the act of playing while that of work lies outside. According to Drever, "In play the value and significance of the activity is found in the activity itself, whereas in work, the value and significance of activity are found an end beyond the activity". In this way, every moment spent in play brings its own rewards in terms of pleasure and amusement, whereas work is accompanied by no such pleasure. Usually, it is the opposite, as work is attended by pain and effort. It attains fruition a long time after it, itself has been completed.

3. Play Gives Immediate and Work Remote Pleasure. Man is by nature an epicurean who turns towards things that bring him pleasure and instinctively turns away from the objects that bring him pain and misery. Hence, in both work and play, the aim and object of the child are obtaining pleasure but while play yields its pleasures immediately and in the present, the pleasures to be had of work, are slower in their coming, It sometimes never comes at all even in the future, and sometimes even brings pain and suffering.

4. Play creates energy while work consumes it. All work and no play makes the proverbial Jack a dull boy. Play is a kind of recreation. It takes away the individual's fatigue and brings him balmy rest. It is for this reason that young and old, none are averse to playing. But this does not mean that play does not result in physical exhaustion. But the fatigue that results out of playing differs in nature from the fatigue that originates in hard work. The fatigue of play is health giving. Of course, excessive practice in competitive games may harm physical progress of the individual and stunt his growth. Playing acts as a tonic both for the body and the mind, provided games are not played in excess of the body's energy. Such a condition can be easily recognised if one observes the physical condition after play. The individual should be refreshed and be enthusiastic about the work before him, and should have the energy to perform it. In physical games, the blood circulates rapidly through the body so that many undesirable elements present in the body are eliminated and the individual feels lighter and more energetic. After the day's tiring routine, most people feel the need for some form of recreation and enjoyment. Play is one form of it. On the other hand, work reduces the efficiency of the individual. Hence games and work should be rationally synthesized.

5. Difference in mental attitudes. Play and work differ in respect of their accompanying mental attitudes. Play is independently indulged in without any hint of compulsion whereas work is associated with the feeling of necessity and inevitability. The necessity may be due to some external compulsion such as the order of a superior or it may be imposed on the self from within. Man naturally engages in and concentrates upon the play, but whereas work concentration is a matter of conscious effort rather than one of effortless ease. The feeling of responsibility is conspicuously absent when one is playing; he is not answerable to anyone and he has nothing much to lose if he makes a mistake as nothing is valuable at stake. But on the other hand, in work, the individual is conscious of a certain burden, and he is answerable to certain other individuals if he fails to perform his functions efficiently. He is responsible for the work he is allotted, and he is very likely to become a prey to boredom easily. It is for these reasons that the child, in his infancy and childhood, is allowed little work and more play. Even the things that he is taught are presented in such a manner that he treats them as a child's play. But when he attains adolescence and adulthood, he is entrusted with work of greater and greater responsibility. He even comes to perform such responsible functions avidly and enthusiastically.

Relationship between Work and Play

Despite the above superficial points of difference between the work and play, there is little if any fundamental dissimilarity between them. There can be no sharp and precise dividing line that demarcates the two and divides them into water tight compartments. The child learns both from play and work; in both he finds material that helps to develop his character, and both are essential and beneficial to him. Then, every individual can obtain some pleasure from the work he is engaged in, by orientation and conscious effort. And in the case of very efficient and capable individuals, it is said that work is a child's play for them. The ease and comfort with which famous authors compose voluminous works appears play to their readers and sometimes even to themselves. In fact, the ability with which an individual introduces the pleasure of play into his work depends upon the efficiency with which he can perform that work. To quote : Sir T.P. Nunn, "An agent thinks of his activity as play if he can take it up or lay it down at choice or vary at will the condition of its exercise; he thinks of it as work if it is imposed on him by unavoidable necessity, or if he is held to it by a sense of duty or a vocation." The person who looks upon it as play and accepts it willingly and freely excels in it both quantitatively and qualitatively. To take a simple example, the gardener engaged in the gardening can choose to look upon his job as play or as a vocation. In the first instance, the work will afford him much pleasure whereas if he chooses to treat it as a vocation he will be depriving himself of considerable pleasure.

What is Work?

Work can be defined as an action performed with the object of achieving some particular objective. Hence work is an action with a particular aim which is fulfilled by the action. Human beings do various kinds of work to earn their livelihood. Apart from the earning of livelihood, actions may have some other objectives such as study, earning prestige, etc. Here it may be objected that play also has an objective and for that reason it would be difficult to distinguish play from work. But two things must be kept in mind. In the first place, the player does get some satisfaction of his physical and psychological needs, but he does not start by considering this satisfaction as his goal. In the second place, it is not possible to draw a dividing line between play and work. The same activity may be a game for one individual and work for another, depending upon the attitude. For example, just as the player devotes his entire attention to playing the game without being overtly conscious of the results, the determined worker may perform some activity with complete concentration and be oblivious to the actual results. On the other hand, every player does think in terms of winning and losing, irrespective of how much sporting spirit he has. Hence, while the definition of work given above shows its relative difference from work, it does not indicate that there is a complete difference between the two. As far as the pleasurable and interesting aspect of play is concerned, the success of many great people lies in the fact that they found as great pleasure in doing work as they did in play.

KINDS OF WORK

Work is broadly divided into two categories — muscular work and mental work. Before going on to a detailed description of these two kinds, it is necessary to remember that the two are so intimately connected with each other that the distinction between the two is merely verbal and a matter of practical expediency. Muscular work requires physical energy. On the other hand, mental work requires the expenditure of nervous energy. But there is no physical work which does not require some mental participation just as much as there is no mental work which does not consume some physical energy. Hence both kinds of work are mutually dependent, not mutually exclusive.

Muscular Work

Every human being performs a multitude of muscular actions everyday in his life. Muscular work, depending upon the difficulty involved, results in more or less fatigue, sooner or later, and one arrives at a stage when one stops work due to the fatigue. This limit differs from individual to individual and from work to work.

Measurement of Fatigue in Muscular Work

The fatigue which is consequent upon all muscular work is measured by the ergograph, an instrument which measures the contraction of the muscles. Although many kinds of ergographs are in use, the most commonly used are Mosso's and Kraeplin's ergographs. In using the ergographing, the right or the left arm of the subject is tied in such a way that he can move only the middle finger. Before starting the experiment, the instrument for measuring rhythm is fixed at 60°. Then the subject pulls the thread fixed to the ergograph at the first beat of the metronome and relaxes it at the second beat. The contraction and expansion of the muscles in the middle finger are recorded on a sheet of a smoking paper through a needle. Since this work of pulling and relaxing the string is continued over a long period and since the relaxing is loaded with some weight, the subject's finger becomes fatigued until a stage is reached when the finger cannot pull the thread at all. As fatigue increases, the height of the markings on the smoked paper begins to fall and at the time of total fatigue, the markings take the form of a straight line. In this manner the ergograph helps in the study of effects of fatigue on muscular work.

Fig. 21.1. Mosso's Ergograph

Effect of Rest on Muscular Fatigue

Muscular work also reads to the exhaustion of muscles and if the muscles are allowed to rest for sometime, the fatigue is reduced. It may even be completely eliminated. Many experiments have been conducted to observe the effect of rest on muscular fatigue. Many important facts as regards the length and the frequency of the rest period have thus been discovered. For example, in one experiment, the subject was given a six-kilogram weight to lift. Having lifted the weight caused fatigue in muscles. The subject was given a ten-second test after every lifting. As a result, the subject continued to lift the weight at ten-second intervals for an indefinite period. After sometime, in a second experiment, the rest interval was reduced from ten seconds to only two seconds and it was found that within one minute the subject became so tired that he could not lift the weight at all. Besides, he had to rest for two hours to get rid of the fatigue accumulated in that one minute of work. It is, therefore, evident from this that it is not only the rest given which is effective in removing fatigue, the rest interval must be given with the right frequency and it must be in proportion to the time spent in work.

Influence of Mental Factors on Muscular Work

The extent of fatigue and time in which it occurs also depends to a great extent upon mental factors. It has been seen that if the individual takes interest in his work, he can produce more work for longer time and still do not complain of fatigue. Generally, mental fatigue has an adverse effect on muscular activity, although there are many exceptions to this. Sometimes individuals are seen performing muscular work with great skill and application despite mental fatigue. Yet, mental factors do undoubtedly influence muscular work.

Other Factors in Muscular Work

In addition to the above-mentioned factors, many other factors also effectively influence muscular work. For example, it has been observed that women get tired more quickly than men in doing muscular work. Lombard's studies had a very favourable influence upon the introduction of rest as well as practice, food and alcoholic drinks. Harley's studies showed that tobacco has a detrimental effect on muscular work.

Study of Muscular Work by the Hand Dynamometer

All the above examples of muscular study were made by the ergography. But it is also measured and studied by the use of hand dynamometer. In this instrument, the subject fits his finger into the dynamometer and pulls it with his entire strength and then relaxes it. The meter is fixed at 60°. An interval of four seconds is allowed between the two successive acts of pulling the handle. The subject performs this function for one minute and in every case the force exerted by the subject is measured in terms of kilograms. If the subject does not take rest but performs this action continuously he tires rapidly and a diminution in his energy is soon apparent. But if he takes rest at regular intervals then he can continue to do this work for a much longer time since he does not become fatigued so quickly.

Value of the Study of Muscular Work

As has been pointed out earlier, the study of muscular work is valuable from the psychological point of view. It is a matter of common experience that output can be increased if muscular fatigue can be prevented. Therefore, many measures are adopted to reduce muscular fatigue in most factories and offices. Generally, the workers are allowed to have one or two rest intervals during the working hours, and the period of rest varies from half an hour to one hour. Arrangements are also made for refreshments. Efforts are also made to make the work interesting. In some organisations, music is played for the workers while they are working. Then, normally only men are employed to do only muscular work while children and women are allowed to do only light muscular work because they become tired much quicker. Studies are still being conducted to discover ways and means of reducing fatigue. In addition to this, bonuses are offered to improve the motivation of workers. It need hardly be pointed out that the worker's efficiency and skill can be vastly improved by these studies of muscular work.

MENTAL WORK

What is Mental Work?

Mental work involves the use of mental energy. All individuals are not endowed with the same amount of mental energy and therefore, all people cannot be expected to perform the same kind of mental work. One common example of mental work is the work of study. In this kind of work, too, some functions are difficult and hard while others are simple and easy. It is, for example, easier to take notes than to write a book. Hence individuals with varying amounts of mental energy are required to perform these simple and complex tasks. Individual differences in respect of mental energy are seen just as they are present in the case of muscular energy. Besides this, some individuals have exceptional capacity for certain specific kind of tasks and takes but negligible capacity for these. For example, the good teacher is rarely a good writer while the good writer may or may not be a good teacher.

Study of Mental Work

Among the many methods adopted in the study of mental work, the more commonly used are :

1. Letter elimination method. As is evident from the name itself, in this method the subject has to eliminate certain words from the list provided. He is made to sit comfortably and then given a list and a pencil with which to eliminate letters. This work can be done for any fixed period, from half an hour to an hour. The subject is informed of the completion of the work a minute or two before it actually ends. At the end of the test, the subject's personal examination is also recorded. Now the letters cancelled by him, the letters left untouched and the letters cancelled incorrectly are counted and an evaluation of his work is made. From this, one can evaluate the mental efficiency of the subject.

2. By addition or subtraction. In this, the subject is required to do some addition and subtraction and his work and its quality are evaluated on the basis of the right and wrong answers given by him.

WORK CURVE

Work curve, as is evident from the term itself, is that line on a graph which indicates the work done by an individual. Work curves can be prepared both for mental work and muscular work. The work curve of an individual's performance possesses the following three features :

1. Initial spurt. Whenever an individual begins to do some work, he sits down to it fresh and, for that reason, his production progresses rapidly in the initial stages of the work. Hence, the work curve progresses quickly in the beginning.

2. Plateau. This initial spurt, or rapidity is not maintained for a long time because the individual invariably, begins to get exhausted as he continues to work. For this reason, his progress begins to fall and then stops increasing.

3. Final spur near to the end. Whenever the individual learns that his work is coming to an end, he puts in a special effort near the end. This also leads to a rise in the work curve although this spurt lasts for only a short time. In this stage, the individual works enthusiastically although he is exhausted.

The above sketch of the nature of the work curve does not indicate the extent and variety of factors that influence the production. But it does suggest that the work curve declines due to fatigue. Fatigue is delayed if the worker has practice in his work. On the other hand, fatigue also has a detrimental effect on the habits formed by practice. Sometimes, the worker produces as much in a fatigue condition as otherwise but, in that case, the quality of the work is definitely inferior to his normal production. All these factors are known as the factors which influence the production of work.

FACTORS INFLUENCING THE PRODUCTION

The factors influencing the production have been discovered after many experiments. Some of these factors help production and increase it while others hinder and retard it. Basically, these factors can be divided into the personal and environmental categories. Personal factors are again of two kinds — the mental and the physical.

(a) Personal Factors

These are the factors which are inherent in the worker himself. Every kind of work is a consequence of the worker's mental and physical application and it needs the use of mental and physical energy. For that reason, the personal factors influencing production are psychological as well as physical.

1. Psychological factors. This category includes all those factors which are part of the worker's psychology and have some influence upon the work produced by him. The main ones are as follows :

(i) ***Motivation*** : Motivation is the most important factor in production because production increases when motivation increases and falls when motivation is reduced to a lower level. Although motivation alone is not enough, it does influence production under more normal circumstances. It is of even greater importance when the work is difficult and complex. The truth of the matter is that motivation will have great influence upon production when the work is more difficult.

(ii) ***Incitement*** : Many experiments have established that production can be increased by incitement. It is difficult to be skilled in one's work if this is lacking. Its influence is not very apparent in work which is done continuously, but it can be seen that all work is done at intervals. This fact has been reasoned. The workers are given incentives in different professions so that they may produce more.

(iii) ***Interest*** : It is a commonly accepted fact that production increases if there is an interest and decreases if there is none. Interest helps to delay fatigue and also to reduce it. Many experiments have shown that interest is the cause of application and dedication to a task and this increases production.

(iv) ***Reward and punishment*** : The consequences of an individual's work influence his production. If the result is reward, he tends to return to his work with even greater enthusiasm. The reward may be material, as in the case of money, or verbal, as in the case of praise, etc. Different individuals react differently to various kinds of rewards but it has some effect, more or less. But the more effective reward is one which is neither too easily available nor impossible to attain. It also should not be so cheap as to have no real value and neither should it be so valuable that the worker may show greed for it. The effect of reward and punishment can be seen clearly in the case of students. It has a very great importance for games.

(v) ***Coordination*** : In any industry, the production achieved by a worker depends upon his coordination with the work. It has been seen in the experiments of Kraeplin that in the absence of coordinations there is much greater distraction of attention. When the coordination improves the loss of attention is considerably less with the result that he can concentrate on he work and produce more.

(vi) ***Established rapport among the workers*** : If many workers are to work simultaneously to complete some work then rapport must be established between them. Besides, production is also better when the relations between the workers are friendly and cordial. On the other hand, absence of such relations leads to loss of production in terms of quantity as well as quality.

(vii) ***Blocking*** : The effect of blocking of production can be seen in the experiments conducted by Bills. According to him, no person can perform some mental work continuously. In certain cases, the frequency of blocking is as high as four or five times within one minute. Sometimes the period of blocking itself may last for one minute. In the duration of blocking, the worker's mental condition is more or less stunned. Although it is impossible to say why blocking occurs at all, it cannot be denied that it does occur and that the frequency and the actual length of blocking vary from one person to another and even from one kind of task to another in the case of the same person.

2. Physiological factors. The physiological factors which influence the production are those which depend upon the bodily condition of the worker. The main factors are :

(i) ***Health and capacity of physical organs*** : Different bodily organs such as hands, feet, eyes, etc., are employed during different kinds of tasks. If these organs are defective or weak then production is very adversely affected. On the other hand, more production can be done if these physical organs are healthy and strong. Hence the total quantity of work done by a worker depends upon the condition of his bodily organs.

(ii) ***Fasting*** : Fasting also influences production. The experiments conducted by Glaze indicate that fasting for more than one day has a distinct influence upon production although fasting for a day or less may have no apparent effect. Glaze experimented upon three subjects and observed that production went down in each case due to fasting. Later on, the skill was regained when the fasting was stopped.

(iii) ***Sleep*** : Sleep has an important influence upon production because lack of adequate sleep leads to a fall in the quantity and quality of production. Adequate sleep has a beneficial effect on production.

(iv) ***Drug addiction*** : Almost all experiments in this connection have proved that drug addiction is bad. Hollingworth has substantiated this view after conducting an experiment on six subjects.

(v) ***Use of tobacco*** : The experiments conducted upon the effect of tobacco chewing on production have not yielded uniform results. In the case of middle-aged people addicted to smoking, it was found that tobacco has a beneficial effect. On the other hand, if tobacco is taken by people not accustomed to it, their production registers a sudden and sharp fall because tobacco renders their mental and physical condition abnormal.

(b) Environmental Factors

The environmental factors influencing production include all those circumstances and conditions which alter production in any way. The more important ones are as follows :

1. Light. In every kind of industry, some degree of light is necessary. But if the intensity of light is more or less than required, then, the production suffers. The quality of light, in addition to its quantity, also affects production. The best light is the natural light of sun. It not only helps vision but also has a good effect on health but in its absence white light is believed to be the best substitute. In addition to the quantity and quality, the distribution of light available is another effective factor. The light should be so distributed over the working area that it should light up and illuminate the machines and other instruments being used by the workers. But it should not fall directly upon the eyes of any worker because this may dazzle him and lead to accidents. If the light is adequate, it will avoid straining the eyes and in this manner contribute to the skill of the worker.

2. Ventilation. If many people work together in the same premises, it becomes necessary to make provision for the flow of clean air into the place and of stale air out of the place. Besides, in many kinds of work, many harmful gases are generated in production. All kinds of experiments have indicated that proper ventilation has a positive effect on production and the absence of such arrangements leads to the ill-health of the workers and a subsequent fall in production.

3. Temperature. In many offices and factories, it becomes necessary to control the room temperature in the premises in order to maintain the efficiency of the workers because excessive heat or excessive cold have an adverse effect on production. The proper temperature can be determined only by the nature of the work, the local climate, the location of the factory and also by the average health of the workers. But it can be said definitely that it is necessary to maintain proper temperature for good production. For this reason, many laboratories are air-conditioned nowadays.

4. Noise. Some experiments conducted upon the effect that noise has upon the production indicated definitely that when noise rises above a certain pitch, it is definitely harmful. The pitch of the noise that can be tolerated depends upon the habits of the worker, his skill and the nature of work. Many experiments have been conducted in this connection and many means devised to reduce the volume of noise in factories. Many modern laboratories are sound-proofed to external noise so that the workers within are not disturbed.

On this account of factors, only the more prominent personal and environmental factors have been taken into account. In actual fact, it is not possible to list the total number of factors. Besides, psychologists attached to different industries continue to study these factors and make experiments. They help in revealing many new facts.

5. Rest pause. It has been found that adequately timed rest pauses of proper duration have a positive influence upon the production. It is possible to determine by experiment the length and frequency of rest pause which will be adequate for a particular individual. Vernon and Bedford conducted an experiment on 17 young girls in which the girls were given a rest of ten minutes after every hour of work. A 20 per cent increase in production was observed. In another experiment in which seven girls were involved, a 13 per cent increase in production was noticed when they were allowed to rest after every hour. In an experiment by Ermaski, it was seen that when a five-minute interval was introduced after every hour of work and a fifteen minute interval after every hour and quarter of work, 25 per cent improvement in production was noticed. Graff conducted some experiments and concluded that production is increased if a rest of two minutes is given after forty minutes of mental work. On the basis of experiments it was found that a rest pause of 6 to 10 minutes after every two hours of work proves useful and beneficial in the case of middle-aged workers. Some other experiments have shown that if the rest pause is more or less than a particular limit then it will hinder production instead of helping it. If the rest pause is too long, it is harmful because the worker's enthusiasm cools down and it amounts to beginning afresh. Besides, it also leads to boredom and disgust. In an experiment by Amberg, a rest pause of 5 minutes was found useful while a rest pause of 15 minutes proved definitely detrimental. In the same way, different length and varying frequencies of rest pauses can be determined for different persons. The basic fact is that the rest pause should be long enough to eliminate fatigue and make the worker fresh but it should not be so long that it may induce boredom, lethargy and disinterest. It is only natural that different rest intervals will be required for individuals with varying personal interests, capabilities, abilities, etc. Hence it is the worker who himself can tell how much rest he requires and after what interval of time. The basic principle governing the timing of the rest pause is that it should be introduced after the period of maximum production because soon after this, production begins to fall. If rest is provided at this time, this inevitable fall in production can be eliminated.

6. Group situation. Psychologists have conducted many experiments to find out whether production improves while working in a group or if it is better when the individual is working alone. Modi induced a group of youngsters to do muscular work on the hand dynamometer first individually and then in pairs, and came to the conclusion that production was 2 percent more in the group situation than while it was done alone. In his experiments on college students, Whitmore saw that production was 26 per cent more when work was performed in a group situation. The main reason for this increase in production in the group situation is that a definite competitive spirit comes into play while working together. As a result, the individual worker is induced to bring into work his entire energies. But this kind of increase in production is mainly quantitative because in terms of quality, the work generally deteriorates. The reason for this phenomenon is that the worker is constantly interested in the total work done by others and in trying to do better than them, fails to consider the quality of his own work. Although, generally the more skilful individuals retain their quality while working collectively, some individuals are found to perform better while working alone. This fact depends on one side upon the individual nature and working habits of the persons, and on the other side upon the nature of work. For example, mental work in which quality counts, the creation of art or literature is better done alone because in a group situation there is too much distraction of attention. But this fact cannot be said to be true for all writers and artists, because much depends upon the working habits of each individuals. On the other hand, mechanical and physical work in which quantity alone is important, is normally better performed collectively.

QUESTIONS FOR EXERCISE

1. Write a short note on Work Curve.
2. Explain the characteristics of a work curve. Prove that the introduction of the rest pauses enhances the efficiency and output of the work.
3. What is work? Explain muscular work and mental work.
4. State, how rest affects work. Illustrate your answer with examples from everyday life.

22

Performance Appraisal

WHAT IS PERFORMANCE APPRAISAL?

1. Shubin. "Performance appraisal is a systematic appraisal of the employee's personality traits and performance on the job and is designed to determine his contribution and relative worth to the firm."

2. Dale Yoder. "All formal procedures used in working organisations to evaluate personalities and contributions and potentials of group members."

OBJECTIVES OF APPRAISAL

1. To serve as a basis for job change or promotion. By establishing whether the worker can contribute still more in a different or a higher job performance appraisal helps in his suitable promotion and placement.

2. To guide training and development programme. By identifying the strengths and weaknesses of an employee it serves as a guide for formulating a suitable *training and development programme* to improve his quality of performance in his present work.

3. To serve as a feedback to the employee. By letting the employee know how well he is doing or where he stands with his superior performance appraisal tells him what he can do to improve his present performance and go up in the management hierarchy. It thus facilitates self-development and makes the employee aware of his key performance areas.

4. To serve as incentive. Performance appraisal serves as an important incentive to all the employees who are assured of the management's continued interest in them and of their continuous possibility to develop. They realise that they being continuously observed and have not been forgotten.

5. To increase observation. The existence of a regular appraisal system tends to make the supervisors and executives *more observant* of their subordinates as they know that they will be expected to fill out rating forms periodically and would be called upon to justify their estimates. This knowledge results in improved supervision.

6. To provide rational foundation for wages. Performance appraisal provides a rational foundation for the payment of piece-work wages, bonus, etc. It estimates of the relative contributions of employees help to determine the rewards and privileges rationally.

7. To evaluate effectiveness of selection devices. Performance appraisal serves as means for evaluating the effectiveness of devices used for the selection and classification of workers. Its knowledge of the characteristics of superior and inferior workers can be helpful in selection and placement of workers.

8. To help planning. Permanent performance appraisal records of employees help management to do planning such as fixing targets, responsibilities, etc. without relying upon personal knowledge of supervisors who may be shifted.

FACTORS AFFECTING PERFORMANCE APPRAISAL

According to Prof. S.K. Chakraborty,[1] before doing performance appraisal it is always advisable to make a preliminary survey of the following factors within which the employees of an organisation are working :

1. Environmental constraints. There are several environmental constraints outside the control of a worker. It would be unjust to ignore this fact in judging his performance. For example, the quality of raw material in an organisation may deteriorate over a period or the machinery may break down unexpectedly. Hence both productivity and quality may suffer. But the performance appraisal of the worker should not be affected if selection of materials and maintenance of machinery are done at higher levels in the organisation.

2. Style of organisational leadership. The style of the leadership of an organisation to a large extent determines the loyalty and commitment of employees to the goals of an organisation. Effective top leadership orients and motivates the entire organisation for better performance. Employees at every level become highly performance conscious. Under such condition performance appraisal is liked by everybody. It is considered an imposition or stricture in the opposite conditions.

1. S.K. Chakraborty, *Managerial Development and Appraisal.* Macmillan: India (1978).

3. Interdependence of sub-systems. A big organisation is composed of a number of interdependent sub-systems, the success or failure of which must be interpreted in the context of all other sub-systems to which it is related. For example, the sub-standard output of the production department may be due to the poor quality of purchases made by the Purchasing Department. It may be at some higher level sub-system where planning for the production and purchase departments has been done.

Because of this interdependence of sub-systems suggestion is often made to start performance appraisal from the apex. This leads to more systematic and logical cause-and-effect tracing of performance at all levels within the organisation.

4. Organisational structure. Burns and Stalker[2] classify organisational structure into : "organistic" and "mechanistic". Organistic structures have quite flexible organisational structure. Elaborate organisation chart or manuals are usually non-existent. In rapidly changing environments such structures can quickly manoeuvre themselves into vantage position to confront new situations. This makes such structures responsive to innovations of all kinds. On the other hand, mechanistic structures tend to be rigid, with clearly defined relationships and responsibilities. As shown by readily available organisation blueprints and the like a formal awareness of the structural pattern pervades such organisations. By implication, these structures tend to be static and are designed to carry out a nearly fixed strategy in a relatively environment. In a mechanistic structure initiative, drive and imagination do not receive encouragement.

CRITERIA OF PERFORMANCE APPRAISAL

1. Job Analysis

It identifies the components of a particular job which helps in distinguishing one job from the other. In performance appraisal the goal is not to make distinctions among jobs, but rather to make distinction among people, especially among people in the same job. Criterion development is the critical intermediary process. In it the important job components identified in job analysis are transformed into a number of performance criteria which may be used to measure the proficiency of an employee. These criteria

---

2. Burns, T. and Stalker, G.M., *The Management of Innovation.* Tavistock: London, 1961.

may be classified into two main categories : objective criteria and subjective criteria.

(i) ***Objective criteria*** : Amount and quality of production, work sample tests, length of service, amount of training necessary, absenteeism, accidents, etc. are all examples of objective criteria.

Although objective measures of performance are intuitively attractive, they suffer from the following weaknesses :

(a) *Contamination* : These measures sometimes become contaminated by several situational factors, which give a wrong picture of employee's performance. Thus employees who are equal in performance may be rated differently on the basis of difference in their outputs which may be the result of differences in the quality of materials handled, the condition of machines, working conditions, supervisory pressure, experience, age, sex, time at which measurements are made and so on. The difference in the rupee volume of sales of two sales persons may be due to the difference in the sales potential of their territories.

(b) *Neglect of behavioural aspect* : Objective measures sometimes fail to take into account the behavioural aspect of performance, *e.g.*, a worker's ability to get along with his fellows.

(c) *Difficult to specify* : Objective measures are difficult to be specified for higher level jobs which are complex and vague.

The weaknesses of objective measures have led organisations to rely heavily on subjective measures of job performance.

(ii) ***Subjective criteria*** : Rating of employee's job proficiency by their superiors, peers and subordinates, extent of upward communication of ideas, degree of knowledge about corporate goals, contribution to socio-cultural values, etc., are all examples of subjective criteria.

However, since subjective measures are prone to certain kinds of errors associated with the rating process as they are dependent upon human judgement.

TYPES OF PERFORMANCE CRITERIA

1. Performance Criteria for classes of employees in an organisation

(i) Quantity and quality of output in a given period

(ii) Work sample tests

(iii) Length of service

(iv) Amount of training necessary

(v) Ratings by supervisors

(vi) Number of accidents in a given period

(vii) Number of absent in a given period

2. Performance Criteria for Frontline Supervisors

(i) Quantity and quality of output in a given period

(ii) Labour cost per unit of output in a given period

(iii) Material cost per unit of output in a given period

(iv) Total cost per unit of output in a given period

(v) Absenteeism rate for a given period

(vi) Turnover rate for a given period

(vii) Manshifts lost due to stoppage of work in a given period

(viii) Number of accidents in a given period

3. Performance Criteria for Middle-level Managers

(i) Quantity and quality of output in a given period

(ii) Labour cost per unit of output in a given period

(iii) Material cost per unit of output in a given period

(iv) Total cost per unit of output in a given period

(v) Rational use of overhead facilities

(vi) Coordination among supervisors

(vii) Degree of knowledge among supervisors about corporate goals and policies

(viii) Extent to which frontline supervisors regard themselves as managers and behave likewise

(ix) Extent of upward communication of ideas, information and queries from frontline supervisors

4. Performance Criteria for Managers

(i) Return on capital employed

(ii) Labour productivity indices (improvements in labour productivity arise from capital investment, better work methods, better personnel policies, etc., all of which originate at the top echelons of management)

(iii) Capacity utilization

(iv) Gain or loss in market share

(v) Degree of knowledge among middle level managers about corporate goals and policies

(vi) Extent to which middle level managers regard themselves as managers and behave likewise

(vii) Extent of upward communication of ideas, information and queries from middle level managers

(viii) Contribution to the socio-cultural values of the environment (a consideration of this aspect is essential to determine whether the organisation has secured a niche for itself as a worth-while institute in society)

Criterion Development

(i) ***Production*** : For a worker engaged on a production job the number of units produced in a given time would accurately represent his proficiency. To make it directly comparable with the output of other workers amount of output should be adjusted for variation in quality, if any. But if the units of measurement differ for different sub-groups of workers or if production in different sub-groups is done under different conditions, direct comparisons of outputs between workers in the two sub-groups are not possible. Hence each worker's output may be expressed as a percentage of the average for his department or sub-group and then the productivity of workers in different groups can be compared.

(ii) ***Work sample tests*** : When accurate output records of workers cannot be obtained, work sample tests can serve as a measure of proficiency. Here the employee performs exactly the same work as that involved on the job. The typing proficiency tests are the most commonly employed work sample tests.

(iii) ***Length of service*** : In many situations the longer a worker has remained on a job the more successful he is considered. His long stay on the job reflects his ability to adjust to the working conditions, get along with his fellow workers, satisfaction with the job and similar factors.

(iv) ***Amount of training necessary*** : Training time can be used as a measure of worker's proficiency when the training period is expensive to the organisation. The worker needing a longer time to learn is considered inferior to one who learns in a relatively short time.

(v) ***Ratings of supervisors*** : Ratings are quantitative statements of opinion of foremen, managers and others in supervisory authority. Ratings are about such characteristics of a worker as job knowledge, about tools and equipment, coordination and speed of body movements, ability to read drawings correctly, interest in work, attendance, attitude toward suggestions, work place set-up and regard for safety, cooperativeness and so on.

(vi) *Weighing* : A weight must be assigned to each of the component measures of efficiency in the following ways :

(a) *Equal weighing* : Cattell objects to equal weighing thus : 'Ten men and two bottles of beer cannot be added to give the same total as two men and ten bottles of beer. Two men with the same composite score may have very different patterns of scores on the criterion elements. The driver whose number of collisions with vehicles and pedestrians is small may achieve the same composite criterion score as another driver whose number of collisions is big but whose number of traffic violations is small. Since these two patterns of work behaviour are so different in nature it makes no sense to assign them the same composite score which would possibly result if the components were equally weighed.

(b) *Weighing according to the judgement by experts* : Here a satisfactory agreement in their ratings is seldom attainable.

(c) *Weighing according to the reliability of the criterion measures* : Here a given measure may be highly reliable and consequently would be given a high weight though it may be relatively unimportant because it is not highly representative of the job requirements. If the measures available are equally representative of the job, then weighing them in terms of their reliability is a very effective procedure.

(d) *Multiple cutoffs* : A minimum standard is set for each measure of proficiency. A worker who is above the standard on every measure of proficiency is deemed successful, whereas a worker who falls below on any one of the measure is considered unsuccessful. Thus workers are classified into two groups — the successful and unsuccessful. Every single aspect is considered essential. For example, no matter how good an aeroplane pilot is on take-offs, navigation, cross-country flying, etc., if he is poor in making landings he must be considered unsuccessful.

(e) *Net contribution* : The contribution that a worker makes to an organisation in terms of output and the costs that result from his activities through wastage, accidents, errors, etc., can be expressed in rupees. The net contribution in terms of rupees made or lost to the company can be determined. As all measures of performance are expressed in the common terms of rupees they are readily combined.

METHODS OF PERFORMANCE APPRAISAL

1. Ranking method
2. Rating-scale method
3. Check-list method
4. Forced-choice method
5. Field review
6. Critical incident technique
7. Confidential report
8. Essay appraisal
9. Assessment centre

1. Ranking method. To compare one man with all other men and place him in a simple rank order is the oldest and simplest method of performance appraisal. In it ordering is done from best to worst of all individuals comprising the group. Though this method is both simple and natural, it has following disadvantages :

(i) It is highly subjective.

(ii) People are compared as a whole. Comparison of the various components of a person's performance is not done.

(iii) The magnitude of differences in ability between ranks is not equal at different positions. For instance, the difference in ability between the first and second individuals may be much greater in absolute terms than the difference between the second and third. In terms of ranks, however, the differences between these individuals are the same.

(iv) Its use is difficult in large groups as the rater cannot compare several people simultaneously. The paired comparison method of ranking has been evolved as an answer to this problem. In it the rater compares each man with every other man in his group, with the final ranking of each worker determined by the number of times he was judged better than the others. The number of comparisons involved in this method is very large. It can be determined by the following formula :

Number of comparisons = $\frac{N(N-1)}{2}$ where N stands for the number of men to be rated. For a 50-man group, for example, there would be 1,225 separate comparisons which is obviously far too great to permit expedient use of the method.

2. Rating-scale method. Ranking methods are unsuitable where the number of persons to be appraised is large and where it is desired to gain information about the size of absolute differences between the rated individuals. Rating-scale methods may be used in such cases. These methods provide some kind of a scale for measuring absolute differences between individuals. The scales used are generally of two types :

(i) ***Discrete*** : Where two or more categories are provided, representing discrete amounts of ability or degrees of the characteristics, the rater can tick mark the category which he feels best describes the person being rated. The characteristic 'Job Knowledge' may be divided into 4 categories on a discrete scale: 'Exceptionally Good', 'Good', 'Average', and 'Poor'.

(ii) ***Continuous (or graphic)*** : Where an uninterrupted line is provided just above the category notations the rater can tick at any point along its length as shown below :

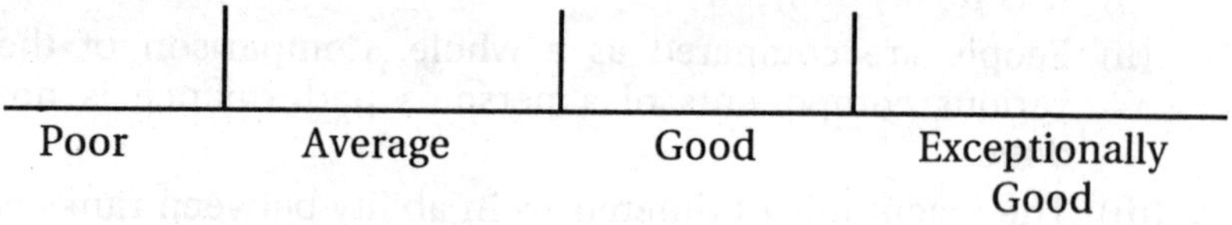

Standards Used in Rating Scales

Four kinds of standards are used in both discrete and continuous types of rating scales :

(i) ***Numerical standards*** : In these a series of numbers is provided. It is supposed to indicate varying amounts of the characteristic being rated. If a person were judged as the best possible workers on a scale ranging from 0 to 10, he would be rated 10. Sometimes 0 is the value assigned to average ability, with a series of positive numbers indicating superior degrees of the characteristic and a series of negative numbers indicating inferior degrees. Sometimes letters are used as standards. In a five-step scale the highest category might be *A* and the lowest *E*.

(ii) ***Descriptive-adjective Standards*** : This is a series of descriptive adjectives such as exceptional, excellent, superior, good, competent, satisfactory, adequate, average, ordinary, fair, weak, poor, etc. These are used to indicate varying amounts of the characteristic being rated.

In both the above types of scales the numbers or alphabets or adjectives used to describe the various categories of a characteristic do not convey the same meaning to all raters.

(iii) *Man to man standards* : These standards are very concrete because there are neither numbers nor alphabets nor descriptive adjectives but persons of varying ability whom the rater has selected and ranked in the ability under consideration. Thus a scale of men is created for each trait. In rating other persons the rater simply looks over this scale and compares them with the persons on the scale. Following are the objections to this scale :

(a) Its construction involves difficult and laborious procedure pre-scaling a group of present employees.

(b) As there is also the very touchy problem of using the names of models without any embarrassment, one must be very careful that the scale is not made public.

(c) The intervals between the men on the scale are often not of equal magnitude.

(iv) *Behaviour-sample standards* : There are a series of actual descriptions of behaviour which is supposed to indicate varying amounts of the characteristic being rated. Its use reduces some of the differences in interpretation usually found among different raters. For example, on a rating scale measuring the trait 'job knowledge', it is highly probable that the agreement among different raters on the descriptions 'unfamiliar with the work', 'works with reasonable accuracy and turns out satisfactory work', 'noticeably better than the ordinary run of men', and 'thoroughly familiar with his work' will be greater than the agreement on the meaning of the adjectives 'poor', 'average', 'good' and 'exceptionally good'.

3. Check-list method. It is a list consisting of a number of statements about the worker and his behaviour. Depending upon its importance each statement on this list is assigned a value. Both statements and their values are derived from preliminary research in which are used the pooled judgements of persons familiar with the job. In rating a person, the rater is asked to place a plus sign, minus sign, or a question mark in front of each statement, depending on whether he feels the description applies, does not apply, or there is doubt, respectively. No restrictions are put on rater about the number of statements he should mark. The worker's final rating is the average of the scale values of all statements that his superior has checked with a plus sign. This method requires only a reporting of facts from the rater. As the values assigned to different statements do not appear on the list, the rater does not know how highly he has rated a given individual. He does not to distinguish among various categories for each of the several traits considered for each of the several employees working under him.

Limitations

(i) It is difficult to construct a good check-list.

(ii) A separate check-list is required for each job because statements used in one check-list to evaluate one category of workers cannot be used in another check-list to evaluate other category of workers.

(iii) As the rater does not know the values given to different statements, he may resent the system as a whole and not give it his whole-hearted support.

4. Forced-choice method. It consists of a number of statements describing an individual being rated. Groups in twos, threes or fours, all groups on the rating form are made of, sometimes favourable statements only, sometimes unfavourable statements only and sometimes both favourable and unfavourable statements. The rater makes two checks in each group one for the statement which best described the individual and one for the statement which is least descriptive.

Advantages

(i) Impartial. This method has built-in safeguards against partiality. The rater does not know which of the statements in a given group has been considered to be critical or relevant for effective job performance and what value it carries.

(ii) Easy rating. The relevance of a statement and its value are determined by extensive preliminary research. Statements which have more discriminative power to distinguish between good and poor workers are given more value. Statements which have no discriminative power are given zero value. A worker's final rating is arrived at by adding together the values of all the statements that have been checked as describing him.

Limitations

(i) Expensive. It is expensive because the statements must be custom-tailored to the demands of the particular job and company.

(ii) Lack of trust. Because the implicit assumption behind it is that the rater cannot be trusted to make impartial evaluation, it is resented by the rater.

5. Field review. Graphic ratings are often combined with a systematic review process if there is reason to suspect rater bias or when some raters appear to be using higher standards than others. In the field review, the personnel officer meets small groups of raters from each supervisory unit and goes over each employee's rating with them to (a) identify areas of inter-rater disagreement, (b) help the group arrive at a consensus, and (c) determine that each rater conceives of the standards similarly.

As supervisors generally resent what they consider the staff interferences, this method is not widely used. It is also very time-consuming.

6. Critical incident technique. In this method one draws up for each job a list of critical job requirements which are vital for success or failure on the job. For example, the following critical factors may be identified in the job of a salesman :

(i) Following up : complaints, requests, orders.
(ii) Planning ahead.
(iii) Communicating true information to managers and customers.
(iv) Carrying out promises.
(v) Persisting on tough accounts.
(vi) Pointing out uses for other company products besides the salesman's own line.
(vii) Using new sales techniques and methods.
(viii) Preventing price-cutting by dealers and customers.
(ix) Knowing customer requirements.
(x) Initiating new selling ideas.

Limitations

(i) It is difficult to identify critical factors.
(ii) It requires the supervisor to jot down incidents regularly.
(iii) It is hardly desirable to confront an employee with a misdeed or mistake which he committed six months or a year ago.

7. Confidential Report. In this method each employee is rated confidentially by one or more senior officers for his performance. Important disadvantages of this method are :

SAMPLE

Confidential Report

Name..................................Division..

Designation and present duties..

Service with the company..............................Years...........Months........

Age..Qualification.......................................

Present scale and salary...

Next increment date..

REPORT ON YEAR'S WORK AND GENERAL OPINION

Describe your estimate of his/her personal qualities and capabilities :

(a) taking particular note on his/her reliability, judgement, adaptability and ability to organise, supervise and co-operate with others.

(b) mentioning any work of an outstanding character carried out by him/her during the year or any failure on his/her part to achieve the standard expected.

Do you consider that he/she is capable of rising to a higher position :

(a) In his/her present sphere.

(b) In another direction, if so, suggest which one.

(c) Whether at an early date after further experience.

(d) What is needed for his/her development.

Date — Manager

Date — Director

Final Review

Date — Committee of Management

Limitations

(i) *Not data-based* : The method is impressionistic. The appraisal is done on the basis of impressions, only minimal data are used.

(ii) *No feedback* : The method does not give feedback to the appraisee on his performance, who never comes to know about his strengths and weaknesses. When one of his junior colleagues supersedes him in promotion, he keeps wondering what he lacks. He loses enthusiasm and motivation.

(iii) ***Closed method*** : A few companies give negative feedback to the appraisal. But these companies do very little to openly discuss the employee why his performance is considered poor.

(iv) ***Evaluation not development*** : The method lays greater stress on evaluating the employee rather than developing him. For getting over his weaknesses the employee never comes to know what opportunities are available to him.

(v) *Loss of credibility*: Personnel department lose its credibility.

8. Essay appraisal. It is very common for appraising individuals for professional positions. In it the rater, who may be the former employer, teacher or associate of the candidate, is requested to give in writing an informed and honest account of the candidate's strengths, weaknesses, potentials, and so on. The biggest drawback of this technique is the account's variability in length and content, due to which it is difficult to compare two essay appraisals.

9. Assessment centre. Many organisations use assessment centres to predict future performance more accurately. An assessment centre is a multiple assessment of several individuals performed simultaneously by a group of trained evaluators using a variety of group and individual exercises. Individuals from different departments are brought together to spend two or three days working on individual or group assignment similar to the ones they will be handling if they are promoted. The pooled judgement of observers leads to an order of merit ranking for each participant.

Advantages

(i) All assessees have an equal opportunity to display their talents.

(ii) All are seen under similar conditions in relevant situations designed to bring out the particular skills and abilities needed for the position or positions for which they are being considered.

(iii) All are evaluated by a team of trained assessors, unbiased by past association, who are intimately familiar with the position requirements and the institutional climate.

(iv) People chosen by this method prove better than those chosen by other methods.

(v) The centre makes it possible for unknown people to compete with people from more well-known departments. This equalises opportunity, improves morale and enlarges the pool of possible promotion candidates.

REQUIREMENTS OF ASSESSMENT CENTRE

(i) Multiple assessment techniques at least one of which must be a simulation.

(ii) Multiple trained assessors.

(ii) Judgements based on pooled information from all assessors.

(iv) Evaluation made at a time separate from the observation of behaviour.

(v) Simulation exercises should first be tested for their reliability, validity and objectivity.

(vi) The dimensions, attributes, characteristics or qualities evaluated by this programme must be determined by an analysis of relevant job behaviour.

From the foregoing analysis of various performance appraisal techniques, it is clear that no single technique can achieve all the goals of performance appraisal. The choice of a technique should always be made in the light of goals. Separate methods may be used for separate purposes.

PERFORMANCE APPRAISAL OF MANAGERS BY MBO

Meaning of MBO

MBO is a popular technique of performance appraisal of managers. The first original work on it can be found in Peter Drucker's book *The Practice of Management,* published in 1954. In 1965 George Odiorne made a major contribution to MBO.

MBO is a process whereby performance goals and objectives are set by each subordinate in collaboration with his superior at the start of the appraisal period. Progress is now tracked and results are evaluated periodically. According to Prof. Reddin "MBO is the establishment of effectiveness areas and effectiveness standards for managerial positions and the periodic conversion of these into measurable time-bound objectives linked vertically and horizontally and with future planning".

Elements of MBO Programme

1. Areas. Each manager identifies his key effectiveness areas where he should show results.

2. Objectives. Each manager establishes his long term as well as short term objectives in such effective areas. The objectives should be:

(i) Qualified and time-bound.

(ii) Horizontally linked up with the objectives of the peers in the department, and vertically aligned with the objectives of the boss and the subordinates.

(iii) Related to and be part of the total organisational plan.

(iv) Established by the job-holder and the boss together. In other words, goal-setting should be participative. Unilateral imposition of goals by the boss is totally alien to the spirit of MBO.

3. Evaluation. Mutually agreed objectives are used for evaluating performance. Periodic review and updating of these objectives is made by the boss and the subordinate together. Data-led objective consideration reveals whether the target was carelessly fixed or whether other reasons are responsible for inadequate performance.

The Elements of MBO in Actual Practice

(i) The document. A document called the 'Management Guide' or 'Management Job Description' is usually prepared to facilitate the administration of MBO programme. It consists of 3 parts. The first part is the Title Page in which there is a concise statement of the purpose of the job, the job-holder's position in the organisation, as well as his responsibilities.

(ii) Key results analysis. This part consists of 4 different columns. The first column names the key result areas of the job. In the second column the agreed objectives or performance standards are mentioned against each identified key result area. In the third column, the job-holder mentions the source and frequency of the control information which he proposes to use in checking his progress against standards. In the fourth column suggestions are made for improving results.

(iii) Job improvement plan. This is a check-list agreed on by the manager and his boss covering the tasks which the manager is going to carry out in the next few months. It is usually drawn up at the performance review, but it can be amended at any time. It is important that each item in this list is given a date by which the manager undertakes to complete the assignment.

Advantages of MBO

1. More effective planning and control. It sparks more effective planning and more effective controls. It forces managers to think of planning for results rather than merely planning activities of work. It also requires the manager to think of the way he may accomplish given results, the organisation and personnel he will need to do it, and the resources and assistance he will require. There is no better incentive for control and no better way to know the standard for control than a set of clear goals.

2. Reveals deficiency. It reveals organisational deficiencies such as overlapping of authority, ineffective delegation and communication, etc.

3. Commitment. It elicits people's commitment for performance.

4. Objectivity. It furnishes objectivity and reduces the element of pure judgement.

5. Positive. It is a more positive technique because in it the emphasis is shifted from the appraisal of an employee's weaknesses to the analysis of his strengths. In this technique, the employee is helped to improve his performance by developing his strengths and by overcoming his weaknesses.

Limitations of MBO

1. Fixing individual goals. It presupposes fixing of individual goals and responsibilities, though all work in an organisation is a group effort where activities are so closely interrelated that no single individual can be blamed or rewarded for any end-result.

2. No comparative ratings. It is difficult to make comparative ratings of individuals because each individual's goals are different from those of others in terms of complexity, etc.

3. No identification of potential. It is difficult to appraise and identify potential as MBO only deals with performance on the present job.

4. Time consuming. The method is extraordinarily time-consuming.

5. Inhibits honesty. MBO presumes a certain level of trust throughout the hierarchy. But the organisational life teaches people to be cautious which inhibits honest dialogue and appropriate goal setting.

6. Narrow applicability. It is especially suitable for managerial, professional and sales people in whose case performance is variable and it is possible to set flexible goals. MBO is less applicable to routine worker-level jobs, such as an assembly line, where performance levels are relatively fixed.

LIMITATIONS OF APPRAISAL METHODS

1. Emphasis on human performance without regard for human values. George S. Odiorne has denounced all appraisal methods for their single inherent weakness that they lay emphasis on alikeness and conformity if human performance ignoring measurement of human values. All appraisal methods, are like quality control systems which force subordinates to conform to certain standards of physical performance without caring for human values. Thus, the appraisal methods rank both the benevolent and despotic managers equal if they are found equal in their physical achievements, though their value systems are widely different.

2. Halo effect. The superior allows his good impressions of one or two important work characteristics of an individual to carry over the total evaluation. He rates all the characteristics of a person much higher than they should be. For example, if he is very fond of punctuality, a punctual worker may get a high rating on practically every factor though many factors have little to do with punctuality.

3. Hypercritical or "Horns" effect. A superior rates people lower than their performances justify. Following are some examples of this effect :

(i) The superior is a perfectionist. As his expectation level is very high, he is more often disappointed and rates his people lower than he should.

(ii) The maverick or the non-conformist gets a low rating simply because he is "different".

(iii) One who has failed may wipe out the effect of years of good work on his appraisal and be rated low on his recent behaviour.

(iv) One who is too meek, too passive or who lacks some trait we attach to good men may suffer in his rating.

(v) One who does not do the job as well as we remember we did it when we held that job may suffer more than those who do work unfamiliar to us.

4. Central tendency and leniency. The superior is guilty of awarding average or more than average ratings to all his workers, on the ground that it will not injure the rate and that it will not expose his lack of more definitive information. Leniency reflects a desire to err on the generous side to avoid controversy by giving each rate the benefit of the doubt. To meet this situation the 'forced distribution system' is used where the rater is instructed about the percentages of cases which should fall in each category on the rating scale. For example, on a scale of 'job knowledge' the following percentages might be used :

Poor 10%, Below average 20%, Average 40%, Above average 20% and Exceptionally good 10%.

5. Reluctance to "play God". Managers are unwilling to "play God" by judging others as accepting the responsibility for being a judge for the future of another person causes severe anxiety in them. The tendency to complete the appraisal form at the last moment when they are due and to treat the entire process casually is necessary to relieve the anxiety of the evaluator in the role of "judge". The aggrieved employee is invariably left with the feeling that the superior is arbitrary in his judgement. This is a very frustrating experience for an honest and impartial superior.

6. Defensiveness of employees. The appraisal process frequently creates defensiveness among employees as the supervisor's appraisal influences the employee's most vital job concerns — promotions, transfers and dismissal — During an appraisal interview the employee's defensiveness often 'makes the procedure unproductive for both the supervisor and the subordinate.

OVERCOMING OBSTACLES TO EFFECTIVE APPRAISAL

Companies generally take a two-pronged approach to overcome the obstacles to effective appraisal : they try to design the kind of system that will counteract tendencies to human errors and biases, and they train managers in the correct use of appraisal procedures. A training programme for managers generally covers :

1. The nature of the halo effect and of central tendency errors, and how to guard against them.

2. The desirability of placing emphasis on observable behaviour, where possible, as opposed to emphasis on personal traits of the rates.

POST-APPRAISAL INTERVIEW

According to Normal Maier, there are three types of appraisal interview 'Tell and Sell', Tell and Listen', and 'Problem Solving'.

1. "Tell and Sell". In this type of interview the interviewer is cast in the role of a judge who comes with the diagnosis and the remedy. But the subordinate who is being judged tries to conceal his weaknesses and if he feels the criticism is severe or the praise faint, he either protests or gives defensive responses. Its objectives are (i) to let the employee know how he is doing, (ii) to gain the employe's acceptance of the evaluation, and finally (iii) to get the employee to follow the plan that is outlined for his improvement.

The skills required for success in this type of interview include the ability to persuade the person to change in the prescribed manner. This may require the development of new needs in the person, as well as a knowledge of how to make use of the kinds of incentives that motivate each particular individual. This type has its greatest potential with young and new employees who are inexperienced and insecure and want the advice and assurance of an authority figure. The superior is respected not only because of position but also because his knowledge and experience are greater than theirs.

2. "Tell and Listen". Its objective is not only to communicate the evaluation to the employee but also to drain off his feelings aroused by the evaluation. Dividing the interview into two parts, the superior covers the strong part of the interview and avoids interruption and controversy by postponing any points of disagreement for later consideration. The second part of the interview is devoted to exploring the subordinate's feelings about the evaluation.

Initially, the reactions to the Tell and Listen method differ radically from Tell and Sell method with respect to the way disagreement and resistance are handled. Instead of the interviewer dominating the discussion to clarify his views, he always listens to disagreements. Actually he sits back and encourages the employee not only to disagree with the evaluation but also to relate his feelings. Thus during the second part of the interview the interviewer becomes a non-directive counsellor.

The skills of the Tell and Listen approach are (i) careful listening, (ii) making effective use of pauses, and (iii) responding to feelings in order to show that one understands them.

Advantages

(i) It creates a good relationship between superior and subordinate during the interview. The subordinate is likely to leave the interview with a favourable attitude toward the superior.

(ii) It tends to encourage upward communication and make management personnel employee-minded rather than production-minded. Listening and learning about the employee needs and aspirations during the interview the superior transmits his knowledge upward to grow a suitable organisational philosophy.

3. "Problem-solving Interview". Technically known as counselling, the objective of this approach is employee development. Here the appraisal of the subordinate is not directly communicated to him because an awareness of a weakness is not essential to development. The "telling" part of the interview is relevant only if this knowledge is a first step in the development process. If, however, the development of an employee can proceed without going through the step of locating and correcting weaknesses or faults, there is no need to communicate the appraisal to him.

This interview takes the interviewer out of the role of a judge and makes him a helper. He sacrifices his right to determine the direction of improvement of his subordinate. He does not specify the area in which this development should take place because this would constitute diagnosis and judgement. He limits his influence to that of stimulating thinking rather than supplying remedies or solutions. He is willing to consider all ideas on job improvement that the employee brings up. Forgetting his own viewpoint he tries to see the job as the employee sees it asking the employee to review the year's progress and discuss the problems, needs, innovations, satisfactions, and dissatisfactions he has encountered. This provides the employee an opportunity to get the boss's ear.

Steps in Problem-Solving Interview

1. Establishing rapport or prepare a case for communication. It generates the necessary confidence in the subordinate. It assures him of his superior's genuine interest in helping him. The counsellor should *carefully listen* to what the subordinate says and *display warmth and responsiveness* from his behaviour.

2. Exploring information about performance. During this stage the counsellor puts to the subordinate various questions which may elicit elaborate information on the latter's achievements, strengths, failures and shortcomings to make the subordinate himself introspect and define his strengths and weaknesses.

3. Helping define the future goal and internalise the problem. After the counsellor has succeeded in making the subordinate reflect on his strengths and weaknesses he can easily make him realise his problems. There is generally a tendency to attribute one's failures, weaknesses or shortcomings to external reasons.

The counsellor has to help the subordinate to internalinse the problem and its causes and in setting his future goals.

4. Drawing action plan. Both the counsellor and the subordinate jointly consider all possible alternative solutions to the problem. Their pros and cons are weighed. The best alternative is selected. A step-wise action plan is prepared along with a time table. The subordinate is allowed to monitor the plan himself. The plan is reviewed by the two parties at regular intervals.

Requisites of Problem-Solving Interview or Counselling

1. Individual's desire to improve. The individual given counsel should be interested in developing himself while superiors usually hold the view that subordinates do not take sufficient interest in their growth and development, subordinates allege that they do not feel free to participate in the process of review and feedback.

2. Continuous dialogue. Not a one-way process of communicating to the employee what he should or should not do. Counselling is a process of continuous dialogue directed toward better understanding of the situation. It presupposes the existence of a general climate of openness, mutuality and trust.

3. Genuine interest of the superior in his subordinates' development. The counsellor should have empathic attitude towards his subordinates. Counselling should not be considered as a burden or an unpleasant task and to be practised half-heartedly or as a compulsion.

4. Mutual participation. Both the superior and the subordinate should whole-heartedly participate in the goal setting and reviewing of goals and performance. Counselling would be a futile exercise without such collaboration.

5. Focus on work-related behaviour. Counselling should focus only on work-related goals and behaviour. Discussion about personal issues and personality problems should be done only in so far it is helpful in understanding the subordinate's difficulties in performing his organisational role more effectively. The feedback given by the superior should be objective and not just impressionistic.

ESSENTIALS OF A GOOD APPRAISAL SYSTEM

1. Understandable. If the system is too complex or too time consuming, it may be anchored to the ground by its own dead-weight of complicated forms which nobody but the experts understand.

2. Support of all line people who administer it. If the line people think it is too theoretical, too ambitious, too unrealistic, or that it has been foisted on them by ivory-tower staff consultants who have no comprehension of the demands on the time of the line operators, they will resent it. A similar goodwill and understanding must exist between the rater and the rates.

3. Open and participative. Not only should it provide feedback to the employees on their performance it should also involve them in the goal setting process. This helps in planning performance better.

4. Both valid and reliable. The validity of ratings is the degree to which they are truly indicative of the intrinsic merit of employees. The reliability of ratings is the consistency with which the ratings are made, either by different raters, or by one rater at different times. Both validity and reliability result from objective data-base.

5. Built-in-incentive. A reward should follow satisfactory performance.

6. Follow up. The system should have genuine follow-up mechanism to identify employee's growth needs. Otherwise, every employee would view the post-appraisal interview as a mere eyewash or as an exercise by management to force its views on him.

7. Supportive. The system should make the employee feel that he has been treated in a supportive manner.

8. Periodical evaluation. The system should be periodically evaluated to ensure that it is continuing to meet its goals. There is a danger that subjective criteria may become more salient than the objective standards originally established. There is the further danger that the system may become rigid in a tangle of rules and procedures, many of which are no longer useful.

QUESTIONS FOR EXERCISE

1. Define performance appraisal and explain its objects.
2. Describe the factors affecting performance appraisal and explain its criteria.
3. What are the methods of performance Appraisal? Which of these would you recommend for appraising managerial personnel in India?
4. Describe the process of establishing a forced choice system of rating. What are its advantages and disadvantages?

5. Compare any two methods of performance appraisal according to their relative simplicity. Specify the conditions necessary to make effective of a result oriented appraisal system.
6. Explain the meaning, elements, advantages and limitations of performance appraisal of managers by MBO.
7. Describe the Limitations of Appraisal Methods.
8. Explain the types of post-appraisal interview and point out the essentials of a good appraisal system.

23
Fatigue and Boredom

Fatigue can be both mental and physical, but to understand their difference, it is necessary first to understand their nature.

1. Physical fatigue. In physical fatigue, as is evident from the name itself, one finds physical characteristics of fatigue. Physical efficiency and capacity fall down and physical co-ordination becomes difficult. A poisonous fluid known as lactic acid is produced in the muscles and the nervous system, and when this increases beyond a certain level, the entire body becomes lax. If it is confined to any one part of the body, then that particular part becomes tired but when exhaustion increases, it is introduced into the bloodstream and steadily spreads over the entire body. In addition to lactic acid, the body also produces ammonia and carbon dioxide during fatigue. Both these elements are poisonous and by their influence, the energizing elements in the body steadily decrease while the poisonous matter increases. Many psychologists have examined the condition of fatigue, the most valuable work having been done by Miller, Helmholtz and Wundt. Miller confined his study to the state of the nerves in a condition of fatigue. Later on, Helmholtz made a study of the function of the sensory nerves and motor nerves and discovered that, in a condition of fatigue, the experience of anything is conveyed to the brain in greater time while the motor nerves take a longer time to react than under normal conditions. Helmholtz invented the Myograph, an instrument used to measure the contraction of muscles. It was later used in 1858 by Wundt in his experiments. This instrument is now used to measure fatigue.

2. Mental fatigue. Fatigue is not merely physical because it is sometimes manifested even when one has no physical work. This is mental fatigue. Mental fatigue is normally apparent after excessive physical fatigue. The symptoms of mental fatigue are an absence of desire to work, emotional condition, lack of interest and concentration, lack of normal efficiency in work of interest and concentration, desire to rest, etc. At times one's efficiency does not suffer despite some mental fatigue. It is boredom in which one experiences mental fatigue. One important cause of mental fatigue is the absence of motivation and of a proper aptitude. In such a case, an individual loses interest in his work even though he is not physically exhausted. People complain of fatigue despite good working conditions if their attitude is not correct and if there is absence of sufficient motivation.

Difference between Physical and Mental Fatigue

The difference between physical and mental fatigue is evident from the foregoing description of their respective natures. When a person complains that he is fatigued, in fact he is suffering from both mental and physical fatigue. The symptoms of the two conditions are different. Physical fatigue is recognised by the condition of the muscles, chemical changes, nervous fatigue, changes in the blood chemistry and in the mental condition. On the other hand, mental fatigue is diagnosed from the absence of exhaustion yet one is averse to work. The removal of fatigue needs the creation of elements which provide the correct motivation and the correct attitude.

Relation between Physical and Mental Fatigue

Despite the differences between physical and mental fatigue mentioned above, the two should not be taken to be entirely different, for they are intimately related to each other. A person who complains of fatigue is, in fact, suffering both from mental as well as physical fatigue. Sometimes a persons does not notice physical fatigue if a strong motivation is coupled with absence of mental fatigue. In most forms of fatigue, one finds both physical and mental symptoms. According to Watson, mental fatigue is caused by the contraction of the vocal cord. It is also caused by damage to the nerve centres in a condition of physical fatigue. Physical work cannot be done well in a condition of mental fatigue. For this reason, it is better to define fatigue as a psychosomatic or psychophysical condition rather than a physical or mental condition. In fact, it is a physical and psychological condition in which the individual's mental and physical efficiency is reduced. The truth of the matter is that the physical and mental aspects of fatigue can be distinguished only superficially, because in actual fact they are dependent on each other.

Occupational Conditions of Fatigue

In different professions, there are different conditions which lead to fatigue which itself leads to a deterioration in the mental and physical health of the workers and ultimately to a fall in production. Such conditions can be briefly summarised as under :

1. Long hours of work. In some industries, the hours of work are so long that the worker becomes exhausted while, in fact, these longer hours of work do not result in a proportionate increase in production. Many researches have thrown light on this fact. Muscio has mentioned the case of one lady worker who worked six hours instead of the conventional twelve-hour day observed by the other workers and still showed a higher level of production than any other worker. In this factory, the working hours were from 6 to 8 in the morning, 8-30 to 12-30, 1.30 to 5.00 and from 8.30 to 12.30. This particular lady refused to work before breakfast and late at night, explaining that by working for such a long time she could not maintain her efficiency. Over a period of one month it was seen that she worked for 237 hours, despite which she showed more output than the others. It is evident from the research conducted in various countries on the methods of work that production is higher in shorter working weeks than in longer working weeks. In the second world war the working hours were increased in England. In the first week of Dunkirk, the work done each week was 36 hours but after Dunkirk, in all factories connected with war production, the time was increased to 69.5 hours. In the beginning, the production increased by about 10 per cent but later on the production in the factories began to fall and the number of accidents and absenteeism began to increase. In a few months it was noticed that the actual working hours fell to 51 hours although the stated working time was 68.5 hours. Before the change, the number of working hours averaged 53 out of a stipulated 56 hours. And in fact, although the working time was increased, the actual production fell by 12 per cent. After six months, the working hours were again reduced, and it was noticed that production again increased. One explanation of this is that fatigue caused a fall in production when the working hours were increased. It is obvious that long hours of fatigue resulted in ex-haustion. Myers made a study of ladies working in a London factory. Their job was to reverse fuses. When their working hours were reduced from 66 hours to 48.5, the production went up by 15 per cent.

2. Absence of rest periods. If a person works for a longer time continuously then he feels fatigued. If he does not take rest and continues to work, then his fatigue increases even more rapidly because he is working in an exhausted condition. If he is allowed to rest as soon as he begins to feel exhausted, then he returns to his work refreshed and his fatigue does not increase. Hence, it is seen that fatigue is eliminated in all working methods where the workers are allowed to rest for shorter periods during their work. Absence of rest period is an occupational condition that promotes fatigue. Even if some workers steal a few minutes of rest where it is not officially provided for, they do not feel relaxed and rested because during that period their aptitude is not correct. In fact, relaxation of this kind results in greater fatigue. Gilbreth's[1] experiments successfully established that production can be increased by providing periods of rest for the workers instead of keeping them at work continuously.

3. Incorrect temperature. Incorrect room temperature is another occupational condition which results in fatigue because in such cases, the room is either too hot or too cold. In both cases, the mental and physical condition of the worker deteriorates and he soon feels exhausted.

4. Absence of proper ventilation. If a person does not get clean air while he is working, he soon gets tired. In an office or a factory in which the air is polluted, the incidence of fatigue will be far greater than in any other factory where there is adequate ventilation.

5. Improper illumination. Fatigue also increases if the illumination in the working area is not adequate and proper because the eyes begin to feel exhausted and dry if the light is not enough or too bright. Hence, it is desirable that there should be proper arrangements for illumination in factories and offices, proper light coming from the right direction. For example, in reading or writing, it is desirable that the light source should be placed behind and to the left of the worker. If this is not done, then the eyes suffer great strain. In working on a machine, it is desirable that those instruments should be lighted up which are to be seen constantly by the operator. Hence, the light provided should neither be too little nor too much, for in both these conditions, the strain on the eyes leads to fatigue.

---

1. Gilbreth, L.M., *Fatigue Study*, New York (1965), p. 297.

6. Design of the machinery. Certain machines are so designed that they too exhaust and tire the operator working on them. Hence modern psychologists give suggestions even in the construction of machines so that they should be designed to minimise fatigue and increase production. This branch of industrial psychology is called engineering psychology. Today, the aim is to design machinery which involves the least possible amount of movement while maintaining the highest level of production. When the workers become used to operating such machines, their fatigue is reduced and their work improves.

7. Absence of an adequate seat. It is a well known fact that a person feels exhausted much earlier if he has to operate a machine while standing. That is why the absence of an adequate seat is one occupational condition which causes fatigue. Another important feature of the seat is that it should not offer too much comfort because in that case, the operator feels sleepy. On the other hand, it should not be so hard that the operator may feel discomfort. Arrangement for a proper seat can help in reducing fatigue.

8. Excessive noise. Another occupational condition which increases fatigue is the presence of excessive noise at the place of work. An individual can work for a long time in an atmosphere which is peaceful and free of noise. Some degree of noise can be tolerated, for it has no appreciable effect on work but when noise rises above a certain level, it creates fatigue. Now experiments are made to find out if the noise produced by the machinery is of high enough a pitch to induce fatigue. If this happens, then efforts are made to reduce the pitch of the sound produced and so reduce the level of noise. Kornhauser[2] conducted an experiment on four typists who worked in a noisy environment for four days. The psychologist came to the conclusion that the work went down by 3.2 per cent while the incidence of errors went up by 23 per cent. In an experiment conducted by Weston workers engaged in peaceful surroundings than when working in a noisy environment produced better results.

9. Unhealthy conditions. Fatigue is intimately connected with health. If the occupational conditions are such that they do not promote good health then they are conducive to fatigue. Unhealthy conditions include such factors as incorrect room temperature, improper ventilation, excessive noise, etc. In addition to these, certain other occupational conditions like excessive humidity,

---

2. Komhauser, A.W., *The Effect of Noise on Office Output Ind. Psycho.* 2 (1927), pp. 62-72.

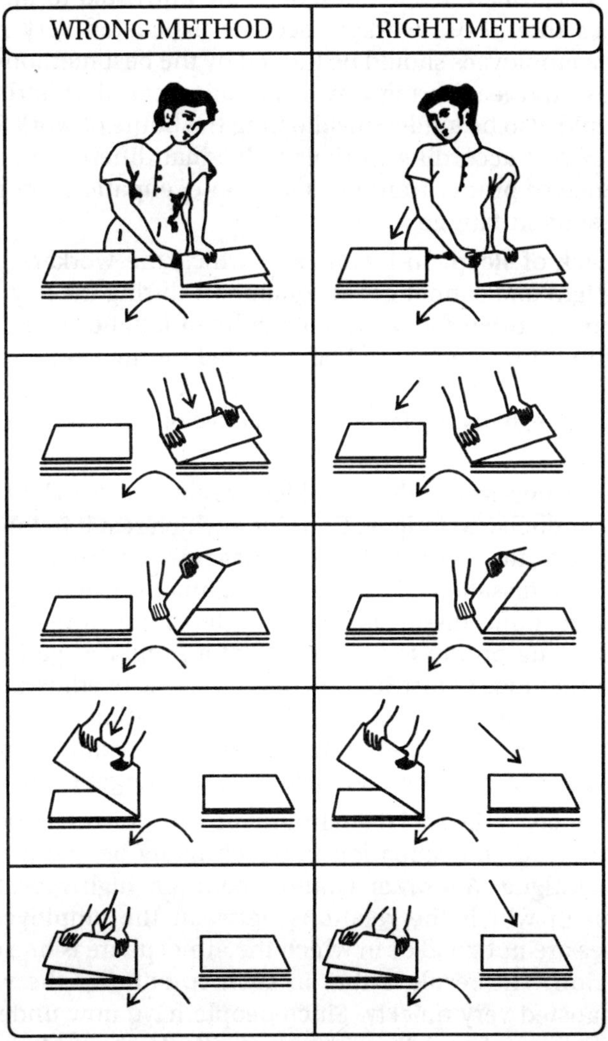

Fig. 23.1. Wrong and Right methods of inspecting the plates from J. Tiffin, *Industrial Psychology*, Prentice Hall, New York, 1952.

absence of rest, presence of some disturbing smell, inadequate arrangements for medicine and medical attendance or the total lack of such facilities also have a bad influence upon the health of the workers with the result that they soon become tired.

10. Absence of proper training. In every profession there are certain functions which require some training before they can be properly performed. If such functions are entrusted to untrained employees then these workers become exhausted very rapidly. Hence the employees should be trained by the best methods about the easiest and least tiring way of handling certain instruments. They should also be guided in adjusting the hours of work and the periods of rest according to their individual differences. Hence, the absence of proper training is also an occupational condition which results in fatigue.

11. Lack of sleep. In factories in which the workers have to work at night and cannot get adequate rest during the day, lack of sleep forms another factor which results in fatigue. To eliminate this, facilities for sleep should be provided for the workers so that they can sleep during their periods of rest. Absence of sleep is invariably an exhausting factor, irrespective of the condition which leads to it.

12. Low morale. Conditions which are conducive to low morale are also conducive to fatigue. Condition which result in low moral are harmful attitudes towards the management, hatred, suspicion and jealousy, dissatisfaction with work and absence of any hope, mental unrest and dissatisfaction, uninteresting work, improper rules governing promotions, absence of a proper wage increase, improper methods of distribution of wages, lack of adjustment; on the part of management, etc. In all such conditions, fatigue also increases rapidly and leads to physical fatigue. Conditions in which high morale can be generated also lead to energetic work.

13. Defects in the social environment. The defects in the social environment of an occupation in which many people work also leads, to fatigue. A worker cannot maintain high morale in a condition in which the relations between the employers and employees are not good or in which the atmosphere is one of hate or suspicion. The result is that in such conditions, the workers feels exhausted very quickly. Since people have now understood the significance of social environment, efforts are made to make the social atmosphere in the place of work, cooperative and refreshing or encouraging. This must be done so that the worker can work for a longer time without feeling exhausted.

In fact, all occupational conditions which have an adverse influence upon the worker's mental and physical condition are conducive to fatigue because in such conditions, mental and physical fatigue is very rapid. Hence all such conditions should be corrected if fatigue is to be avoided. But for this all the workers, the managers and the government will have to work co-operatively.

MEANS FOR REDUCING FATIGUE

Roughly speaking, the chief method of reducing fatigue is to eliminate all occupational conditions which increase it. Hence, mention will here be made of those means by which fatigue can be reduced. It should always be kept in mind that work invariably results in some degree of exhaustion and that there can be no ways of eliminating fatigue completely. One can only hope to devise means by which fatigue can be reduced or controlled before it becomes excessive. Briefly, this can be done in the following ways :

1. Reducing the hours of work. One way of reducing the fatigue is to reduce the hours of work. It has been seen in many experiments that fatigue is reduced when working hours are reduced, whereas the production does not fall proportionately but in many cases actually increases. In 1928, Sheppard pointed out that for the previous thirty years, workers were made to work ten hours a day for six days a week in all American industries. On the other hand, the workers are now made to work eight hours, besides which, on Saturdays they are required to work only for four hours, while Sunday is a day of rest. But actually production has increased as a result of this decrease in the hours of work. Many other experiments have substantiated Sheppard's conclusions. Hence, one way of reducing fatigue is to reduce the hours of work. But at the same time, care should be taken to avoid reducing working hours to such an extent that the worker's energy is not fully utilized. The most appropriate method is to have sufficient working hours in which the worker can continue to work without feeling totally exhausted. Evidently, the working hours will differ from industry to industry, according to the nature of work.

2. Provision of rest periods. Another way of reducing fatigue is to introduce appropriate and properly timed periods of rest. An appropriate period of rest involves calculation of the total rest period allowed in proportion to the work expected from the worker. And a properly timed rest period implies the time at which this rest should be allowed and the frequency with which it should be allowed. After every hour, according to Sheppard, the worker who works for eight hours a day should be allowed to rest for 16.6 per cent of the total working time. It is evident that in providing rest periods, one must consider the total rest period in proportion to the working hours as well as the frequency and duration for which it should be given.

3. Arrangements for maintaining the correct temperature. In order to reduce fatigue, it is necessary to maintain the correct room temperature in the place of work. Arrangements should be made to raise the temperature in winters and to lower it in summers. If the temperature is adequate then the workers can work for longer hours without experiencing the fatigue. For this reason, many modern factories have air-conditioned rooms or other means of reducing the heat during summers while heaters and other contrivances are used to increase the temperature in winter months.

4. Proper ventilation. Fatigue can also be reduced by improving the ventilation so that the polluted air is eliminated and fresh air admitted into the factory. Most factories make use of exhaust fans designed to push out such a polluted air out of a room or a hall.

5. Arrangement for proper lighting. Fatigue can also be reduced to some extent if proper provision is made for lighting up the area in which the workers work. For this, it is necessary that the light should come from the right direction and it should be of a particular intensity. The advantage in this is that the eyes do not suffer strain and hence the workers do not become tired quickly.

6. Improvements in the design of machines. The shape and the size of a machine operated by the worker also influences fatigue. If the machine is so designed that it can run efficiently by making the minimum possible movements the worker will not feel exhausted.

7. Proper seating arrangement. A proper seating arrangement for the worker also helps to reduce fatigue. As far as possible, the workers should be allowed to work while sitting. The seat should provide normal comfort to avoid fatigue but it should not be too comfortable, for in that case it will induce sleep. But it should also not be too hard.

8. Control over noise. Since excessive noise also induces fatigue, it is desirable to have some control over the amount of noise in or near the working place, if fatigue is to be avoided. This can be done in many ways. It is more difficult to reduce the noise made by the machines installed in the factories but efforts should be made to control the noise produced. If the noise in the factory or a office is less, the workers' fatigue will also be less.

9. Healthy working conditions. If the working conditions are conducive to health then fatigue always remains at a low level because the worker's health and his fatigue are directly related to each other. In order to create healthy conditions, it is necessary to pay attention to ventilation, sufficient light, absence of noise, proper room temperature, control over humidity, medical facilities, adequate arrangement for rest and food, etc. All these things help to refresh the worker.

10. Arrangements for industrial or professional training. The worker feels less fatigued in manipulating a machine for which he has been trained because he does not make any unnecessary movements. Hence professional training can also help to reduce the fatigue.

11. Proper arrangements for sleep. In many kinds of work, it is necessary to provide some arrangement for sleep. Even if the worker is given a chance to sleep or comfort for only half an hour out of the total working time, much of his fatigue disappears. Such an arrangement is particularly useful for the workers working in shifts.

12. High morale. High morale can also help to reduce the fatigue among the workers. Maintenance of high morale requires an attitude favourable to the management, self-generated discipline, group administration, enthusiasm, mental satisfaction and peace, respect for and confidence in the management, etc. If these factors are present, the incidence of fatigue is much lower.

13. Proper social atmosphere. Even the social atmosphere plays an important role in reducing the worker's fatigue. The worker's enthusiasm can be easily maintained and fatigue kept at a low level if good relations with the management can be created and if the general atmosphere is one of the co-operation.

14. Special means of reducing fatigue. In addition to the factors explained above, many other means are now being adopted to reduce the worker's fatigue. For example, in many factories, arrangements have been made to play music to the workers while they are engaged in their work because the workers feel less tired if they sing as they work. Many new experiments are being conducted on this aspect these days. Besides, change in the nature of work also helps to keep the workers' interest alive. Efforts are made to make the work interesting in many different ways. As industrial psychology progresses, many new ways of reducing fatigue will definitely be discovered.

CRITERIA OF FATIGUE

The criteria of fatigue implies the symptoms by which its presence can be diagnosed and recognised. In order to understand this it is essential to keep in mind the various aspects of fatigue. Since fatigue is a psychophysical condition its symptoms are both mental and physical. It can be recognised by the following factors :

1. Feeling of exhaustion. The chief symptom of fatigue is the feeling of fatigue even if the individual is not feeling physically exhausted. In a state of exhaustion, the desire to work is noticeably reduced and the desire to rest is clearly heightened. Generally, it also leads to a fall in the individual's production, though this is not universally true. In the state of exhaustion, the individual's feelings about work changes and he evinces no desire to do any kind of work.

2. Muscular condition. In a state of fatigue, the muscles lose their power to contract and expand. Hence, physiologically, fatigue is a muscular condition and the failure of the muscles to contract and expand is one criterion of fatigue.

3. Chemical changes. As a person works, the proportion of acetic acid and other poisonous chemicals in his body increases. In a healthy body, the oxygen is properly distributed through the blood stream with the result that poisonous matter is eliminated from the body. When the muscles become tired, this process of elimination does not work efficiently. This leads to a fall in the quantity of glycogen in the body along with an increase in the quantity of poisonous matter. In this manner, many chemical changes occur in the body during fatigue, and it can be recognised by these chemical changes.

4. Nervous slackness. One criterion of mental exhaustion is nervous slackness. Sometimes it is caused by muscular fatigue but it also has many other causes. In a state of nervous exhaustion, the nerves lose their power to react with the result that the individual cannot work efficiently. Many experiments have established that, in a condition of exhaustion, the nerves and muscles do not have the power to react properly or to achieve the normal state of excitation. As a result of this slackness, the sense organs do not react properly. The sense of smell is particularly influenced while the powers of seeing, hearing and touching are also adversely influenced.

5. Changes in the blood chemistry. Some symptoms of exhaustion can also be found in the tired person's blood. If some of this blood is introduced into the blood of some healthy person, one will find the symptoms there too. The same is true for muscles too. On one hand, the blood stream helps to eliminate poisonous matter from the body, but on the other hand, it also helps to distribute the fatigue all over the body. For this reason, the whole body shows symptoms of exhaustion even when only one part of the body is bearing all the strain. If any one part of the body is put to excessive use then that part shows signs of fatigue early but soon these symptoms can be seen all over the body because exhaustion is communicated by the blood.

6. Changes in the mental condition. One criterion of fatigue is the change in the mental conditions because in an exhausted condition, the individual experiences deterioration of his mental powers and a loss of interest. He cannot concentrate upon anything for a long time and becomes bored with work. Because of this influence upon the mind, fatigue is considered a psychophysical phenomenon.

7. Increase in the number of accidents. An analysis of accidents in industry has revealed that majority of accidents occur either in the morning or late in the evening. This fact has been generally substantiated by studies in Germany, England and America. A study of fatigue has also shown that it is greatest early in the morning and late in the evening. Hence one can estimate the extent of industrial fatigue from the number of accidents. For this reason now provisions are made for introducing rest periods in the early hours and in the late evenings. This pattern of accidents can be seen in almost any industry. While the morning accidents are uniformly present, the late evening accidents follow various patterns in different industries. Accidents in the late evening take place more rapidly but the total number is not much more than that of the accidents in the morning. One can see a difference in the number of accidents that take place during the morning and the night shifts. Hence, the relationship between fatigue and accidents is obvious.

It should be kept in mind that despite the clear relationship between fatigue and accidents, fatigue is not the sole cause of accidents and for this reason an increase in accidents is not a criterion of increasing the fatigue. Many other factors apart from fatigue often prove far more important in causing the accidents.

For example, women are more accident prone than men because women tend to tire easily and more rapidly. It cannot be denied that in a state of exhaustion, the individual becomes restless, he cannot control his movements properly, he may even go to sleep, he lacks concentration. Despite this, fatigue cannot be accepted as the sole cause of accidents.

8. Fall in production. Sometimes fatigue is defined in terms of the fall in production. As has already been mentioned in connection with accidents, the early morning shift and the late evening shift result in accidents and also in a fall in production. The cause of this fall in production is believed to be fatigue. During the first hour in the morning, the production rate rises steeply because this is the warming up period. This warming up can be due to numerous mental and physical causes. And the period consumed in warming is up to the individual differences between one worker and another. Two factors which are responsible for the rate of worker's output are health and the nature of the conditions under which he has to work. It is normally seen that production reaches its highest peak in the third hour, after which production again begins to fall due to fatigue. It is for this reason that a rest period is provided after the third quarter of the day. The phenomenon of warming up is not seen at all for the work starts at a high speed. But this rate of work declines steadily till it reaches the lowest level of production in the last hour of the day. Apart from fatigue, many other factors may also account for this. Sometimes the workers begin to put away their tools quite just before the closing hour, which is one reason why the production during the last hour is much lower. It is evident from the above explanation that the fall in production after the first two hours and again in the afternoon can be accepted as a criterion of fatigue.

In addition to the above factors, all other symptoms of physical and mental fatigue can be accepted as the criteria of fatigue. Fatigue can be recognised by such mental and physical conditions as changes in the respiration, blood circulation, blood pressure, disinterest, lack of concentration, slackness, etc. Nowadays many scientific instruments are employed to measure the fatigue.

DIFFERENT ASPECTS OF FATIGUE

In order to fully understand the nature of fatigue, it is important to consider its objective, physical and mental aspects :

1. Objective aspect. In its objective aspect, fatigue can be defined as a fall in the efficiency to perform some function. This occurs when some work has been done for a long time. Fatigue does not occur if the worker interupts his working periods with short rest periods. In the laboratory, the decline in the ability to work is measured by the ergograph while the decline in the mental ability to work is measured by the word elimination method. Fall in efficiency is evinced not only through the fall in production but also through the deterioration in the quality of the work because the worker begins to make more mistakes when he is exhausted.

2. Physical aspect. The physiological aspect of fatigue is concerned with its influence upon the body. Many experiments in this connection have revealed that in a state of fatigue, the poisonous substances in the body increase in quantity while the energizing elements fall in number. From the physiological point of view, in a condition of fatigue, one can observe an increase in the rate of respiration, blood circulation, blood pressure, etc. Many other chemical changes also occur within the body.

3. Mental aspect. The mental symptoms of fatigue are exhaustion, lack of desire to work, emotional instability, lack of concentration, slackness, etc. All of these are expressed through lack of interest in work and a desire to rest.

A complete definition of fatigue cannot be produced by placing stress on any one of the above aspects of fatigue. The objective aspect is not the best method of recognising fatigue because fairly often people do not show any deterioration in the performance of work despite some mental fatigue. Despite fatigue the production does not fall nor do the number of mistakes go up. Poffenberger conducted an experiment on twelve college students. In this experiment, the students were required to make sentences, and the scientist showed that over a period of five and a half hours, the ability to make sentences did not deteriorate despite increasing the fatigue. On the other hand, Robers' subjects showed a decline in the quality of work despite an absence of any feeling of fatigue. Hence, the objective definition of fatigue is incomplete.

Separate explanations of the mental and physical symptoms of fatigue may lead one to the conclusion that they are completely disconnected, but this is not true. Hence it is incorrect to believe that fatigue can be exclusively mental or exclusively physical. Fatigue of all kinds is manifested by physical as well as mental symptoms, a fact which has been established by experiments. Watson has proved that the contraction of the vocal muscles leads to mental fatigue. In the same way, any damage to the nerve cells in the higher parts of the brain leads to mental fatigue. It is a matter of common experience that one cannot efficiently perform physical work in a condition of mental fatigue, or mental work in a state of physical exhaustion.

Briefly stated, fatigue can be defined as a psychophysical condition in which the individual's mental and physical ability to work deteriorates. It is apparent from this definition that the mental and physical symptoms or aspects of fatigue are verbally differentiated only for convenience because in actual fact they are not independent of each other. And while on the subject of ways and means of removing fatigue, it is necessary to remember that only unnecessary fatigue can be eliminated by these means. There is some necessary fatigue which accompanies every kind of work, and this cannot be eliminated completely. To put it differently, it is not possible to create conditions in which fatigue can be eliminated completely. It is, on the other hand, possible to reduce it.

MEASUREMENT OF FATIGUE

As far as the measurement of fatigue is concerned, it is essential to remember that the measurement can be definite only if all the other factors and their influence are shown. For example, fall in the production curve is an incontrovertible proof of exhaustion because it can also be caused by changes in aptitude, excitement or interest, etc. At present, we have no means of knowing whether fatigue is the cause of the fall in production or whether it is caused by any of these other factors. For this reason, the psychologist Muscio believed that the measurement of fatigue is unscientific. Dhers said. "Fatigue can neither be scientifically isolated nor measured." Despite this, fatigue has been measured with varying degrees of accuracy, and most of the methods employed have proved of some practical value. Mosso, Greff, Kraeplin and other psychologists have discovered some valuable scientific facts by the measurement of fatigue. Hence, it would be in keeping with the context to give a brief account of the methods of measuring fatigue. Generally, the methods of measuring fatigue are divided into three parts according to the three aspects of fatigue. They are objective methods, physical methods and mental methods :

1. Objective methods. These include mainly those methods which measure variation in the quality and quantity of production. Such tests as word elimination method may be included in this category. But it should be kept in mind that these tests do not determine whether fatigue is present or not because the fall in production may even be caused by such other factors as opposite motivation, lack of enthusiasm or excitement. On the other hand, the normal level of production may be maintained through habit, despite the presence of fatigue.

2. Physical methods. These include the methods which measure the physical symptoms of fatigue. Methods involving the chemical analysis of urine and saliva, the measurement of pulse, heart-beat and blood pressure are included in this category. The ergograph, hand dynamometer and Martin's spring balance can also be included in this group. But the symptoms measured by them may have some source other than fatigue.

3. Mental methods. This group includes the methods which measure the mental symptoms of exhaustion. Such symptoms are the deterioration in attention, memory, imagination, mental decision, emotional analysis and power of reasoning. As in all the other methods, these methods too cannot determine the true source of the change, because it may be caused by something other than fatigue.

Fig. 23.2. Instrument for Measuring Value of the Work in Terms of Fatigue

It is evident from the above brief account of the methods of measuring fatigue that the results arrived at may not be valid. Even eminent scientists have their doubts about the validity of such experiments. But it cannot be denied that these methods have helped in practical situations and it is possible that the future may bring more accurate methods of determining the fatigue.

ERGOGRAPHIC STUDIES

The ergograph is used in the measurement of fatigue. The instrument was invented by Angelo Mosso, a famous Italian psychologist. With the help of ergograph, he studied the relation between fatigue and the functioning of any particular part of the body. He studied the working of a particular part of the body. He studied the working of a particular muscle and induced fatigue in it. In this manner he eliminated the influence of such complex psychological phenomena as boredom and monotony, and studied fatigue in its more simple manifestation.

Ergograph is a simple instrument in which the hand is placed on a frame in such a way that it is not exerted or pressed in any way, but it cannot move. All the fingers except the middle one are tied in such a way that they cannot be used. Then a string with some weight on the other end of it is tied to the middle finger. This weight is lifted by the middle finger. In the ergograph, this string passes over a pulley and has a weight attached to it. In the more modern adaptation of this instrument, arrangement is made to expand and contract the finger without lifting the weight. The finger is made to perform various functions according to the pattern determined by Metronome, and then these movements are studied. The most important thing to be noted is the frequency of contraction and expansion of the muscles. For this reason, only this contraction and expansion are controlled. The graph of the fatigue is prepared by a moving string attached to a needle which moves on a revolving drum and draws straight lines. The frequency of contraction and expansion in the muscle is shown by the irregularity in these lines drawn by the needle.

Conclusions Reached through Ergographic Studies

Ergographic studies provided many results which have proved useful for application in industries. Mosso reached the following nine conclusions about fatigue on the basis of ergographic studies :

1. If the frequency of muscular contraction, in lifting any weight, is once every two seconds, then the rate of contraction gradually falls, till at the end there is no contraction. With a weight of six kilos, this state is reached in approximately one minute. If the weight is then reduced,

the contraction of the muscle can be started again but even then fatigue will be induced soon.

2. If the muscular contraction is induced after a long time period, such as ten seconds, for the same weight, then there is no external manifestation of exhaustion. In such conditions even the weight of six kilograms can be lifted for an infinite number of times.
3. If work done is measured in terms of quantity of weight, then the work done for smaller weights is definitely much more than for heavier weights. Hence, a weight of three kilograms can be lifted more than twice the number of times than that a weight of six kilograms can be raised.
4. If the given weight is raised rapidly a number of times, then the fatigue induced is greater than in lifting it once. But if the weight is lifted slowly, then fatigue is less.
5. Time taken to regain energy increases with an increase in the intervals between periods of work. For example, if the time required to regain energy for sixty contractions is two hours, then the time required to regain energy for 30 contractions may even be 30 minutes. When a situation is reached that the finger cannot be moved at all, then the fatigue which has been induced by the attempts to lift weight cannot be easily eliminated. It requires a very great time to regain energy, and this cannot be done by providing the normal intervals of rest. Putting it another way, as fatigue accumulates the effect of fatigue in contracting the muscle also increases rapidly and cannot be overcome easily.
6. If other muscles of the body also function at the same time as the finger, then the finger loses its ability to lift weight to some extent. If the individual has performed some strenuous exercise before the ergograph experiments, than the state of total inactivity is arrived at much sooner than under normal circumstances. In this way, the ergograph exercises indicate that fatigue is communicated to those parts of body, through the blood stream, which are not being used at that time.
7. Such factors as lack of sleep, mental causes, hunger and the shortage of blood in the muscle reduce the efficiency of the muscle. In fact, any factor which is an obstacle to

nourishment or tends to reduce it, will also tend to increase the fatigue.

8. The efficiency of the muscle can be increased by massaging it, by increasing the quantity of sugar in the blood, by giving nourishment to the body and by improving the general health.
9. Different people get exhausted at different rates but the principles governing fatigue which have been mentioned above hold true despite all individual differences.

Industrial Applications of Ergographic Studies

Psychologists applied the findings of the ergographic studies to industrial situations, although some objected that this should not be done because the conditions prevailing in an industry and in the psychological laboratory differ to a very great extent. Besides, in ergographic studies, only the finger is made to work, while in a factory the worker has to exert his entire body. For this reason, the laws governing fatigue in the two cases may not be the same. But these objections against the conclusions obtained through ergographic studies were not found to be valid because the conditions in the psychological laboratory and in an industry have some common features, although there are many differences. The application of these conclusions to industry has provided many beneficial results. Despite this, it should be kept in mind that ergographic studies that have been conducted in the laboratory and the results obtained should not be applied exactly as they are without testing their validity in the industrial situation, because in a factory the worker has to exert his whole body, not only his finger. Besides, the production of some workers may suffer or change not only because of the work done or the number of hours of work but also as result of his attitudes and motives. If the worker wants an interval in his work, it is not only because he wants rest but also because he may wish to have a chat with his colleagues over a cup of coffee. Sometimes workers ask for an interval soon after arriving in the factory, or soon after the lunch interval. It also happens that some workers utilise the lunch interval to do some personal work and then use the rest interval to take lunch, in which case the purpose of the rest interval is defeated.

One difficulty in applying the results of ergographic studies to industry is created by the attitudes of the industrial trade unions. It has been seen that once the working hours are reduced and the rest periods increased, the workers do not easily agree to an increase in working hours and a reduction in the rest periods. Many industrial organisations are not prepared to increase the rest intervals for the simple reason that despite all such increase, the workers always demand for a further reduction in the working time and an extension of the rest hours. If some company reduces the working hours from nine to eight, the workers immediately demand that they should be reduced to seven. Even if the company accedes this, the workers do not stop but go further and demand that the working hours should be further reduced to six. For this reason, an industrialist prefers to control the workers from the very beginning. In addition to this, it is a generally known fact that, according to their individual qualities, each worker becomes tired after different time and he requires a different time to recoup his energies. Hence, it is apparently unscientific to give the same time of rest to each worker and also to provide it at the same fixed time. On the other hand, if differing periods of rest are given to the workers according to their individual differences, then the workers immediately voice protest against the apparent injustice and inequality in treatment. No trade union is prepared to accept the fact that the worker doing the same work and obtaining the same wages should be allowed to have varying amounts of working time and rest time. All these factors greatly hinder the application of ergographic conclusions in industries, but this does not imply that it is impossible to be benefited by their application. At many places, the workers and the management have co-operated with each other and thus introduced many reforms in the conditions of work and rest.

Now, we must turn our attention to the extent to which ergographic conclusions can be applied to the industries.

One general fact which can be derived from the first five conclusions of the ergographic studies is that more work can be done if the limited energy of the muscle is consumed slowly, rather than rapidly. In fact, the principle governing the expenditure of muscular energy can be applied to the use of energy in any form. If, for example, a car is run at high speed, it consumes more fuel than when it is runs at low speed. Hence, if one wants to travel the greatest possible distance by using the least possible fuel, then one must run the car at a low and steady speed. Another example of this kind is the long distance runner, because such an athlete must learn to control his energy. If he runs fast in the earlier stages of the race, then he consumes most of his energy very early and fails to complete the race. The long distance runner must begin the race at low speed, increasing it gradually, till he attains the highest speed near the end of the race. He can run fastest near the end of the race because he then loses nothing by becoming exhausted at this stage. But, if he becomes fatigued in the beginning, he cannot hope to complete the race, let alone to win it. Here one must keep it in mind that the general tendency is against such a careful utilization of one's energy. Generally, a person likes to work quickly when he is fresh, without realizing that although he is working faster, he is, in, fact wasting a good amount of energy. If a person has to complete some big project, he must learn how to husband his strength and to expend his energy gradually because if he finishes his stock of energy in finishing half the work, he will never be able to complete it. Another difficulty in keeping one's work at a steady pace is the human tendency to retire for rest only when one has become tired and restless, although actually the period of rest should come much earlier. As has been pointed out earlier, a person can do much more work by interspersing the working hours with short periods of rest in which he can recoup his energies. This happens because once a man is completely exhausted, he needs much more time to regain his energy. For this reason it is believed that the worker should be allowed a shorter period of rest after some period of work, if one is to put the worker's energy to the best use.

Muscio has proved the validity of the above ergographic principle by giving another example of its application to industrial conditions. In this experiment, one individual was made to lift six kilograms of weight three times on the ergograph under different conditions. In the first condition, he was made to contract his muscles every two seconds till he could not lift the weight at all. Then, he was allowed to rest till he could regain all his energy. In working by this method, the individual contracted his muscle thirty times and then rested for two hours. In this way he could sit for the experiment four times in an eight-hour period and in each session he contracted his muscles thirty times, a total of 120 times in the entire period.

In the second condition, the individual was allowed to rest for half an hour after every fifteen muscular convulsions. The result was that he could put in 16 sessions of muscular exercise, in each of which he lifted the weight 15 times. Consequently, he convulsed his muscles a total of 240 times. It is, therefore, evident that the individual doubled the quantity of his work because he was given rest at more frequent intervals.

In the third condition, the individual was allowed a rest of ten seconds before each muscular exertion. This speed of working was so slow that he did not experience fatigue at all. He took two seconds to convulse his muscle and ten seconds to rest it, with the result that he performed one unit of work in twelve seconds. Consequently, he could contract his muscles three hundred times in one hour and twenty-four hundred times in eight hours. The quantity of work thus achieved was twenty times the work done in the first condition.

By comparing the first and second conditions of work, we come to the conclusion that in the first condition, the individual took half an hour to regain the energy he had spent in contracting his muscles fifteen times, an average of two minutes to each muscular contraction. But, it took 90 minutes to regain the energy spent in the other fifteen contractions, an average of six minutes for each contraction. Under the third condition, it only took ten seconds to regain the energy spent in each contraction. It is evident from this that more time is taken to regain energy after work if the periods of rest are far apart. And, the most expensive movement is that in which the individual tries to lift some weight when he is almost completely exhausted.

An experiment of this kind cannot be applied to industrial conditions in precisely the same way because in this experiment only some particular muscles were called into play and were used till they were completely exhausted. In an industrial situation, neither of these two conditions holds good because, neither is it necessary to use any one particular muscle nor it is used to such an extent that it becomes completely exhausted. Despite this, the experiment provides a guideline that the intervals of rest should be distributed in such a manner among the working hours that the energy spent can be regained as rapidly as possible. And if the intervals of rest can be increased and they do lead to even a 15 per cent increase in production, the change should be considered significant. As is evident from the other ergographic principles explained earlier, if the intervals of rest are distributed between small units of work, it is possible to work for longer periods without becoming exhausted. This fact has also been substantiated by the experiments of Gilbreth. He made a study of time and motion, and concluded that fatigue can be reduced by reducing the load, increasing the intervals of rest and balancing the movement in the work. But it depends upon the nature of the work as to which load should be reduced, where the interval of rest should be increased and which movement should be controlled. Concerning the use of a spade, the experiments of F.W. Taylor revealed that more work can be done by using of the spade will depend upon the nature of the work and the individual using it. A larger spade is needed to lift a light weight and a smaller spade to lift a heavier weight. Yet, it is possible to decide the size of the implements to be used by workers in some particular industry. Large spades induce fatigue, while smaller spades do not. But less weight can be transported by a smaller spade, and if the weight transported is less than the weight of the spade itself, then the amount of work done declines sharply. And since the quantity of work done is measured by the total weight carried by the spade, not by the weight of the spade itself, it is perfectly possible to have a spade so small that the work done by it is negligible. Still, between the extreme limits of a very big and a very small spade, it is possible to decide upon some practicable size of spade which can be used efficiently in some particular industry. By making experiments of this kind, it is possible to decide the best possible size and weight of the tools used by different artisans.

Certain functions can be performed by two people working together, and in all such work it is seen that the result of the combined effort is always better than the sum total of the work done by each individual separately. Whenever it is impossible to reduce the load to be lifted or to allow them to work together, efforts should be made to reduce their fatigue by giving them more periods of rest. In certain industries, instead of lifting heavy loads, the workers have to make some movements rapidly. In such industries, the speed of movement should be regulated or the work should be divided into small units so that intervals of rest can be given between each unit of work. Although it is difficult to determine the speed of work in any kind of performance, it can generally be said that the speed of work should be slow in the first half hour of work, normal in the later hour and the fastest near the end. Maintaining slow speed in the beginning is necessary because it gives the worker time to warm up, after which the speed of work can be increased to the normal level. This normal level should be maintained. The purpose behind increasing the working speed near to the end is to finish the work which has been leftover and thus avoid the adverse effects of fatigue on production. Certain people begin the day by working as hard as they can with the result that their speed falls as time passes. This method is supported by the argument that the worker tries to achieve as much as he can while he feels fresh. But, in fact, the worker tires very rapidly if he begins working fast too early in the day, and then he continues to work in a state of exhaustion with the result that the working speed declines steadily. This always results in lower production.

Fatigue covers the entire body. Among all the conclusions drawn from the ergographic studies, the sixth is that fatigue is general although only one part of the body is employed. Fatigue is communicated from one part of the body to all the body by the blood stream. It is evident from this that fatigue can be eliminated by giving rest to the whole body, not only to one part. Hence, it is not enough only to stop work, if one wants to rest. The worker must get complete rest during his interval for rest. Arrangements should be made to provide comfortable beds and easy chairs for the workers' use during the lunch and rest intervals. It is essential to have proper arrangements for drinking water. Briefly, fatigue cannot be eliminated merely by stopping work. Arrangement for complete rest should be made.

Importance of Health and Nourishment

The seventh and eighth conclusions drawn from the ergographic studies of work fatigue indicate the value and importance of bodily health and proper nourishment for reducing fatigue and increasing output. Hence it is desirable that the conditions even outside the factory should be such that they promote healthy living and proper nourishment. In this connection, H. Gartner, a German scientist, has suggested that attention should also be paid to the distance a worker has to travel from his house to the place of work. If this distance is so great that the worker becomes exhausted in travelling, then the quality and quantity of his production will be below normal because he will be working for the entire day in a condition of exhaustion. It has been suggested that the residential districts of the workers should be within the vicinity of the working place. Nowadays there is a great demand that factories should be located outside the city to avoid pollution of air. It therefore becomes even more necessary to pay attention to the aspect of distance from home to factory. Visualizing the problem one can see that the worker should be provided a house near the factory, and in addition arrangements should be made for the schooling of his children and for purchases which he requires from day to day. The importance of this factor has been realized by many industrialists, and consequently they recruit only such people who live within a reasonable distance from the factory. In Gartner's opinion, the worker should live at such a distance from his place of work that he can reach it within thirty minutes.

Arrangements for the worker's rest should be made within the factory so that his health can be maintained. But the time that should be given for rest is a controversial subject. Two factors that should be kept in mind are that the period of rest should not be so long as to induce lethargy and not so short as not to provide adequate rest. Gartner has suggested that the worker should sleep for thirty minutes in order to get adequate rest. If the workers are allowed to sleep for more than thirty minutes, it is possible that their sleep at night may be disturbed.

Food plays an important part in removing fatigue, and hence arrangements should be made to provide cheap, wholesome and appetizing food for the workers. Even if the organisation has to spend some money to provide this facility, it stands to lose nothing and to gain much by maintaining the health of its employees. It has been seen that the food brought by the workers themselves for their lunch is more often than not neither nutritious nor adequate. The place provided for lunch, should not be too far from the place of work, because if the worker becomes tired in travelling to the place reserved for eating, the organisation will lose because the production will fall. If, on the other hand, canteens are attached to the factory premises, the workers enjoy taking their food, with the result that their health does not suffer. Their fatigue is reduced both by the nourishment and by the pleasure they derive in taking good food. The organisation benefits by the consequent increase in production. Food can be provided both in the morning and in the afternoon.

The health and nourishment of the worker depends not only upon the rest and the food which are provided to him. Certain other factors also play an important role in it. For example, economic worries have a detrimental effect on health. For this reason, it is desirable that the employer should provide facilities for small short term loan so that the workers can tide over a difficult period. Medical facilities provided at low cost also help the worker to great extent.

Healthy recreation is another factor that helps to build up the mental and physical health of the worker. For this reason, most modern industrial organisations provide healthy recreation by opening clubs, cinema halls and other forms of entertainment near to the industrial complex.

Importance of Individual Differences

The last conclusion drawn from the ergographic studies places stress upon the importance of individual differences insofar as they have some influence upon fatigue. It is generally known that some people become tired quicker than other people and also take a longer time in recovering their strength and energy. Other people tire less easily and also regain their energy more quickly. This fact of individual differences has special importance with respect to work in which more than one person work together. If, for example, all the people are deputed to perform a single task, they tire easily, and the task will be completed only with great difficulty. For this reason, the fact of individual differences should be kept in mind while selecting people to perform different functions in a factory. Difficult work should be assigned to people who do not tire easily. Certain kinds of work require a lot of hard work in the beginning, but at the end they can be performed without too much effort. For such work, it is better that it should be started by a person who is capable of greater effort. It can then be completed by another person who is weaker.

The importance of ergographic studies has been made clear by the application of their conclusions to actual industrial conditions, an account of which has given above. Many industrial organisations have benefited by introducing lunch and rest intervals. Wherever some difficulty has been experienced as a result of introducing these intervals, it has been caused by those workers who return late to their work, or collect in great numbers in the coffee shops, factories and offices or even in the elevators. As a result, organisations do experience some difficulty, but nobody complains that the introduction of such intervals is harmful or that it is not beneficial. Some of the important researches and studies conducted on these subjects are outlined here.

1. Haggard's research.[3] According to W.S. Haggard, a 10 per cent increase in production resulted when the workers were provided two additional lunches. The workers also reported that they are helped in recovering their energy and that despite the increased work they experience less fatigue. The provision of comfortable chairs and beds in some other industrial organisations also resulted

3. Haggard, W.S., *Work and Fatigue, Mech. Engin.* (1936), 58, pp. 298-301.

in an increase in production. The truth of the matter is that if the management does not make provision for rest, the workers themselves take time out for rest, unauthorisedly or without permission. In some offices the clerks are seen sleeping on their chairs while in others, the workers leave their desks by inventing some or the other excuse. Sometimes the worker seeks relief only in reducing the tempo of his work. If the worker can think of no other excuse, he gees and stands in the queue outside the lavatory. It is therefore better that the management should itself provide a rest interval for the workers. Not every worker can think up excuse to get rest and neither can one actually feel relaxed by stealing rest in this way.

2. Mezerik's research.[4] On the basis of his studies Mezerik has written that in one particular case, a 32 per cent increase in production was seen merely by providing sitting stools for women workers. Women are employed in many modern industries to perform the lighter functions. The management's attention has been drawn towards providing rest to the female workers because it is realized that the feminine body is naturally softer. Wherever female workers are employed in modern industries, provisions are made for rest intervals, beautiful and comfortably furnished rooms for resting, reasonably comfortable working seats, etc. If this is not done, the workers experience a feeling of dissatisfaction which, in the long run, harms the employer. The expense incurred in providing such basic amenities is recovered manifold through the increased production.

3. Bonmann's studies. The researches of E. Bonmann, a German scientist, have thrown light on the ergographic conclusion that the effect of fatigue continues to increase if the individual continues to work. For this reason, he has suggested that the lunch intervals should be provided after one-third of the total working time has been consumed. By doing this, the persistent increase in fatigue can be avoided.

It is evident from the above discussion that the application of ergographic principles to industries has benefited most of the people, but the extent to which intervals of rest should be introduced can be determined only through further experimentation. The kind of arrangements for maintaining the health of the worker, the

4. Mezerik, A.G., *The Factory Manager Learns the Fact of Life,* Harper's (1943), pp. 288-97.

extent of rest, the kind of food, will depend upon the nature of the work done in a particular industry, upon the age and sex of the worker, and upon numerous other factors. The maximum advantage can be derived only after sufficient thought has been devoted to these factors.

REST PAUSES

1. Studies by Viteles.[5] M.S. Viteles proved by his studies that increase of 10 to 20 per cent in production can be seen by the introduction of rest pauses. For example, in one industry employing female workers, a 20 per cent increase of production was noticed when they were provided a ten minute rest pause in their morning work. These girls pasted labels. This example has been cited by H.M. Vernon and T. Bedford[6] in their essay on rest pauses.

2. Studies by Farmer and Bevington.[7] Explaining the conclusions arrived at as a result of one experiment, Farmer and Bevington have pointed out in their essay that an appreciable rise in the production curve was seen when seven-minute rest pauses were introduced in the morning and afternoon working schedules.

In addition to the above experiments and studies, the benefits of rest pauses have been noted in many other industries. It has been seen that it is advantageous to give a five-minute rest after every hour of work.

Experiments can be conducted to determine the length of rest pauses which will suit different industries and different kinds of work. This is so because the rest pause will depend upon the nature of work, the length of the working time, the length of the working week, the age and sex of the workers, the level of nutrition and the individual differences between the workers. For example, women workers require a longer rest interval than male workers. Similarly, workers who do not enjoy good health require more frequent and longer rest periods. While some people require many and long rest intervals, other people can continue to work for a long time without experiencing fatigue and can also recover their energy in a comparatively short time. Motivation also influences the rest pause because in cases of strong motivation, individuals

5. Viteles, M.S., *Industrial Psychology*, pp. 470-82.
6. Vernon, H.M. and T. Bedford, *The Influence of Rest Pauses on Light Industrial Work* (1924).
7. Farmer, E. and S.M. Bevington, *An Experiment in the Introduction of Rest Pauses*, Nat. Institute, *Indus. Psychol.* (1922) 1, pp. 89-92.

continue to work for a long time without fatigue. Some laboratory experiments have brought useful facts to light in this connection. G. Shepherd[8] conducted an experiment on educated university students to determine the influence of light and heavy work on the muscles. These students were studying at the Purdur University and were given wages for the work performed by them. They were required to spend eight hours a week under working conditions. They were also given a bonus so that the working conditions should resemble actual industrial conditions. The nature of the work was such that they were required to go towards a machine, to stretch away from it and lift and drop some heavy weight. In order to avoid, the accumulation of fatigue, they were given a 19-hour rest on the previous day, besides which they were provided with comfortable cots to be used during the rest intervals. The work varied between 25 and 60 minutes while the rest pauses varied between 7 and 16 minutes. In other tests, the rest pause of this changed while the work was kept constant. As a result of this experiment, it was discovered that the best results were achieved when the rest interval extended over 16.7 to 20 per cent of the total working time. It was also discovered that it is better to provide a short rest pause after less work than to provide a long period of rest after continuous work over long periods. The maximum distribution of the rest pause was tested with two students. While experimenting with a rest pause of 18.2 per cent, it was observed that the greatest benefit of the rest pause was derived when rest pauses of one-minute were given in the working schedule. Under these conditions, it was also seen that there was no deterioration even near the end of the work schedule, although falling off of production near the end of a working day is normal. Here it should be kept in mind that such frequent rest pauses can be introduced only in that work in which there is no system or organisation. In this experiment, another fact observed was that whenever the distribution of rest period was left to the students themselves, they could not use it properly but when they were trained in the underlying principles of the distribution of rest pauses, they could place them more beneficial in the work schedule.

As has been pointed out earlier, the existence of the rest pause does not depend upon the sweet will of the employer. Even if no such rest interval is officially provided by the management, most

8. Shepherd, G., "Effects of Rest Pauses on Production," *Person. Jour.* (1928), 7, pp. 186-202.

of the workers do manage to take sometime off for rest. Many workers work at such slow speed that they take some rest at regular intervals. For example, most workers engaged in house building in India sit down for a smoke after few minutes, a kind of rest interval in addition to the normal time taken off for lunch. This fact is true of almost all kinds of workers. Some labourers and office clerks make a habit of leaving their place of work or desk every few minutes. Some leave the work in order to drink water or to urinate, and very often they do not even trouble to switch off the machines on which they are working. Hence the only way in which the management can prevent such unofficial intervals is to introduce an official rest pause because when the worker resorts to such actions, it does not imply that he does not want to work. In fact, he is only trying to avoid fatigue and get some rest. People who have to work for a long time normally work at a slower rate than those who have to work only for a short time. Some important experiments have been conducted in this connection. In one of the studies H.M. Vernon[9], made a study of the working methods of workers who worked for six hours. When the working day was eight hours, an average rest period of 12.50 minutes per hour was observed by the workers. Hence in the six-hour working day, the rest period was 17 per cent of the total working time, but when the working day had eight hours, the rest pause was 20.8 per cent of the working time. But it should also be remembered that this rest pause was not taken after every hour. In fact, the average is obtained by dividing the total working time with the total rest period taken by the workers. The managers of industry should try to find out the length of a rest pause required after a particular stretch of work so that maximum production can be achieved while the motivation of the workers is maintained at a high level. When such rest pauses are provided by the management, the number of unofficial rest intervals will decrease.

Numerous studies were conducted to solve these industrial problems. These studies have revealed a vast fund of interesting and useful facts. For example, ergographic studies have indicated that the rest pause should be given at a time before the production begins to fall due to fatigue. If the rest interval is given before production falls then the worker can regain his energy and continue to work at the same rate. Sometimes rest pauses can also lead to obstruction in the work. For this reason, the workers should be

9. Vernon, H.M., *Industrial Fatigue and Efficiency*, pp. 107-10.

consulted while determining the rest interval. Besides, it should not be rigorously imposed. For example, it is foolish to force a person to rest when he is working at high speed with complete concentration because in that case production will fall while the individual will not get any real rest also. Hence the working pattern of the workers should be carefully studied before the rest interval is introduced. The work and rest should be divided only on the basis of this pattern of work. The best way, of course, is that the workers should be trained to distribute the work and rest themselves so that they can make this distribution on the basis of their own individual capacities and abilities.

Another beneficial effect of officially providing a period of rest is that the workers gain confidence in the management since they feel that the management is conscious of their welfare. This helps to develop a positive attitude to the work, and this attitude helps to increase production. Hence, the total effect of giving a rest period depends upon the rest and also upon the positive attitude generated by it. This benefit cannot be derived when the workers take unofficial rest because the attitude of the work does not favour the management since he has stolen the rest. It has not been provided to him. Besides, some of the workers are not capable of such disloyalty with the result that they have to bear the maximum burden of the work. Hawthorne's experiments have also yielded useful results concerning the rest pauses. It has been seen that a fifteen-minute rest pause during the morning, a lunch interval and a ten-minute rest pause during the afternoon have great advantages.

Many experiments have been conducted to find out the maximum work that a worker should be forced to do so that he gives the maximum production. In one organisation, the workers worked ten hours a day at packing apples while in another organisation, the workers put in eight hours a day at similar work. By comparing the total amount of work done, it was seen that the workers who worked for eight hours a day packed on an average five cases more every day. Evidently, production had fallen with an increase in the working time. Hence, in most of the modern industries, the management takes care not to increase the working schedule to such an extent that it should prove harmful.

EQUIPMENT DESIGN

After making a study of fatigue, boredom and accidents in industry, it has been concluded that in addition to the environmental and personal factors which influence industrial loss, the design of the equipment also plays an important part. In fact, it would not be wrong to say that equipment design is a comparatively more important factor than environmental and individual factors in causing industrial production. It is natural that industrial efficiency should be influenced by equipment design, if the equipment is so designed that the worker becomes tired rapidly, out of all proportion to work, or if he cannot work without some interruption or if he can achieve only a very low level of production. As far as automatic machines are concerned, they are usually designed to avoid accidents. It is necessary to see in such a case how the worker will sit, the amount of light he will get and the direction from which it will come, and the movement he will have to make in order to control such a machine. It is essential that the light should fall on the instrument panel and not on the eyes of the worker. If the light disturbs his vision, he will not be able to see the instrument panel, thus increasing the chances of an accident. He may even be dazzled by the light and thus operate the machine incorrectly.

While operating different kinds of machines, workers have to make different kinds of movements with their hands and feet. Fatigue is directly related to the kinds and extent of such movements. If some specific muscles are brought into play in operating some machines, then it is only natural that the muscle will suffer extreme fatigue. That is why psychologists have assisted in designing of equipment which will result in maximum production while inducing the least possible amount of fatigue. Motion studies are of great value in the designing of this kind of equipment. In recent years, psychology has been able to help machine designing to such an extent that a branch of psychology known as engineering psychology has come into existence.

Equipment design is concerned not only with the shape and size of machines and tools but also with the order in which they are placed within the factory premises. It is common knowledge that the tools and machines required by a particular worker should be placed within easy reach so that he can pick them up by extending his hand. In addition to this, the tools should be placed in the order in which they will be required. Even this arrangement of the tools is the work of the psychologist.

If a worker has to stand and work, he will naturally become tired more quickly and thus his industrial efficiency and output will both suffer. For this reason, psychologists have suggested the construction of machines which the worker can operate while sitting. A study of physical fatigue has revealed the various positions of the body in which the individual tires rapidly. On the basis of this knowledge, the psychologists have given suggestions for the construction of machines in which the worker's body is placed in such a position that he does not tire easily. When machines are designed in this way, the worker can increase his production without becoming extremely exhausted.

The importance of equipment design for industrial efficiency is evident from the above exposition. Psychologically considered, if the machine design is adequate, the accident rate falls, fatigue declines, enthusiasm is maintained and industrial efficiency increases.

MUSIC IN INDUSTRY

Effect of Music on Production

Today music is provided for the workers while they work so that their boredom and monotony can be kept at a low level. B.E. Benson believes that music is of great importance in industry. The first experiments on this aspect were conducted in England. Music was provided to reduce boredom. When music was played to the workers while they were doing normal mechanical work, a 6 per cent increase in production was observed. A marked difference between production on ordinary days and production on days in which music was provided was thus seen. It was also seen that the duration of music was not very important. More benefit can be derived by providing music in the morning than in the afternoon. In explaining the importance of music for industry J.F. Humes[10] has mentioned one particular study. A study of fast, slow and mixed music programmes was conducted in a factory making radio tubes. It was noticed that when the music was either fast or slow, the loss of time was much less. But the loss was much greater either when there was no music or when fast and slow music programmes were broadcast alternately.

Influence upon Mental Condition

Music programmes influence the worker's mental condition and also the production. W.A.W. Kerr made a study of the effect of music on industrial workers and concluded that it has a positive and useful effect on the mental condition of the workers. H.C. Smith saw in his research that music has a good influence

10. Humes, J.F., "The effect of occupational music on scarppage in the manufacturing of Radio Tubes", *Journal Applied Psychology*, 25, pp. 573-87.

upon the attitudes of the workers, upon the production and upon the prevention of accidents. Smith has given a detailed account of the varying influence of music on various kinds of work and the different work shifts. He indicated that the provision of music resulted in a 7 per cent rise in production in the day shift and a 17 per cent increase during the night shift. It was also observed that music has the greatest influence in those operations in which memory of recall plays an important part and conversation is possible. Mcghee and J.E. Gardner[11] showed by their experiments that music did not result in any increase in production but in this case music was provided for workers engaged in some complicated operations. These operations necessitated the use of decision making, constant attention and thought and determination. But even though the production did not increase, the workers were under the impression that they had produced more while music was played.

Influence upon Boredom

Music has the most beneficial effect upon boredom. Although it takes the attention of the worker away from his work for a short time, it does not force him to use his mind. Besides, the provision of music helps to maintain the interest of the worker in functions needing recall.

Effect on Accidents

Many valuable studies have been conducted to study the effect of music on accidents. It was generally taken for granted that music would cause more accidents because it would distract the attention of the worker. And this would hold true in the case of operations in which constant attention to the work is essential but in many functions, such constant attention is not necessary. In all such operations, music has a beneficial influence. Music helps the mind to wander a bit thus reducing boredom and monotony. By allowing the mind to wander, music does not let the mind become lethargic. Distraction caused by music is not the same as lack of attention which results from fatigue. The latter kind of disinterest normally leads to accidents but the distraction of music does not. For example, the car driver can allow his mind to wander a bit, but as soon as any obstacle presents itself or another vehicle comes within range, his mind immcdiatcly snaps back to car driving and despite the distraction accidents do not take place. This wandering

11. Mcghee, W., and J.E. Gardner, "Music in a Complex Industrial Job", *Person. Psychology*. (1949), 2, pp. 405-17.

of the mind helps the driver because it reduces the monotony of car driving, which becomes mechanical after long practice. Wherever industrial operations are of a similar nature, functions in which the worker can afford to let his mind wander a bit without leading to accidents, music has a positive influence because it maintains the interest of the worker and avoids monotony.

Positive Effects of Music in Industry

Briefly, it can be said that music has a beneficial effect on an industrial situation. Most workers also testify to the fact that music gives them pleasure. Although 1 or 2 per cent of the workers oppose the introduction of music, they do so because of some individual attitudes or difficulties. Almost 75 per cent of the workers are in favour of music. The kind of music and pitch of the sound at which it should be played can be determined by experiment and study, and it can be made to suit different kinds of functions. Some of the major facts in this connection are the following :

1. Music at low pitch is more useful than music played very loudly.
2. The music should also be changed after sometime.
3. Instrumental music distracts attention less than vocal music. It is also more satisfying.
4. Music should not be provided all through the working hours. It should be provided at a time when fatigue is maximum.
5. Music provided during the night shift has proved more advantageous than music given during the day shift.

BOREDOM AND MONOTONY

Meaning of Boredom and Monotony

In the context of psychological fatigue, insofar as it pertains to industry, the words boredom and monotony are used in addition to fatigue. Monotony is a mental condition which is produced by the constant repetition of some function over a long period of time. On the other hand, boredom is a mental condition in which the individual evinces negative attitudes and aptitude for a particular work. In other words, he does not want to do that work. Both boredom and monotony contribute to fatigue but neither is the result of physical fatigue. Both of them are caused by mental attitudes. Boredom is caused more by the personality of the worker, his aptitude, his emotional condition and the apparent importance of the function he is performing. When these factors are varied, one person will feel no boredom in some particular function which bores another person. Some people become bored rapidly with some work requiring repetition but many other people adapt themselves very quickly to such work. For these reasons, the workers have completely divergent opinions about work which is boring and other work which is not. Some important facts connected with this subject were revealed in the study of S. Wyatt, J.H. Langdon and F.G.L. Stock.[12] This study was conducted on ten individuals and five kinds of work. Each individual was required to do each kind of work for one month, and at the end of the period each individual was required to point out the extent of boredom experienced in each kind of work. The worker was to award zero points to the work which contained no boredom and five points the work in which he felt consistently bored. When this evaluation was analysed, it was seen that all the workers considered two kinds of work consistently boring, although some awarded five points to one work and some awarded them to the other. Apart from this, the ten individuals showed no unanimity of opinion. The average evaluation for the five kinds of work was 4.2, 2.4, 2.3, 1.7 and 1.7. It is evident that different individuals made a separate evaluation of boredom according to their individual differences. The scientists conducting the study pointed out that boredom was evinced by workers with a higher intelligence quotient and an extrovert tendency. But this fact has not been substantiated by other studies.

Fig. 23.3. Instrument for Measuring Boredom

12. Wyatt, S., Langdon, J.H. and F.G.L. Stock. "Fatigue and Boredom in Repetitive Work".

Causes of Boredom and Monotony

Factors which cause boredom and monotony have been revealed through many studies. Some of the factors leading to boredom and monotony, briefly stated, are :

1. Individuality of the worker. As has already been demonstrated above, boredom and monotony are closely connected with the individual traits of the individual workers. It is commonly seen that one particular kind of work will strike some people as boring while others will find no boredom in doing it. In an experiment on 400 students of Munsterberg's college, it was seen that boredom depends upon the individual's particular personality traits, not upon the nature of the work. Different individuals take interest in different kinds of work, and that is why the pattern of boredom in each case is different.

2. Intelligence of the worker. Among the different qualities that make up individual differences, intelligence is important and it has a close relation with boredom and monotony. As has been pointed out earlier, the more intelligent individual is inclined to be bored by mechanical repetition of some activity. On the other hand, the less intelligent individual makes a better adjustment with his work. But in this connection it would be better to give a brief review of some of the studies conducted on this subject. The more important studies are the following :

(i) ***Thomson's study*** : Thomson experimented upon 32 people and came to the conclusion that boredom has nothing to do with intelligence.

(ii) ***Viteles' study*** : Viteles conducted an experiment on girls working in the salary section and concluded that the more intelligent girls experience more boredom with the result that majority of such girls are among those who leave this kind of job.

(iii) ***Kornhauser's research*** : A.W. Kornhauser conducted an experiment on office workers and supported the contention of Viteles. He also found that the more intelligent people soon become bored with the work and run away. The less intelligent continue to retain their interest in their work.

(iv) ***Burnett's study*** : Burnett came to the same conclusion when he conducted an experiment on four girls. He also concluded that the less intelligent girls achieved higher production than the more intelligent girls.

(v) ***Studies by Wyatt, Frazer and Stock*** : These psychologists also came to the same conclusion. It was observed by them that the less intelligent girls take more interest in their work than the average or exceptionally intelligent girls.

In his book *The Iron Man in Industry,* A. Pound has remarked, "A morone trained in habits of doing regularly and obedience; is, for many practical purposes, more valuable to his boss for good production than one in higher mental state."

3. Attitude to the work. Many studies have established that workers with a negative attitude to their work experience boredom and monotony much sooner than those with a positive attitude. People with a positive attitude can maintain their concentration in their work for a much longer time.

4. Satiation. Some people soon become fed up with doing work that needs recall, and they do not want to continue doing it. Their attention in the work gradually decreases as their mind becomes more and more satiated. As a result, the quantity and quality of the production also decline. Satiation is a psychological condition in which physical fatigue is at a very low level. A. Karsten conducted an experiment in this connection with some college students. When they had become completely bored with the work of writing they were asked to write names on a sheet of paper, in which they experienced no difficulty at all. In an experiment with poetry, it was seen that some individuals who did not want to utter one more line of poetry were willing to continue talking for a long time when the subject was changed. They, too, did not experience any fatigue. It is evident from both of these experiments that only those muscles were being exercised which already appeared to be fatigued. But this apparent fatigue was due to boredom and when the subject was changed they again began to function normally because the boredom was removed. Obviously, the difficulty in working was not due to muscular fatigue but due to satiation, a psychological condition. Satiation is caused by doing the same kind of work. It does not imply fatigue. This was also proved by the fact that some workers complaining of fatigue resumed their work when they were allowed to change their position.

5. Feeling of progress. Many experiments have also yielded the fact that if the worker is aware of the progress he has made in his work, he does not experience boredom or monotony. In fact, as the work progresses, the worker becomes excited at the prospect of achieving his target and works with renewed energy. An individual becomes bored very quickly with some work, the end of which he cannot see or which leads to no tangible result. For this reason, it is always better to have recognisable targets at shorter intervals in any work. The desire to finish the day's work can itself be an aim. In such a case, one can observe the increase in the speed of working. But the feeling of having achieved some target or of being near to the end also depends upon the individual's attitude. If the attitude is negative, this feeling of achievement is weak. Fairly often, the boredom of the individual can be reduced if he can be convinced of the value and importance of his work for others.

6. Other qualities. In addition to above, individual qualities of the worker also influence boredom. The more important ones are leaning of attention, emotional condition, peculiarities of nature. If these are in favour of the work, the work will produce less boredom. But if these are negative, the individual will soon become bored with his work.

7. Feeling of leaving something uncompleted. One particular worker was lying on his death-bed. He was asked to mention the last wish he would like to have fulfilled. He said that he would like to have a board on which the screws were only half tightened. He wanted to complete the work of tightening those screws. This individual had spent all his life fixing screws on a board and half-tightening them. But he was always filled with the desire to tighten these screws fully. Similar phenomena have been observed in many studies. A worker feels dissatisfied and deprived if he is not allowed to complete his task. In another example, it was seen that one foreman ordered a worker to leave the work in hand and go on to something else. The worker did not want to leave his work incomplete, so he refused to obey the foreman. Using his position, the foreman ordered him to leave it. This led to an exchange of words and a scuffle in which the worker pushed the foreman who fell against a machine and was killed. The only thing at the root of this incident was that the foreman wanted to take the worker away from his work, which the worker wanted to complete. It is also seen that many workers do not want to start some fresh assignment near the end of the day. They know that they will not be able to complete it, and it is against human psychology to leave the work incomplete. A refusal in such conditions does not amount to disobedience, disrespect or obstinacy, and should not be interpreted as such. Man has a natural desire to finish anything that he has begun, and if he is prevented from doing so, he loses his balance, a fact which has been established by many psychological experiments. Many experiments have shown that man first of all shows the desire to complete any work which has been left incomplete. When the worker enters the factory, he first of all wants to complete the previous day's work before going on to something fresh. While working, an individual enters a psychological state in which he wants to leave some work only after he has completed it. This motivation can differ in degree from person to person and from work to work. And providing an opportunity to complete the work is an important element in job satisfaction. This tendency of completing unfinished work is seen more particularly in those kinds of work which influence the emotions, irrespective of their inherent interest or the lack of it. If the worker is indifferent towards his work, he will show no desire to complete it. A worker is seen working rapidly only because he is pressed by the desire to finish it. For this reason the desire to finish some work has an important influence upon boredom or monotony. If this desire is present, the individual does not become bored. In this way, this tendency is directed against boredom because it creates motivation. In industrial conditions, it is desirable that the work should be divided in such a way among the workers that they get an opportunity to complete their part of the work. This increases motivation and reduces boredom.

8. Conditions of work. From the above account of causes of boredom and monotony, it should not be taken for granted that only individual and personal factors are responsible while the external environment plays no part at all. In fact, the truth of the matter is that the manager or the employer can do more to remove boredom and monotony by changing the external conditions of work than he can by trying to condition the worker's mind or to control his attitudes. Monotony can be reduced and production increased by making adequate changes in the working conditions. This can be done by making the following changes :

(a) ***Provision for rest*** : Boredom or monotony increase in the absence of any rest period. In a study conducted by Mayo, it was seen that the workers in a cloth-mill suffered from boredom because they did not have any rest interval in their working hours. When provision was made for rest, an immediate decline in the level of boredom was noticed. This has also been substantiated by the research of other psychologists.

(b) ***Arrangement for wages*** : The salary system plays an important part in creating interest among the workers. They feel dissatisfied and bored if the wages are not paid at the correct time or at the correct rates. Shaaz saw in his studies that the worker experiences less boredom and achieves a higher level of production if he gets proper wages.

(c) ***Working method*** : Wyatt Frazer and Stock studied the work technique of three girls working in a factory making cigarette boxes. One of these girls had to work three times as much as the third girl, with the result that they regularly exchanged their positions. The scientist, instead of allowing one girl to work at one position for the whole day, made the girls interchange their respective positions six times a single day. It was noticed that their boredom grew less and they produced an extra 10 per cent of work.

9. Nature of work. One cause of boredom is the nature of work because if a particular function does not vary at all, the worker becomes bored very soon and experiences monotony. If the work is varied and changed frequently, the worker's interest in it is maintained. Many experimental results have confirmed this view. Wyatt and Frazer conducted experiments in which six girls were asked to pack soap, fold handkerchiefs, gather cycle chains and to do a variety of other kinds of work. It was noticed that production went up and monotony declined.

10. Social factors. Boredom and monotony also depend to a large extent upon some social factors because the worker works in a social environment which has a decided influence upon his mental condition. If the mutual exchange between the management and the worker is entertaining and cooperative then the boredom is quickly done away with. Then the worker takes an interest in his work. As long as conversation and laughter do not interfere with the performance of work, the workers should be allowed to indulge in conversation. This helps to maintain the worker's interest in his work. It has also been noticed that less boredom occurs if men and women work together. On the contrary, if the atmosphere is one of mutual suspicion and distrust in which the management goes out of the way to scold the worker, the worker soon loses his interest in work, thus adversely affecting production.

MEANS OF ELIMINATING BOREDOM AND MONOTONY

Many psychological means have now been evolved in industrial psychology to relieve boredom and monotony. Since monotony depends upon the nature of the work and upon the individual differences of each worker, different means are adopted to remove monotony from different kinds of work. But even then the following general measures can be useful in eliminating boredom :

1. Exchanging job. The most important single measure in removing boredom is to exchange the jobs of the workers among them. Since different kinds of work exhaust different muscles of the body, a change of position often helps to give rest also. Besides, a change of job helps to maintain the novelty of the work and thus monotony is avoided. Again, the worker also gets an opportunity to gain experience about different kinds of work, while repetition of the same work does not provide any variety of experience. In addition to an exchange of jobs, the worker should be allowed to do the same job in many different ways since this helps to reduce mental and physical fatigue and maintains interest in work. In case of girls working in a telephone exchange, it was seen that they took more interest in their work and complained of boredom less frequently when they were allowed to exchange their jobs. By his studies, J.R.P. French has shown that job exchange has a positive and beneficial influence upon morale. In his study, the working girls were allowed to change the rate and method of working.

2. Relating the job to the large picture. Some people become bored with their jobs only because their function is not connected with a comprehensive picture of the job. If a woman who cleans dishes treats each dish as nothing more than another dish, she will soon become bored and will experience monotony. Norman R.F. and Maier[13] has described the case of a subnormal boy who cleaned all the dishes in the house, irrespective of the number of guests. And as there were already fifteen members in the household, he should ordinarily have become bored and tired very soon. But he never required any help in his task because, for him, each dish had individual characteristics and he could identify each dish by some mark on it. He treated each dish as a friend and found pleasure in cleaning the face of each friend. Some of them he liked more than others and therefore he had reserved special places for them. He found interest in his work because he experienced the feeling that he was rapidly meeting one friend after another.

It has been seen that working girls soon become bored in their office work if they do not have interest in it. On the other hand, a typist will not experience monotony if he finds the official

13. Maier, Norman R.F., *Psychology in Industry*, George G. Harrap & Co., London (1955), p. 477.

correspondence interesting or if the office's functions interest him. For this reason, it is desirable that all the workers should have sufficient knowledge of the work of their organisation. As long as they are ignorant of this, they cannot gauge the importance of their own contribution to it. Once they realise this importance, their own job can be seen in the right perspective as part of the larger picture. Then the sense of responsibility increases and better work is done. Sometimes the worker is told to mind his own business and to carry out orders as they are given to him, without taking interest in the working of the organisation. The consequence of this kind of management is that the worker is not interested in the quality of his own work and neither does he make any effort to improve his method of working.

3. Use of sub-goals. In order to reduce monotony, it is desirable to create sub-goals within the work which can be achieved quickly. One such goal is the completion of the day's work with the result that the worker feels he is making progress as the day wears on. If the goal is too far away or can be achieved only after a long time, it does not serve to inspire the worker in this way. In addition to this goal of completing the day's work, his rest intervals can also be made sub-goals. The worker is inspired to complete his work because he feels that soon he will get the chance to rest. It is often seen that the speed of working increases as the time of rest comes nearer. In this way, the rest period provides relaxation and removes monotony.

Another way of creating goals is to divide the work into larger units. For example, if we start reading a book with the intention of finishing it chapter by chapter, then the book can be completed without loss of interest or creation of boredom. Besides, the reader experiences a feeling of progress as he moves from one chapter to the next.

In order to enhance this sense of achievement in industry, the various units of production should be distributed among the workers and each one should be encouraged to complete his own unit. Production can thus be increased by making production itself a goal. The unit of production is between two periods of rest, and the desire and enthusiasm to complete the unit tend to reduce monotony.

4. Use of pacing method and automatic work habits. Psychological analyses have revealed that monotony is a repeated activity. It is not caused by recall but by repeating the work. Nowadays efforts are made to turn all repetitive functions into automatic activities, as far as is possible. When this is done, the work becomes natural and continues to be done without any attention being paid to it so that the worker can allow his mind to wander here and there. Work of this kind does not cause monotony. For example, people do not notice the distance they have walked if they are talking to another person at the same time. But if the individual concentrates his attention on the activity of working, he will soon find it monotonous. Hence, if the work is of the same nature as walking, then the worker should have the liberty to talk to others or to daydream, if he so desires. Many studies have shown that, given the liberty to daydream, monotony can be kept at a low level.

Improvement in performance can be seen when some repeated activity is made rhythmic. It has been seen that when many workers are performing the same function, they tend to follow a rhythm. Men who carry heavy loads can be seen working in this way. Similarly, less boredom is experienced when walking in step rather than in walking without any rhythm.

5. Provision of industrial music. Another means of reducing boredom is to provide music to the workers in industry. This measure has proved of great value in all work situations which do not require the constant attention of worker. And it should be noted that instrumental music proves more useful than vocal music.

6. Increase of experience of completion. The awareness of having completed some work provides natural motivation and stimulation. For this reason, boredom can be reduced by allowing the worker to have a greater sense of having completed his work. The managers should try to avoid interruption of the worker at his work and in particular not to interfere with him before he has completed his task. The consciousness of completion is created when the worker is aware of the progress he has made. Leaving the work in hand as soon as ordered is not a sign of effective administration or obedience in industry. No intelligent manager will stress that the worker should suspend his work as soon as he is ordered. The manager will allow the worker to complete the work in hand and then ask him to report. By doing this, the manager can help to maintain the motivation of the worker and avoid boredom. In addition to this, the work can be divided into small units so that it gives more frequent experience of completion and achievement. These smaller units themselves become the goals for the worker and he gets a feeling of completion and the satisfaction when he achieves even this smaller goal. The total work and the working hours should be divided in such a manner that there should be the satisfying experience of completing each unit. The job of preparing records and maintaining accounts can be made more satisfying by dividing the work into separate files so that the worker can feel relieved after finishing work on one file. Job satisfaction increases as the work is seen coming to an end.

7. Attending to individual differences. In dividing the work among the workers attention should be paid to their individual differences. If this is done the incidence of disinterest and boredom will be less. As far as possible a worker should be given a task which suits his intelligence, attitudes, spheres of attention, nature and emotional conditions.

8. Improvement of working conditions. Generally, boredom and monotony can be kept in control by providing a properly timed and sufficiently long period of rest, payment of wages at the correct time, by introducing the proper methods of working, permitting freedom to laugh and enjoy, and generally improving he working conditions.

9. Proper social environment. Finally, the most important method of reducing boredom is to maintain an atmosphere of love and confidence, cooperation and faith among the workers and the management. If the social environment is encouraging and pleasant, boredom normally does not occur.

QUESTIONS FOR EXERCISE

1. Distinguish between physical and mental fatigue. How can fatigue be eliminated?
2. Describe the causes of mental fatigue in an industry. Suggest ways and means to remove mental fatigue.
3. Explain the physiological and psychological aspects of fatigue in detail.
4. Distinguish between different types of fatigue in industry and show how these are assessed.
5. What are the industrial circumstances in which fatigue is produced? What measures should be adopted to minimise fatigue?
6. What are the industrial circumstances in which fatigue is produced? Distinguish between physical and mental fatigue and point out the relation between them.
7. Examine the general concept of fatigue, and discuss the factors that underlie its causation in industry.

8. What is the nature of fatigue in industry? What measures would you recommend for the elimination of fatigue?
9. Explain the concept of industrial fatigue and discuss the factors that underlie its causation.
10. Critically examine the concept of fatigue in different aspects.
11. Examine the concept of fatigue, and comment on the statement that in testing fatigue we "tend to measure that of which we have only the adequate knowledge by procedures which are not altogether valid".
12. Describe the different types of measurement of fatigue. Is fatigue curve in any way related to accident frequencies?
13. Briefly describe the various tests of fatigue and explain their importance in industry.
14. Write a short note on Ergograph.
15. Indicate the industrial application of the ergographic studies of work and fatigue.
16. What are the main findings of ergographic studies of work and fatigue? Consider their implication for industry.
17. Write short note on Industrial music.
18. Write critical note on Importance of music during work.
19. Write critical note on Music and job performance.

24
Industrial Accidents

ARE ACCIDENTS ACCIDENTAL?

When the scientific attitude had not been adopted by the industry, it was believed that accidents were accidental. But when scientific research began in the sphere of industry, it was soon learnt that if there were provisions for safety, the number of accidents fell. Where safety methods were introduced, a downward trend in the number of accidents was soon noticed. When people were trained to avoid accidents, a marked improvement was observed. Hence, it is no, longer believed that accidents are accidental. The Workmen's Compensation Laws have played an important role in this change because once this legislation was introduced, the industrialists in England and America had to pay very heavy compensation to any worker injured or incapacitated in an accident. The consequence was that accidents became very undesirable as far as the management was concerned and they tried to prevent them as far as possible. With the passing of time it was noticed that the sum spent on introducing safety devices proved to be far less than the total compensation paid out in case of the accident. Hence safety devices proved to be more economic, and the industrialists stood to gain by introducing them and increasing them. Finding these safety measures a paying proposition, the industrialists in every sphere sought to introduce them and also trained their employees to avoid accidents and become more safety-conscious. Another advantage of introducing safety measures was that the loss of working hours through accidents decreased and led to a further increase in production. Besides, the workers now developed a more trusting and confident attitude towards their employers and thus worked harder, again benefiting the industrialist. Many subsequent researches and studies have established beyond doubt that the introduction of safety measures led to the saving of millions of dollars. And the production everywhere went up in proportion to the safety measures introduced, besides the improvement in human relations between the workers and the management. For this reason, great attention is now paid in all industries to the prevention of accidents. This proves that accidents are not really accidental.

Causes of Accidents

If accidents are not accidental, it is obvious that they must have some cause. What, then, is the cause of accidents? Psychologists have undertaken numerous studies of the working conditions, the methods of working, the mental condition of workers, to locate the causes of accidents. They can be briefly enumerated as follows :

1. Improper working conditions. Factors such as the improper temperature in the factory, the intensity and the quality of illumination, the working hours, the extent of humidity, the arrangement of machines, the work shift, are responsible for accidents. Factors which are directly responsible for increasing accidents are following :

(a) ***Absence of proper temperature*** : Many studies have established that the number of accidents goes up if the temperature rises or falls far above or below the normal. This fact proves to be most truthful about the labourers working in mines. It was seen that the number of accidents in the hottest mines was three times as much as the number of accidents in the coldest mines. The frequency of accidents increases with any extreme variation in temperature. Even when the temperature falls below the normal, the number of accidents increases. Women can adapt to higher temperatures better than men. One cause of this can be the different kinds of clothing used by men and women. Yet, it is necessary to determine the normal, the highest and the lowest temperatures differently for every country because of the different climate. The normal temperature in a very cold country may still be sufficiently cold to cause accidents in an otherwise hot country because for people of hot and temperate climates that temperature may still be too low to be tolerated easily. Hence it is necessary to make experiments to determine the normal temperature in a factory in a particular location. Then efforts can be made to maintain that level of temperature so that accidents are avoided and the highest possible production maintained. Osborne and Vernon conducted an experiment in a shoe factory, and they came to the conclusion that the least number of accidents occurred when the temperature was between 55° and 59° Fahrenheit. This conclusion was further substantiated by the studies of Bedford and Vernon.

(b) *Amount of humidity* : If the humidity in a particular factory is far above normal, then the bodily health of the worker is adversely affected with the result that the possibilities of accidents increase. This has been proved to hold true of mines. Hence it is now considered necessary to control the amount of humidity in working areas.

(c) *Absence of proper light* : The absence of proper illumination is another cause of accidents because excessive or too little light strains the eyes and leads to fatigue. Natural light is always better than artificial light. It has been seen that accidents increase by about 25 per cent when natural light is replaced by artificial light. The relationship between accidents and lighting is further proved by comparing the number of accidents in the day and night shifts. By making this comparison, Osborne and Vernon[1] have shown that there are fewer accidents during the night shift than in the day shift. More railway accidents take place at night than during the day because at night, the light is far less than it is during the day. But it should be remembered that the quantity of light is not the sole cause of accidents because fewer road accidents occur, at night, despite less illumination. This happens because during the day roads are more frequented than during the night.

(d) *Work shift* : Vernon[2] has shown by his studies that fewer accidents take place during the night shift than during the day shift. This is explained by the fact that during the day shift, the worker arrives at his work after a night's rest and is also well fed at time. What happens is that after working for sometime he becomes careless. This leads to accidents. On the other hand, the workers in the night shift have already been awake for a number of hours before coming to work, with the result that they pay more attention to their work and thus accidents are avoided. Some studies have given results which contradict the findings of Vernon because it was then seen that more accidents took place during night shift than during day shift. Some workers were involved in accidents during night shift either because they could not get adequate sleep during the day or because they came to work in an intoxicated condition. Railway workers have more accidents during the night because they become inattentive due to sleep. In view of the

1. Obsborne, E.E. and H.M. Vernon, "The Influence of Temperature and Other Conditions on the Frequency of Industrial Accidents".
2. Vernon, H.M., *Industrial Fatigue and Efficiency*, London, p. 264.

contradictory findings, most scientists do not agree about the number of accidents during the night and day shifts. While during the day there is more light and the workers are better rested, they have accidents because they become careless. But the workers in night shift tend to be more careful and attentive.

2. Work methods. Work methods are also sometimes responsible for accidents. It has been seen that factors, such as lengthy period of work, severity of work, the rapidity of production, fatiguing work methods, play an important role in causing accidents. Among the more important factors relating to work methods responsible for accidents are the following :

(a) ***Length of work periods*** : Long working periods have more accidents because fatigue tends to increase and to accumulate over a long period of work. In one of the studies conducted by Osborne and Vernon, the number of accidents in a day shift fell by 10 per cent when the working time were reduced from 59 hours to 56 hours. A decrease of 25 per cent in the number of accidents was observed when the working time of one particular night shift were reduced from 63 hours to 48 hours. It has also been seen that more accidents take place when the worker works in overtime in addition to his normal working hours. Hence, it can be said that when the working period extends beyond a definite limit, the number of accidents increases.

(b) ***Severity of work*** : Any work which needs extreme physical endurance and leads to physical exhaustion can be called a severe work. Severe work of this kind is more prone to accidents than other kinds of work. Goldmark made a comparative study of severe work and other kinds of work and also of accidents taking place in the morning and evening. He came to the conclusion that severity of work is one cause of accidents, and as fatigue increases, so does the possibility of accidents.

(c) ***Speed of work*** : Vernon's studies have shown that the possibility of accidents increases with an increase in the speed of work. One main cause of this is that fatigue increases when the speed of work increases. Miles proved the truth of this statement with the help of the pendulum test. He demonstrated that the frequency of accidents increases with the speed of work. But, on the other hand, many studies have not led to similar conclusions. For example, the American Engineering Council conducted a survey of safety measures and production on an estimated ten lakh employees and came to the conclusion that accidents fall as the speed of work increases. In actual fact, much depends on what is considered as the most appropriate speed of working in a particular industry. And this speed may even vary from one individual worker to another. Some people have the capacity to always work faster than others, and such people may in fact have more accidents if their speed is reduced. In the same way, the speed of working will also depend upon the tools and instruments being used. Then again a tired worker cannot work at top speed for a long time while a healthy and fresh worker may be able to work much faster without being involved in any accident. What has been established is that if the speed of work increases beyond the appropriate level, then the possibility of accidents becomes greater, but the appropriate speed of work can only be determined by many factors such as the nature of work, the construction of machinery, the health and motivation of the worker, etc.

(d) ***Methods which increase fatigue*** : Any method which increases fatigue will also increase accidents because increasing fatigue leads to accidents. It has been seen in motor car accidents that they occur most often when the driver of the vehicle is exhausted. The same has been found to be true in the case of railway accidents.

Absence of safety devices. Conditions of work which do not make provision for safety devices also contribute to accidents. In some factories, the machines used have no safety devices attached to them, while in some other cases, the machines are provided with safety devices but the workers ignore them because they want to show that the devices are superfluous and that they can work without them. In order to forestall all such tactics, it is better to have the safety devices integrated with the machinery so that the workers cannot avoid using them. As the safety devices increase, the accidents become fewer while the absence of safety devices leads to an increase in the accidents.

3. Factors concerning the worker. In addition to the conditions and the methods of work, there are certain factors concerned with the worker which lead to accidents. Such factors are mainly :

(a) ***Immature age*** : Many studies have indicated that as compared to mature workers, immature worker; are involved in a greater number of accidents. In this connection, Lippman, Gates and Schmitt have conducted valuable studies. Now, most modern industries do not encourage immature people to become workers.

(b) ***Inexperience*** : Among all those who operate machines, the experienced worker is less inclined to cause or become involved in an accident than the inexperienced worker. For this reason, inexperience is an important contributing factor for accidents.

B. Fisher[3] conducted a study on this aspect with the Carnegie Steel Company, Youngstown Steel Company and some other similar organisations and came to the conclusion that workers having experience of one month have six times as many accidents as more experienced workers. From this, it is obvious that inexperience is an important factor.

(c) ***Bad state of health*** : If the worker's health is not good, if he constantly complains of head aches or stomach aches or back aches or generally suffers from one complaint or the other, then he is more accident prone than a healthy worker. In the course of a study, Farmer and Chambers observed that there was a direct correlation between the number of accidents and the presence of workers in the hospital. E.M. Newbold established a relationship between accidents and the less important disease. By conducting a study of 135 workers of the Philadelphia Electric Company, Viteles[4] came to the conclusion that the suffering workers had a record of three times as many accidents as the healthy workers. Bingham[5] made a study of workers suffering from blood pressure and came to the conclusion that this disease was one cause of accidents. In this way, ill-health has been established as a cause of accidents.

(d) ***Physical defects*** : Different kinds of work require different kinds of efficiency and capacity from the different physical organs. For example, if a worker has to work efficiently on some machines, it is desirable that his eyesight should be normal. If it is not, he may cause some accidents. For this reason, the eyesight of a person is especially checked before he is allowed to take up a job with the railways. The nature of the work determines the most important part of the body and the necessary level of the efficiency it must possess. A worker using a heavy hammer with his hands must necessarily have strong muscles in his arms. Otherwise he will cause some or the other accident. On the other hand, if a particular part of the body is not used in any particular function, then it does not matter if that particular part is damaged or otherwise

---

3. Fisher, B., *Mental Causes of Accidents*, New York, p. 34.
4. Vitals, M.S., *Industrial Psychology*, p. 352.
5. Bingham, W.V., *Prone to Accident Driver, Proceedings 17th Annual Conference on Highway Engineering*, p. 4.

handicapped. If a person is to work as a script writer, it matters little if his feet are deformed.

(e) ***Influence of sex differences*** : It has been seen that because of sex differences, both men and women are better fitted for some particular kinds of work. Generally, women cannot perform dangerous and very severe work as efficiently as men, and for this reason if they try to do so they soon meet with accidents. The number of female car drivers involved in accidents is normally larger than the number of male car drivers. In severe work, women workers normally have three times as many accidents as male workers.

(f) ***Unfavourable mental and emotional conditions*** : The possibility of accidents also increases if the worker's mental and emotional condition is unfavourable when he is working. It is for this reason that mentally unhealthy and emotionally unbalanced individuals are involved in more accidents than the more normal workers. That is why, in most factories no workers are, allowed to enter the premises in a drunk condition. Alcoholic drinks tend to disturb the mental balance and thus make work impossible. Hersey's studies indicate that almost 50 per cent of all accidents are caused by the mental imbalance of the workers.

In addition to the above, mentioned causes of accidents, there are certain momentary factors which lead to accidents. For example, such conditions as failure of the safety devices, inattention of the workers, ignorance, being intoxicated or exhausted, arguments between the worker and the manager, etc., can also cause the accidents. For this reason, it is always considered necessary to go into the causes of an accident so that the responsibility for it may be placed. It is best to pay attention to the conditions of work, the method of working, the individual qualities of the workers involved in the accident, but even more to the social conditions, the relationship between the management and the worker and the conditions existing at the time of accident.

MEANS OF PREVENTING ACCIDENTS

The only means of preventing accidents is to remove all the causes of accidents that have been mentioned earlier. Generally speaking, accidents can be avoided or prevented if the following measures are adopted :

1. Reform of the working conditions. If accidents are to be prevented, then the conditions of work should be improved. The temperature in the working premises should not be such that it may lead to discomfort. This helps to improve the health of the worker and thus prevents accidents. The illumination provided should also be only strong enough and not too intense. Besides, the light source should be installed at the correct angle. Only those parts of a machine should be well lit which are to be constantly in the eyes of the worker. The light should not fall directly on the eyes of the operator. Besides, the machines in the factory should be so arranged that the workers should be able to get maximum production by making the minimum possible movements, so that there is not waste of effort. If some particular machine is likely to cause accidents or if it is dangerous to go near some particular machine, then safety devices should be installed to keep the workers away from it.

2. Provision of safety methods. Nowadays engineers and psychologists cooperate to design safety methods by which even dangerous machines lead to fewer accidents. Engineers have been responsible for designing safety devices, special kinds of gloves, special kinds of spectacles which shield the eyes, and other gadgets by which machine can be operated from a safe distance, without ever being touched by the human hand. Methods of keeping the operator away from the machine while working have also been adopted but sometimes operators wish to show that they are not afraid of the machines and they deliberately avoid using these devices. In such cases, devices have been developed to ensure that the worker cannot operate the machine efficiently. If it is not possible to install such devices on some particular machines, the workers should be trained and encouraged to use these devices.

WHICH IS BETTER?

Fig. 24.1. Two Approaches to Safety

And if it is not possible to make provisions for training the workers, then they should be paid some compensation in lieu of this training. In short, the workers should be encouraged in every possible way to adopt these safety devices.

The left-hand figure shows the foreman instructing his man to work safely. If the man learn his lesson well, he will not fall over the pipe. This is a way of preventing accidents by changing the obstruction. The right-hand figure shows a runway built over the pipe. In this instance, the hazard is reduced by a change in the obstruction.

One basic condition of safety device is that it must be 100 per cent safe. If it is not completely safe then accidents will increase because the workers depend on it and in their own way become careless. If the device offers only 50 per cent safety factors, it proves actually harmful because accidents increase. On the other hand, if there are no safety devices, the worker naturally pays more attention and tends to be cautious with the result that fewer accidents occur. Actually, the worker makes his own adjustment with every kind of condition. If he is asked to operate a dangerous machine on which there are no safety devices, he operates it with extreme caution. Workers working in the night shift tend to be more cautious than workers in the day shift because they realize that lack of caution will lead to accidents. The result of this is that while more accidents should occur during the night under artificial light, in actual fact more accidents take place during the day. But if the machine is fitted with safety devices, the worker himself does not take so many precautions and if the device fails, an accident occurs immediately. This fact can be seen in the case of car accidents caused by speed. Fewer accidents take place at slow speed because no driver has the opportunity to speed up, and besides the presence of other cars makes it dangerous. But when the driver finds an empty and clear road he tends to drive much faster, with the result that many accidents take place on rural roads, and only 5 per cent on the urban roads in America, although the rural roads are generally deserted while the urban roads are far more crowded and carry much more traffic. Similar examples can be found in different industrial conditions.

In addition to the adoption of the above measures, every new worker in a factory should be carefully warned about the dangerous machines. In many modern factories, such machines have a danger sign printed on them so that the workers may be constantly warned.

Sometimes a device installed for safety in one particular direction becomes the cause of an accident in some other. For this reason, engineers and psychologists should design safety devices in such a way that they do not disturb the normal pattern of working. In fact, even safety devices should help the worker in his work. If such machines are designed, then production increases along with safety, while fatigue is reduced. The worker tends to become tired if he is aware of danger because then he is always tense. But if safety devices are provided, this mental tension is avoided and fatigue is reduced.

3. Pay attention to individual differences. Many accidents take place because the worker is required to perform some work which is beyond his physical capacity. Women, for example, cannot do heavy work, and if they are asked to do it, accidents become inevitable. Hence it is desirable that before allocating a particular task to a particular worker, information about his age, experience, mental health, emotional condition, sex, nature, intelligence, physical qualities and defects should be collected. If, after all this information has been collected, he proves to be capable of performing the particular task, he should be entrusted with it. Besides, if one worker has proved a failure at a particular task and is involved in many accidents in doing it, he should immediately be taken away from it and put to some other work. And before putting a man on some dangerous machines, it is better to test his accident proneness.

4. Training in right work methods. Many accidents occur because the operators using machines have not been trained in the correct use of them. It is always better, therefore, to train a person in the use of a machine, in its maintenance, before allowing him to handle it. Another reason why accidents occur due to wrong methods of work is that in such a case, the worker becomes tired very rapidly. And once a person is exhausted, his tendency to commit mistakes and cause accidents increases rapidly.

5. Means of removing fatigue. It has already been pointed out that one important cause of accidents is fatigue. Hence one important measure of avoiding accidents is to remove fatigue. The most important method in this connection is to provide properly timed rest at frequent intervals so that the worker can regain his energy and avoid reaching a stage of complete exhaustion. Besides, the hours of work should not be too long so that complete exhaustion should not occur at all. Fatigue can also be prevented by providing a worker with a job which suits his mental and physical capacity.

Fatigue can also be reduced by allowing the worker to have a sense of satisfaction by completing his job, by creating an atmosphere of cooperation and happiness, by creating cordial relations between worker and management, by making arrangements for timely payment of salary, etc. In addition arrangements should also be made for providing drinking water, wholesome and cheap food, and comfortable furniture for resting during the working hours.

6. Proper speed of work. Accidents frequently occur when the work is performed at a speed much greater than that which is desirable. Drivers who often drive at high speeds are very frequently involved in accidents. Therefore, the speed of the worker in an office or a factory should be controlled. Accidents can also occur if the workers make a habit of putting in overtime, in addition to their normal working hours. If the worker tries to work rapidly as soon as he starts working, he becomes tired very quickly with the result that he works for the rest of the day in an exhausted condition, thus increasing the chances of accidents. Hence the workers should be encouraged to work at such a speed that they can maintain their efficiency and work throughout the day without unnecessary fatigue.

7. Organisation of safety committees. Another measure for preventing accidents suggested by psychologists is the formation of safety committees. There should be one such committee in each factory, or even in each department of the factory, should the factory be exceptionally large in size. In addition to the workers, even safety officers and psychologists may be asked to function in this committee. In this committee, the suggestions and complaints of the workers are recorded and considered so that the possible areas of accidents can be known and measures for preventing them instituted. At the same time, such an organisation helps to interest every worker in preventing accidents. Such safety committees can also be organised on a national scale, so that representatives from different industries can take part in them. Such committees help to train the worker, make him more safety conscious, and also help to develop or invent new safety techniques. Another benefit which can be derived here is that the worker who is negligent of safety measures or who habitually pays no attention to the possibility of accidents can be criticised and even socially ostracised.

8. Safety campaign and posters. Safety can also be promoted in another way, by organizing a campaign, in factories and offices. Posters and slogans can also be used in such a campaign, but normally the slogans should not be negative. For example, a slogan like 'The careless worker is a fool', is not a proper slogan. Instead one can have more positive slogans such as 'Beware of danger', 'Keep the hat on the head', 'There is a danger of poisonous gases here', Cross the road here', 'Smoke, if you must, but in the next room'. These slogans will help the worker to control his actions. Such slogans can be printed and hung up in various places within the factory premises. They will help to drive away the worker's fear, awaken his sense of safety, and direct him to act in the correct way. Any poster concerned with accidents should not contain only a mention of the accidents possible because this will serve only to frighten the worker. Posters should tell him not only that accidents are possible but also how he can avoid them.

9. Habits of safety. Despite all the safety measures adopted, by far the best and the most successful method is the creation of habits of safety. If some worker has made a habit of operating his instruments improperly and of not using the safety devices, he may have an accident despite his efforts to prevent it. Different kinds of safety devices are built into different machines, and it is necessary that the worker should be trained in the use of them. But he must also be in the habit of using them. At times, the workers resist the installation of some new safety device. In such a case, they should never be forced to use the new device. They should be psychologically convinced that it is to their own advantage to make use of the safety devices. Once they are convinced they rarely have any hesitation in using it. If such habits have been formed, it is no longer necessary to remind the worker to be careful of accidents because caution becomes part of his thinking. This is why training is considered to be so important in all industries. Experience also has importance precisely for the same reason.

10. Motivating safety. Unless the worker is motivated to exercise caution and to make use of the safety devices installed for his benefit, accidents cannot be prevented. Therefore, nowadays workers are motivated and encouraged to work cautiously. One way of doing it is to increase the salary of those workers who follow the safety regulations. Another way of doing it is to counteract opposite kinds of motivation. For example, if a worker is encouraged to adopt safety measures on the one hand and is also forced to increase production on the other hand, then the work will defeat its purpose. Sometimes safety devices are not adopted by the workers because they cause discomfort. In that case, efforts have to be made to make these devices more comfortable and endurable. Sometimes workers are even punished by fines if they do not make use of the safety devices but this method is harmful in as much as it does not encourage the worker to make use of the safety device but only forces him to find ways of concealing his practice. To put it briefly, the best way of encouraging the use of safety devices is to make use of the psychology of motivation. In the first place, contradictory motivations should be removed and then useful safety devices should be sought out. Workers should also be rewarded for making use of them. Even safety committees encourage the use of safety devices.

It is evident from the above description of the means of preventing accidents that the goal can be achieved only by the willing cooperation of the management, the workers and the psychologists. The government too can make a valuable contribution in this effort. Nowadays great efforts are being made to avoid industrial accidents in all progressive countries.

ACCIDENT PRONENESS

What is Accident Proneness?

Generally more accidents take place in some industrial circumstances as compared with the others. Most psychologists feel that a particular pattern can be seen in accidents. For example, once a person has been involved in one accident, he is inclined to get involved in another because the first accident makes him lose his self-confidence. In other words, his accident proneness increases. Another proneness is that tendency due to which some particular person gets involved in more accidents than some other person. Accident proneness is found is industrial circumstances which lead to more accidents, while there are certain individuals who, because of their psychological and physiological structure, are inclined to be involved in more accidents.

Laws of Accident Proneness

Psychologists have made a study of accidents in order to discover the laws governing accident proneness, and in this connection it is possible to make the following remarks :

1. If the accidents are accidental then some people are only rarely involved in them. While some are involved very

frequently, the majority of people are at a stage somewhere between the two extremes.

2. If the accidents are due to circumstances then it will be seen that people who suffer from many accidents in a particular period, will be comparatively free of accidents in the following period.
3. If accident proneness increases because of accidents, then the particular individuals found involved in accidents in a particular test will also be found to be involved in accidents at any later test.
4. If the accidents are due to some particular qualities of the individuals then people obtaining a particular grade in a particular accident will obtain the same grade in future accidents also.

Psychologists have been able to come to some conclusion about the causes of accidents. Most studies have indicated that some individuals are so constructed that they are involved in more accidents than others, and are also the cause of involving other people into the accidents. Individuals of this kind are called accident prone. Normally there is always some scope for more or less accident proneness in every sphere where human beings work. It has, therefore, come to be believed that instead of throwing out the accident prone worker, it is better to analyse his accident proneness. This phenomenon can have many causes, and it may be possible to remove some of them. It has been found, for example, that accident proneness is definitely reduced if the individual is imparted training in some specific job. Then there are certain kinds of work which naturally lead to a greater number of accidents than other kinds of work. Experience also takes care of accident proneness because the individual becomes less prone to accidents once he gets experience. Besides, the basic cause of accident proneness is some fault in the working conditions, such as improper illumination, lighting which is either too strong or too dim, or lighting which is directed from the wrong angle, or improper arrangement of machinery, etc.

Tests of Accident Proneness

Psychologists have succeeded in evolving certain tests by which it is possible to discover accident proneness. These tests have been developed after extensive study of accident proneness. It is sometimes noticed that the more skilled workers are more accident prone than the less skilled ones. One cause of this is that they work with such speed that the probability of accident increases rapidly, and for this reason accident proneness cannot be taken as an indication of lack of skill. In the second place, identical characteristics are not found in all individuals who are accident prone. Despite this, it has been possible to identify certain characteristic qualities which tend to promote accident proneness. The tests for determining these qualities are as follows :

1. Sensory motor tests. Accident proneness and muscular coordination are intimately related. Individuals whose muscular coordination is not good suffer from more accidents. It has been observed that the relation between accidents and results obtained in sensorymotor tests increases with experience. In the second place, skill and accident proneness have been found to have a definite relationship. If the individuals who achieve the lowest scores in tests for accident proneness are selected, there are fewer accidents and the standard of the workers rises. It is a commonly accepted fact that lack of skill, slackness of motor reaction cannot escape from a situation with an accident potential without sustaining some injury and in certain situations they cannot escape accidents. They may just be accident prone without being careless or irresponsible. Hence, it is evident that accidents take place due to lack of proper muscular coordination.

2. Emotional stability tests. Emotionality and accident proneness are also intimately related and it has been found that highly emotional taxi drivers are involved in more accidents than other drivers while people with more stable emotionality have a lower accident proneness. Lower accident proneness is found in those individuals who are capable of controlling their reactions even in situations which distract attention or which disturb the individual. Briefly said, individuals obtaining high test scores in emotional stability tests have four times the probability of avoiding tests as compared that with accident proneness. It has been seen that depression was the cause of almost two hundred minor accidents out of four hundred such accidents.[6] On the other hand, production went up by 8 per cent in a mood of happiness which proved that this mood not only prevents accidents but actually promotes production. Himler[7] made a list of 28 personality traits which were

6. Hersey, R.B., "Emotional Factors in Accidents".
7. Himler, L.E., in *Psychological Factors in Industrial Accidents*.

the causes of accidents and more than half of them were connected with emotional coordination or stability.

3. Intelligence tests. Tests which indicated a relationship between accidents and muscular coordination or emotional stability did not indicate any relationship between accidents and intelligence. But some other researches indicated a relationship between accidents and intelligence. But some other researches indicated a relationship between accident proneness and mental traits. And in these studies it was found that the test scores of intelligence and emotional stability showed more valuable conclusions about accidents than the test scores of emotional stability alone. In another study, the relation between intelligence and accidents was discovered in tests as some professional individual avoided an accident because of his intelligence rather than as a result of his better skill. In a study concerning motor car drivers, it was found that generally individuals with lower intelligence were involved in more accidents than people with more intelligence. But generally it is believed by most people that intelligence is an important factor in avoiding accidents.

4. Sensory and perceptual speed tests. In certain tests it was seen that people with greater perceptual speed, meaning people who could rapidly observe even minor differences in perceptible pattern, were less inclined to be involved in accidents. On the other hand, individuals whose perceptual speed was less than their muscular reaction showed a higher degree of accident proneness. In this manner, accident proneness is increased if perceptual speed is less than muscular reaction because such people react faster than they can observe.

5. Tests of visual skills. Since the use of the eyes is very important in almost all industries, it is natural that defects of vision result in more accidents. In a study of this kind, it was seen that 63 per cent of people who did not cause accidents passed the eye test while only 33 per cent of the people causing accidents could pass them.[8] Nowadays, in many modern industries, efforts are made to find out the minimum level of visual skill which is needed for the successful performance of a particular work. For example, the visual skill of people applying for jobs as signallers in the Indian Railways is tested particularly because if they have

8. Kephart N.C. and J. Tiffin, "Vision and Accident Experience", *Nat Safety News*, pp. 90-91.

some visual defect they may endanger the lives of thousands of people. And the truth of the matter is that as the efficiency of all the sense organs, not only the eyes, increases, accidents decrease in number. They increases when such defects also increase.

Psychologists nowadays emphasize that the difficulties of the accident prone individual should be examined with great care and measures of eliminating them should be evolved and suggested. With the adoption of such an attitude, the rate of accidents of 44 accident prone motor car drivers fell from 1.3 to 0.75 over a distance of one thousand miles within one year.[9] For a study of this kind, it is necessary to find out and to isolate the particular individual factor which has been responsible for accidents. For example, in connection with motor car drivers it has been seen that about 64 per cent of accidents take place due to a defective aptitude, failure to anticipate the possibility of an accident, incorrect judgement of speed and distance, excessive impulsiveness, irresponsibility and failure to keep attention for a long time, or a combination of these factors. Studies of this kind can help to reduce the accidents in many kinds of jobs but it must also be kept in mind that the analysis of accidents often becomes subjective. Besides, mistakes can be made by an error of human judgement. Again, analysis of this kind cannot take the place of the tests described earlier in establishing a relation between accident proneness and individual traits. But as far as one is concerned with the influence of emotional instability on accidents, such an analysis can be useful.

Causes of Accident Proneness

The major causes of accident proneness can be enumerated on the basis of the above description of the various tests :

1. Low degree of muscular coordination. As has been pointed out in the first test of accident proneness, people with a low level of muscular coordination are more prone to accidents.

2. Absence of emotional stability. One major cause of accident proneness is lack of emotional stability, as is evident from the earlier description of the second test of accident proneness.

3. Absence of an appropriate mood. Generally an unhappy and depressed mood leads to more accidents and lower production than a happy and effervescent mood.

4. Weak intelligence. The Traffic Court of Detroit ordered the examination of some drivers for mental hygiene. About one-third

9. Viteles, M.S., *Industrial Psychology*, pp. 376-89.

of the cases referred were found to be mentally feeble. In this way, feeble-mindedness increases accident proneness.

5. Lack of coordination between perceptual and motor speed. In English there is a proverb that 'One should look before leaping'. Obviously, individuals whose speed of jumping is faster than their speed of observing will be involved in accidents. In other words, accident proneness increases when the perceptual speed is less than the motor speed.

6. Visual defects. Visual defects are a major cause of accidents in all kinds of work in which vision is to be used extensively and relied upon.

7. Frustration. An increase in frustration definitely leads to an increase in the level of accident proneness. For example, aggressiveness with frustration and aggression is a major cause of many accidents.

8. Lack of experience. In the modern age only trained individuals are employed to perform complex tasks because lack of experience is another factor causing accidents. Experience leads to an increase in a person's skill with the result that fewer accidents take place.

9. Immature age. Generally accident proneness is reduced when age increases because there is an increase in experience, skill, muscular coordination, perceptual speed, emotional stability, intelligence, sensory-motor reaction, with an increase in age. For this reason, certain industries prohibit the employment of individuals below a certain age. Individuals working in coal mines should be between 30 and 39 years of age, while people doing kinds of work below the earth's surface should be between 20 and 29 years. It must be remembered that accident proneness increases not only with immaturity but also if the worker is above the maximum age limit because older people become fatigued more easily and their powers weaken. Yet sometimes the younger people are involved in more accidents than their older counterparts. This is explained not only by their lack of skill but by the desire to work faster and to fake unnecessary risks.

10. Sex. Women, in general, are more accident prone than men. Even in a work like motor car driving, in which no physical force is necessary, it was seen that women were responsible for three times as many accidents per mile as men. Nevertheless, in the present situation, it cannot be said definitely that this difference between men and women is based on difference of sex or is caused because women tire more quickly than men.

11. Lack of health. It is generally believed that accident proneness increases with ill-health. High blood pressure has been found to be a definite cause of accidents caused by motor car drivers. But accident proneness also increases if a person suffers from mental ill-health. Individuals suffering from nervous and mental disorders or individuals having feeble minds are prone to accidents. The accident rate also increases if the individual is accident prone because it encourages antisocial tendencies.

It is evident from the above description of the causes of accident proneness that psychological means can be used to reduce accidents to a very great extent. If the causes are removed, accidents will definitely decrease. There are certain causes which can be eliminated in all individuals. For example, the lack of experience and training can be eliminated by providing training. But in addition to all these causes of accident proneness, some accidents take place in industry due to human relations. Some people cause accidents because they are completely irresponsible or because they deliberately want to cause damage. In such cases, it is necessary to keep an eye on such individuals so that they can be removed. In this respect, the foreman can play an important part. On the one hand, he can keep an eye on the antisocial elements and thus avert accidents, while on the other hand he can guide each worker in his work and in this way also avoid accidents. Bad behaviour on the part of the foreman leads to frustration and aggressiveness in the workers, with the result, that accidents increase. On the other hand, pleasant and mutually respectful behaviour on the part of the managers generates a happy peaceful atmosphere in the organisation with the result that accidents are kept to minimum. Therefore, the management should assume the role of friend, guide and assistant rather than that of the leader or the judge. This will help to create a group atmosphere in the factory so that the antisocial elements will be suppressed while the other people will cooperate with each other. They will be able to maintain sound mental health so that accidents will not occur so frequently.

QUESTIONS FOR EXERCISE

1. Define accidents. Discuss the environmental causes of industrial accidents.
2. Describe the main causes of industrial accidents.
3. "Accidents do not just happen". Explain this and bring out the major causes of accidents.

4. 'Accidents do not happen accidentally.' Discuss this remark and say how accidents in industry can be prevented.
5. Analyse the causes of industrial accidents in the light of modern research. Do these support the concept of accident proneness?
6. Attempt an analysis of the phenomenon of accidents in industry.
7. Discuss the main factors causing accidents. Are accidents accidental?
8. Elucidate the question of individual differences in susceptibility to accidents, and show how far the attention to the same has been useful in accident prevention programme in industry.
9. Explain with the aid of factual evidence how far accidents in factories are really accident in the accepted sense of term.
10. Describe various causes of accidents and state the measures that may be taken to prevent them.
11. Write short note on Accident Proneness.
12. Explain the evil consequences of accidents describing researches done on accident proneness.
13. Critically evaluate the theories of accident proneness.
14. What do you understand by accident proneness?
15. What is accident proneness? Are psychological tests useful in identifying accident prone individuals?
16. Describe the psychological factors in accident proneness? What measures should be taken to reduce accident proneness?
17. State the factors associated with accident proneness and discuss their relative importance.
18. Evaluate the concept of accident proneness and show to what extent the individual's liability to accidents may be predicted on the basis of psychological tests.
19. Examine the hypothesis of accident proneness. How will you deal with the human factors with a view to reducing accidents?

25

Maladjusted Industrial Worker

KINDS OF MALADJUSTMENT

Workers with a nervous temperament are maladjusted because normalcy of personality is an essential condition of proper adjustment. Before turning to the proper adjustment of the maladjusted worker, it is necessary to understand his main problems. The maladjustment of the worker with a nervous temperament is essentially an emotional maladjustment. It can either be mild or serious. Fisher and Hanna[1] have pointed out six main problems in mild maladjustment and twelve main problems in the more serious manifestations of it.

1. Mild emotional maladjustment. In this form, as is evident from the name, the emotional maladjustment is mild and its symptoms are jealousy, self-pity, absence of cheerful cooperation, fault finding, strong instincts, conflict with labour, abnormal desire to attract attention, etc. A worker with this problem is jealous of the other workers over very minor issues and at times believes himself to be a victim of other's enmity. He does not cooperate with others cheerfully and is constantly engaged in finding faults of the management and other colleagues. In attaining his own interests, he pays no attention to the propriety or impropriety of means and fights with others to gain all kinds of advantages. He wants to attract the attention of others towards himself for no reason and is not bothered about the propriety of the means he adopts for this purpose.

2. Serious emotional maladjustment. The main symptoms of this are the following :

(a) Frequent change of jobs,

(b) Extreme reticence and withdrawal,

---

1. Fisher, V.E., and J.V. Hanna, *The Dissatisfied Worker*, New York, p. 280.

(c) Tired feelings,
(d) Spasmodic and irregular application,
(e) Daydreaming,
(f) Deficiency in power of attention,
(g) Extreme irritability,
(h) Indigestion,
(i) Fear,
(j) Feelings of being spied upon,
(k) Hearing voices,
(1) Miscellaneous symptoms.

Workers with serious emotional maladjustments are seen changing jobs frequently. They are not very serious about many things in their minds and experience exhaustion after very little work. Their behaviour does not follow a definite pattern. They are not very practical and are inclined to be lost in the world of imagination. They find it difficult to concentrate their attention in any work. Small things irritate them. They also suffer constantly from indigestion. They are unnecessarily afraid of many things and feel that their friends are making complaints about them. Sometimes they also hear voices which do not actually exist. There is little synthesis between their emotions and feelings. They are victims of self-pity on the one hand and jealousy on the other. They do not turn their attention to their own shortcomings, instead they blame others for their own failure. They try to hide reality but despite this they feel inferior to others.

Explanation of the Causes of Maladjustment

In the opinion of Fisher and Hanna, mild and serious emotional maladjustment is caused by three main factors, as follow :

1. Emotional immaturity,
2. Exaggeration or over-expression of one or more drives,
3. Abnormal expression of emotions.

Maladjustment can also have causes other than these three factors. Many important researches have been conducted on this subject. H.M. Adler[2] examined one hundred patients in 1917 and pointed out the following three causes of professional maladjustment :

2. H.M. Adler, "Unemployment and Personality : Study of Psychopathic Causes", *Mental Hygiene*, 1 (1917), pp. 16-24.

1. Paranoid personalities,
2. Inadequate personalities,
3. Emotional instability.

Maladjustment is a common feature in industry. In addition to its adverse effects on the quality of production, it also injures the social environment. According to E. Toulouse, industries have to suffer much damage because of emotional maladjustment. V.E. Fisher and J.V. Hanna[3] have pointed out that in an industry employing five hundred individuals, half the expense lay in selecting and training new employees. Maladjustment is found to be a widespread phenomenon. In one study conducted by M.C. Jarrett[4] half the number of workers suffered from emotional maladjustment but this fact seems to be untrue. The studies of H.W. Stevens[5] appear to be more correct on this subject. Stevens studied four thousand workers working in a store over a period of six months and found that 10 per cent of them had problems of emotional maladjustment. V.V. Anderson[6] examined the twelve hundred employees of the R.H. Massey Company and concluded that 19 per cent of the sales workers and 23 per cent of the other workers suffered from emotional maladjustment. He made a list of the best and worst of the first kind of workers and after testing them demonstrated that 22 per cent of the best had personality defects while 54 per cent of the worst suffered from elementary forms of personality maladjustment while 24 per cent of the worst had acute defects of the personality. In a study of 41 maladjusted wire workers, M. Smith, M. Culpin and E. Farmer found that 31 of them had symptoms of mental diseases like anxiety, manic depression, etc. twenty-six workers suffered from neural defects.

Tests of Maladjustment

While the reports furnished by the authorities are useful, many scientific methods are used to test maladjustment. The more extensively used methods are ergograph test, McDougall-Schuster Dotting Test, Graphic Pursuit Meter, Pressure Test, Medical Examination, finding out the emotional nature and development of the worker by examining his external behaviour, etc. All these

3. V.F. Fisher and J.V. Hanna, *op. cit.*, pp. 233-34.
4. M.C. Jarrett, "The Mental Hygine in Industry," *Mental Hygiene*, pp. 867-84
5. H.W. Stevens, *The Psychic Aspect of Industrial Disability*, Bulletin : Massachusetts Department of Mental Diseases, pp. 6-7.
6. V.V. Anderson, "The Problem Employee".

methods should be used to discover the maladjusted worker in industry.

CAUSES OF MALADJUSTMENT

Before trying to find out the ways of removing maladjustment, it is necessary to discover the causes. Briefly, the main causes are :

1. Bad health. Physical health is directly concerned with mental health, as a result of which the adjustment begins to deteriorate if a person falls ill. As has been pointed out earlier, most of the maladjusted workers suffer from indigestion. Bad health makes a person irritable and he takes offence at the smallest things. Decrease in physical energy has an adverse effect on skill which, in turn, saps him of his self-confidence. All this leads to emotional maladjustment.

2. Marital disorganisation. The worker's maladjustment is intimately related with his marital condition. If his marital adjustment is upset then he finds it difficult to be balanced in his behaviour even in the factory. That is why in modern times stress is laid on making his home life happy.

3. Bad condition at home. If the worker's domestic condition is not good due to economic imbalance or any other cause, he suffers from anxiety, which is never good for emotional health.

4. Bad conditions of work. Broadly speaking, all the working conditions have some or the other effect on the worker's mental health but this, is most susceptible to the effect of the social environment. And in this the foreman's and the manager's behaviour is a very important element. If the social atmosphere of the factory is one of sympathy and cooperation, the worker can maintain a proper mental balance. If it is not of this kind, he immediately succumbs to maladjustment.

5. Wrong methods of work. There are many methods of working which tend to increase fatigue, boredom and monotony. They also do not satisfy the worker's desire to complete his work or to learn the results of his work. Besides, he himself feels that he is of no consequence in that particular job and he reduces himself to a cog in the machine. In this way, working conditions of this kind encourage maladjustment.

6. Painful experience of leaving other jobs. If a worker has the experience of giving up jobs at a number of places, then this painful experience spoils his mental balance and he cannot adjust himself.

7. Low income. Poverty is at the root of all kinds of maladjustment because a poor man finds it difficult to retain balance of mind. Because of low income, the worker continuously lives in a state of anxiety. His needs are not satisfied and hence his emotional adjustment is destroyed.

8. Old age. Viteles believes that in addition to the above-mentioned seven causes of maladjustment, old age is another cause. According to E.D. Smith, in old age an individual cannot change himself according to the conditions of work and for this reason, his power of adjustment is reduced. In the opinion of E.L. Thorndike,[7] the worker's ability to learn is reduced in old age and he cannot adopt the new and more efficient ways of doing work. H.L. Hollingworth[8] opines that, maladjustment in old age is caused not by the inability to learn but by the inability to put the learnt techniques to proper use. Many psychological investigations have indicated that people suffer in old age because they cannot adopt the modern ways of doing things. Their physical vitality is reduced and the desire to learn new things also declines. According to Viteles,[9] in old age the individual cannot adjust with his old fixed habits, ideas and mental attitudes. His balance is disturbed also because his physical and mental vitality is run down. He tends to ramble in his conversation and criticises others for no good reason. Loss of skill also induces loss of self-confidence. Smith points out that in old age, the worker cannot employ the skills and methods he has learnt because more modern methods have come into use by that time, which he is unable to acquire. Hence his adjustment is upset.

READJUSTMENT OF THE MALADJUSTED WORKER

It should not be assumed from the above description of the causes of maladjustment that it cannot be corrected. Not only in the case of maladjustment due to many causes, even maladjustment caused by old age can be remedied. L.J. Martin[10] made use of special experiments to establish proper adjustment in the case of a man of 61 years of age. This worker was the oldest employee of

---

7. E.L. Thorndike, *Adult Learning*, New York (1928), p. 335.
8. H.L. Hollingworth, *Mental Growth and Decline*, New York (1927), p. 396.
9. M.S. Viteles, *Industrial Psychology*, London (1962), p. 602.
10. L.J. Martin and C. de Grochy, *Salvaging Old Age*, New York (1930), p. 173.

the company and was receiving the highest wages. His production had declined by 39 per cent over a period of five years. On investigation it was found that he was alone at home and he had to cook his own food. When his domestic condition was changed, it was found that his production increased by 10 per cent in the first month, 22 per cent in the second month, fourteen per cent in the third, 19 per cent in the fourth month and by 21 per cent in the fifth month. It is evident from this that adjustment can again be established if some of the causes of maladjustment are removed to some extent. The following measures can be adopted for this purpose :

1. Improvement of health. If maladjustment is to be removed, the mental and physical health of the worker should be improved. If necessary, arrangements should be made for his medical treatment. If his economic condition is not satisfactory, it should be changed. He should be given proper and nourishing food at the correct time and allowed to rest as long as necessary.

2. Marital adjustment. In modern nations personal guidance is offered to the workers to improve their marital adjustment because this helps to improve their general adjustment.

3. Family adjustment. Nowadays it is believed that attention should be paid to the family requirements of the worker. If he has a large number of children, the government should provide facilities for free education and medical otherwise long as adjustment cannot be expected.

4. Improvement in the working conditions. In every industry, effort should be made to study the working conditions and to improve them wherever necessary. In addition to the working hours, lighting, clean air, water, correct temperature, etc., the industry must provide security of employment, proper wages, security of future, a desirable social climate, sympathetic and cooperative attitude towards the worker, etc. The worker's adjustment is improved if the level of morale is kept high in the industry.

5. Improvements in working methods. Sometimes the wrong method of working can lead to maladjustment. This can be certified by corrected examination and improvement of the working methods.

6. Individual carc and treatment. Many workers suffer from maladjustment which is caused by some individual factors. In such cases each worker should be examined separately and efforts should be made to solve his problems. He may benefit by personal guidance. Some people carry with them bitter experience of past jobs which they have had to give up. Old age is also an individual state. Some people suffer from some physical or mental illness. The problems of some workers have their source in their marital or general family life. If all these problems are to be solved then each worker must be guided individually and helped in his efforts at adjustment. According to E.D. Smith,[11] one cause of the worker's maladjustment is that he may be forced to do something he does not wish to do. For this reason the doctors and the organisers should make a study of these workers.

7. Committee for mental hygiene. E.E. Southard[12] has suggested the establishment of a committee for mental hygiene to eliminate maladjustment in the worker. This committee should include psychologists, doctors for mental disorders and social reformers in addition to the company organisers. According to H.L. Stevens,[13] the psychiatrist should study each worker and cure symptoms of mental disease if he finds any.

It is evident from the above description of the means of curing maladjustment that in the first place, the individual should be carefully examined so that the causes of his maladjustment can be located. For this it is necessary to win his confidence. Once the causes have been discovered, they can be cured by the cooperation of the organisers, psychologists, the psychiatrists and most of all, the worker himself. It is improper to neglect this problem of maladjustment because this disturbs the adjustment of other people also and creates a social climate directly injurious to work and production. Many serious industrial difficulties are caused by maladjustment nowadays. Hence, if arrangements are made to analyse and cure this problem, the industrialists stand to benefit quite as much as the worker himself.

QUESTIONS FOR EXERCISE

1. Who is a Maladjusted Industrial Worker?
2. What can be the possible problems created by the worker with a nervous temperament? How far is it possible for a psychologist to solve these problems?

---

11. Smith, E.D., "*What are the Psychological Factors of Obsolecence of Worker in Middle Age*?" Assoc. Personnel Series. No. 919, 10, p. 3.
12. Southard, E.E. The Modern Specialist in Unrest.
13. Stevens, H.L. *Psychiatry in Industry*, Monthly Bulletin of the Massachusetts Society for Mental Hygiene, Vol. 6.

26

INDUSTRIAL TRAINING

ADVANTAGES OF INDUSTRIAL TRAINING

It is a matter of common experience that the trained worker takes less time to produce more goods of a better quality than the untrained worker. Where the operation of certain kinds of machinery requires trained personnel, it becomes impossible to do anything without any training. Even in the case of machines which are not so complex, training definitely helps to improve the skill of the worker operating it.

The advantages of training in industry can be briefly summarised as under :

1. Increase in production. The studies of R.J. Greenly[1] show that while no progress was seen over a period of six years in the work of changing knives on one machine, a reduction of one-third was noticed after training was imparted. As a result, it became possible to save twenty thousand eight hundred and eighty dollars within one year. C.H. Lawshe[2] conducted a survey of one training programme. Here it was seen that as compared to the untrained employees, the trained employees showed the positive results of their training within eight weeks.

2. Prevention of breakages. Industrial training leads not only to an increase in production but also to considerable savings in breakages and wastage in other forms. It was discovered by L.G. Lindhahl[3] that a definite reduction in breakages was seen after training had been imparted for twelve weeks. When the quantity of breakages falls, the machines can work for a longer time and raw material can be saved. In this way, training

1. Greenly, R.J. *Job Training, Nat. Assn. Manuf,* Labour Relation Bill.
2. Lawshe, C.H. "Eight ways to check value of a training program".
3. Lindhahl, L.G. "Movement Analysis as an Industrial Training Method".

results in very comprehensive advantages and benefits to the company.

3. Prevention of accidents. Another advantage of industrial training is that it leads to a prevention of accidents. Although it has not been possible to collect accurate data on this subject through research, it can still be asserted that the trained employees as a rule are less prone to accidents than the untrained workers.

4. Reduction in absenteeism. Apart from the more direct advantages of industrial training as outlined above, it also helps to reduce absenteeism. Training makes it easy for the individual to perform even fairly difficult tasks, and because he can produce goods faster and better he wins esteem and sometimes even concrete rewards. This helps to encourage him so that he is less inclined to absent himself. In this manner, training increases morale and job satisfaction in industries.

It is obvious from this brief description of the advantages of industrial training that it promotes the interests of the industrialist. Although no definite conclusions have been arrived at in this sphere despite extensive research, nobody can or does deny that industrial training is really beneficial. In fact, some people believe so implicitly in the advantages of training that they do not think it necessary to investigate it. For example, although teachers have been teaching in colleges for centuries, nobody has ever seen reason to ask whether this teaching has any advantages at all. Neither has it been found necessary to prove the utility of teaching through research. Hence, the importance of training is self-evident.

The Criterion of the Correct Training Method

Having established the importance of training in industry, the next thing to be decided is the method and the time of the actual training imparted to a particular worker in some specific industry. The extent and the method of training vary with the individual differences of the workers and the nature of their functions in a specific industry. The advantages and disadvantages of the various training methods such as the lecture method, or teaching by the use of charts, pictures, sketches and motion pictures, or classroom teaching, etc. have been explained. But before deciding upon a particular training method, it is necessary to determine the objective of that training programme because one method which is good for achieving one objective may prove useless if applied in a training programme with a different objective. While the use of cinema slides, pictures or charts may prove valuable in one particular sphere, it may be better to make use of the discussion or lecture or classroom teaching methods in another sphere. No particular method can be said to be the best for every kind of training programme. So one criterion of the correct training method is the objective to be achieved. Another criterion is the extent of training actually imparted by it, meaning the extent to which the worker has learnt. Some people believe that the importance of training should be evaluated in terms of what has been taught, not by what has been learnt. But this attitude is hardly correct, because the best measure of a training method is the extent of learning absorbed by the trainee. If the trainee has learnt very little, the method cannot be called good, irrespective of the quantity of information which should have been communicated by that particular method. One additional quality of the training method should be that it should teach a trainee only those things which he can easily apply to the job he has to perform. If this cannot be done, he will not benefit very much by the training.

Any training programme will be a failure if the method employed in it does not possess the qualities outlined above. But the failure of the training programme may be caused by many factors such as the wastage of the training time, the futility of the training method used, difference of opinion about the working method between the organiser and the teachers, inaccurate method of testing the training achieved, etc. Sometimes a training programme fails simply because the training is suspended a little earlier than it should have been stopped.

AREAS OF LEARNING IN AN INDUSTRY

Generally, industrial jobs are divided into the skilled and the unskilled. Skilled work is that which normally requires knowledge of some kind and this knowledge is gained through training. Unskilled work, on the other hand, does not require the acquisition of any special skill. So, it is believed that skilled work requires both knowledge and craftmanship, the ability to use one's hands to the best advantage. For example, mere knowledge of the particular trade is not enough to make a man a skilled carpenter, mason or electrician, because he must also possess the ability to efficiently perform the tasks of his trade. No worker can be called skilled unless he possesses this craftmanship. Knowledge of the trade is one thing and craftmanship another. It is for this reason that certain skilled craftsmen produce work which an educated worker can never do, despite all his knowledge. What is this skill? It is a training in the performance of specific movements made in some particular work. Different parts of the body have to make different and specific movements in the performance of different functions. If one can correctly perform the functions required for some particular job, and can also show evidence of coordination of movements, then one is called skilled at that particular work. Hence one objective of industrial training is to impart knowledge about the particular job while the other objective is to create skill in the particular movements required for that job. Industrial training thus requires the following kinds of training :

1. Association. In different industries, efficient work requires that there should be association between the various actions which are performed one after the other. If there is association then they can be performed spontaneously and in the correct order. This association works in the memory and also functions as conditioned response.

2. Selection in learning. In the actual work situation, it is necessary to pay more attention to certain things than to any other. This involves two kinds of selection — sensory and motor. In sensory selection, the individual must learn to distinguish between different sensations and to recognise the correct ones. For example, among all the other kinds of lights that the car driver sees, he must learn to distinguish the red and the green lights and also to understand the meaning implicit in these two signals. Different motor activities are required in different industrial conditions, and these activities should be performed with economy, while aiming at maximum output. This leads to a reduction in fatigue on one hand and an increase in the total time saved on the other. Time and motion studies can be undertaken in different industries to discover the facts concerning each industry.

3. Sensory discrimination. It is necessary for the worker to learn to distinguish between different sensations, as a part of industrial training. Sometimes the worker becomes involved in an accident simply because he cannot discriminate between different sensations. The skilful individual can distinguish between subtle variations in the same thing or between various objects. Some people can recognise the car models at a glance, and therefore it is impossible to deceive them in this respect.

4. Acquisition of skill. Workers who work in factories where they have to use their hands in different kinds of work must acquire craftsmanship. What is this manual skill ? It is the result of training the muscles of the hand. If he has this kind of training, the worker can tell merely by feeling a thing with his hand how far the work has progressed and whether it is progressing satisfactorily. He needs no more than a glance to distinguish between good and bad work. He continues to do his work only by touching things with hand. The movements of the muscles cannot be measured. Hence, skill of this kind is a matter of practice only. The more skilful tennis players know exactly how much strength to use to throw the ball to a particular spot in the tennis court or how far to bend in order to retrieve a particular ball. All these facts are concerned with the player's skill.

5. Understanding and insight in work. Another aspect of industrial training is to instil understanding and insight into work. In the absence of this, simple kinds of functions can be performed but more complex problems cannot be solved. For example, only that engineer can be called skilful who can discover the fault in a machine at a glance and also be able to point out how and why that defect has occurred. The basis of the engineer's skill is his knowledge of the machine's construction and his understanding and insight into technological principles. Hence it is desirable that training should not lead to parrot-like repetition and rote learning but instead to insight into the particular job. If this is done then the workers themselves can evolve the most effective methods of performing their jobs. Although insight and understanding depend, to a large extent, upon the intelligence of the worker, they can be improved to a certain extent by training.

6. Change of attitude. As has been indicated earlier, industrial training helps to improve the morale of the worker. A trained worker can easily perform a function which the unskilled worker finds a great burden. Training thus helps to change the worker's attitude to his work because after training he has a more positive attitude to this work.

Nowadays, various methods are used to impart training in the field of industry — lecture method, propaganda through books and pamphlets, the use of audio-visual aids and the exhibition of films, on-the-job training, discussion method, role playing, etc. Now a brief explanation and evaluation of each training method will be given here :

1. The lecture method. As is evident from the name itself, in this method, the more learned individuals inform the trainees about their jobs by delivering lectures. Thus it becomes possible to acquaint the trainees with various aspects of the work in a short time. These lectures can be made more objective and concrete by the use of charts and tables. In many industries, lectures by eminent authorities on various subjects are frequently arranged. The lecture method is of eminent value in subjects like industrial organisation but it has the following shortcomings :

(a) ***Inappropriate method*** : The lecture method is not apt for changing the attitudes of the workers, for establishing simple association, for increasing skills, etc.

(b) ***Boring method*** : Generally lectures on industrial and technological subjects are not entertaining with the result that the audience cannot concentrate on a lecture for more than 45 minutes at a stretch. And since it is boring, only the discriminating and intelligent listener can benefit by it.

In spite of its above-mentioned shortcomings, many organisations make use of the lecture method for some specific kinds of work. On special occasions, the new employees of the company are acquainted with its policies and its traditions through lectures, so that they know the company. The effectiveness of a lecture can be improved by making it more powerful, which can be done by using forceful words and frequent and violent gestures. It is a common psychological fact that something heard is remembered more than something read. Hence, the importance of the lecture method is obvious.

2. Books and pamphlets. Very often books and pamphlets are distributed during exhibition so as to promote know-how about some particular industry. By reading this, people can know where the industry is located and how it is functioning. This method can also be used for spreading information among the workers.

But it is not possible to calculate the effectiveness of this propaganda by counting the number of books and pamphlets distributed or by recording the number of people who receive them. Majority of people accept them because they are attractive and also free. Some people do open the pamphlets but they go no further than glancing at the colourful pictures or bold slogans. Only a very few people take the trouble of actually reading the pamphlet in detail. It has been seen that most of the workers pay no attention to the books and pamphlets distributed to them.

Despite all these shortcomings, this method has certain advantages over others. Once a lecture has been delivered, it cannot be repeated, with the result that if a listener has forgotten something, he has no way of getting that piece of information again. This shortcoming is overcome by the pamphlet since it can be read any number of times and at any time. People can be encouraged to read the pamphlet by making it more attractive by the use of colours. Besides, the very fact that the company gets such pamphlets printed and distributed is proof of the fact that it wants to train its employees. This, in itself, is a fact which has its own significance.

3. Motion pictures. Although the exhibition of motion pictures is more expensive than lectures or pamphlets, it has many advantages and for that reason this method is extensively used. While many organisations take the trouble of producing their own films, many companies buy them from the producers. The most important quality of the motion picture is that it can be shown repeatedly and, to a very large audience, simultaneously. Besides, most audiences generally tend to pay attention to what is going on the screen. Motion pictures are the best medium of training and instruction. They can be used to show the various machines and tools employed in a particular industry, and it is also possible to realistically show their actual usage. Motion pictures of this kind are no less effective than a guided tour of a real factory. In fact, they are more useful because they can be seen repeatedly, while it may be difficult to arrange a guided tour more than once. It hardly needs to be pointed out that this method is a fine amalgam of the lecture method and the exhibition method.

In spite of this, there should be no misunderstanding about the value of this method because it also leaves untouched certain aspects of training. While it is possible to show human relations through this medium and also to appeal to the emotions of the viewers, it is impossible to improve skill through it. A worker does not become more skilful merely by viewing a motion picture. The most that can be said is that the motion picture method is an unavoidable part of any training programme.

4. Demonstration and audio-visual aids. It is cheaper to collect audio-visual aids than to produce motion picture for training. But it has the same benefits as the motion picture. It helps most obviously in visual training, but it can be most effective if the material used is adapted to the intelligence level of the audience. Hence, the use of such aids is considered a necessary part of industrial training nowadays.

5. On-the-job training. The major difficulty in most training methods is that tacts learnt and acquired in artificial circumstances cannot be easily transferred and put into practice in the actual conditions of work. For this reason, on-the-job training is introduced, and it can be imparted easily in all work which is not done at very high speed. In some factories, new employees are trained on the actual machines after normal working hours. In other cases, the employees are trained on simpler machines which gives them practice but minimise the chances of accidents. For example, the telephone operator can be trained in his work by this method. In factories, the functions of the supervisor can be taught by role playing in certain conditions. The major quality of this method is that training is done through actual work. Besides, in this each trainee is trained individually so that he gets a chance to practise and his shortcomings and difficulties are separately attended to. Naturally, this method is more expensive and it is used only in those kinds of work where it is necessary to pay attention to each worker.

6. The case method. In this method of industrial training, the managers are employed to give training. In this, the trainees are asked to solve some concrete problem and are required to discuss the means by which it can be solved after understanding the factors involved in the situation. It has the advantages of a group discussion in addition to the practice gained in solving actual problems. But it does not help very much in increasing skill. It only inspires the individual to increase his knowledge of human relations.

7. Discussion method. This is another method employed in industrial training and in this many workers get together to discuss some specific problem. Some experts are also present during the discussion. This exchange of ideas improves the worker's understanding and provides practice in problem-solving. This method is of particular use in those subjects where the problem has become complex because of emotions and negative attitudes.

8. Role playing. In industrial conditions many workers have to play many kinds of roles. In this method they are given the opportunity of playing a role by which they can improve their ability to perform the task pertaining to that role.

Industrial training makes use of all those principles of learning which are used in training of any other kind. Modern psychologists have found out many means of economizing in the process of learning. These methods of economy are used extensively in industrial training.

FACTORS ASSISTING ASSOCIATION

Formation of many kinds of association is an important aspect of industrial training. Association is helped by the following factors :

1. Frequent repetition. One common method of making some association firm is the frequent repetition of the subject learnt. This method is particularly useful in the learning acquired through memory. The association between various parts of the subject matter will become more sound as the subject matter is repeated more and more often. Even when something has been learnt by trial and error, repetition can be of some use. This assistance is rendered in two ways — in the first place frequent repetition provides more opportunities of selection while it also helps in forming some association and making it permanent. Works of skill can be also improved through repetition because the association between the various movements becomes more sound. Repetition also saves time in learning. Nowadays the method of repetition is used in advertisement, propaganda, etc. Advertisements are repeated so frequently that the people who see it remember the subject matter of the advertisement and as soon as the need arises, it is easily remembered. For example, the name Aspro is repeated so often in connection with removing headaches that a person thinks of it automatically as soon as he gets a headache. Hence, repetition is an important method in industrial propaganda. In fact, repetition is sometimes used to propagate some object which is not commonly used.

2. Presence of attention and intention. Attention and intention play an important part in learning. If a person is doing something with the intention of learning it, he will inevitably pay more attention to it. Hence, in industrial training, it is of primary importance to generate intention in the trainee. If this is done, he automatically attends to what is being taught to him. And a subject can be easily mastered if one pays attention. In this manner, attention and intention assist each other. In the field of industry, the psychology of attracting attention is used extensively in all kinds of advertisement. If one wants to turn the trainee's periodicity, etc., his motivation should be such that he should be compelled to attend to the training.

3. Spaced repetition. It is always better to repeat some object after some interval than to repeat it continuously because if the repetition is continuous, the listener may become exhausted. In this connection, Woodworth has pointed out that interval between repetitions should be of one or two days' duration. In this way, there should be an opportunity to repeat the subject after intervals. The method of spaced repetition is better in all complex subjects because they lead to boredom and inattention if teaching is continued for a long period. This does not imply that continuous repetition is bad in all cases, because in fact sometimes the method of unspaced repetition is better than spaced repetition. For example, the interval should not be introduced so quickly that the individual cannot even warm up to his work. If this is done, then the individual will only be hindered in his learning. On the other hand, the interval should also not be so long that the individual may actually forget all that he has learnt.

Despite the above advantages, these principles are not followed in actual industrial circumstances. For example, an individual who works would not like to be made to work only for one or two hours each day. Therefore, many other methods are followed. For example, students are imparted training during their period of study itself so that as soon as they have completed their studies, they can quickly acquire the necessary skill. This method is used very much in training bank employees. Another method provides opportunity for training the worker in all aspects of the job, one after the other. In another method, training for some complex function is given while the individual is normally performing a simpler function.

4. Benefits of whole method. Generally the whole method proves more useful in teaching than the part method. In the part method of teaching, the entire subject matter is divided into small units, and each unit is taught in a single sitting. On the other hand, in the whole method, the entire subject is learnt at once, the advantages being that some association between the various parts of the subject is created and this assists the trainee in learning the subject. While teaching the use of some machine, it is better to make use of both these methods. In the beginning, the trainee should be told about the operation of the entire machine that followed up by a detailed account of the function of each part he understands it. Hence, industrial training makes use of both the whole and the part methods of teaching. The subject is introduced by the whole method and detailed training is then given through the part method.

5. Active repetition. Many experiments have proved that the method of active repetition is more effective than the inactive method. The inactive method implies a condition in which the learner does not pay full attention to what is being taught while in the active method he participates in the teaching with his whole mind. If this is done he derives all the benefits of attention and also intention of learning. Hence, in industrial training, it is desirable to employ a method in which the trainee can take an active part. Otherwise the training will not be really beneficial.

ECONOMIC METHODS OF SELECTION IN LEARNING

In certain types of industrial training, it becomes necessary to pay the greatest attention to some particular aspects. If this is not done, then learning becomes more difficult. Many methods are nowadays employed to help in this kind of selection, for example, reward for proper reaction and punishment for incorrect reaction, positive selection and negative selection, etc. Norman Meyer has suggested that attention be paid to the following things in learning :

1. Use of positive selection. Normally, positive selection should be preferred to negative selection. The trainee should be trained both in training and in administration. When there is provision for reward and punishment, the trainee learns to discard one thing and select the other. It is better for the trainee to learn what he has to do rather than what he must avoid doing. That is why the positive method is more beneficial and economic than the negative method. Sometimes mistakes and faults can be rectified if they are repeated consciously and deliberately. Positive selection proves more valuable in removing such defects.

2. Knowledge of results. Many experiments have established that if the trainee is aware of the results of his work, he learns better than otherwise. If he is unaware of results he shows no progress in learning because he does not know his good points or the mistakes that he may have made. Hence it is better that the trainee should be informed of his progress.

3. Clarification of cause-effect relationships. During training the trainee must be made to understand what happens if something is done. For example, if a trainee is being told about the operation of a particular machine, he must bc clcarly told of the results of his actions in operating a particular part of the machine. This will help the trainee to understand how far he can use a particular machine to get the desired results.

4. Personal training. As a result of individual differences, the same tasks present varying degrees of difficulties to different individuals and they commit all kind of mistakes. Hence, during training, provision should be made for individual guidance and rectification of mistakes.

Discrimination Between Sensations

In industrial work, there are certain functions in which it is necessary to distinguish between various sensations. In training for this kind of work, it is necessary to remember that different individuals have varying powers of distinguishing sensations. Hence, before beginning training of individuals for work of this kind, it is necessary to determine whether the trainees have the requisite ability to distinguish between sensations or not. If they do not have the ability, all the training will probably be wasted. This fact is of extreme importance in the selection of inspectors for various functions.

In the second place, the methods used for teaching how to distinguish between sensations should be favourable to the specific sensory capacity or ability. In every kind of work, one or the other specific sensory ability is required. If vision is the most important factor then it is better to use machines which help vision. Similarly, if the auditory powers are most important then only those instruments should be used which help the power of hearing.

Factors Favourable to the Acquisition of Skills

Most kinds of industrial training concentrate upon giving some special skill to the workers. Psychologists have discovered many methods which help in the acquisition of skills and if these methods are used it becomes much easier to impart these skills. The most important factor in acquiring a skill is the training of muscles because expert craftsmanship requires coordination between the speed of working and sensations. And this is a matter of practice. Only the training of muscles can determine how hard a particular instrument should be pressed. This cannot be learnt only by imitation. The trainee should not only know what the work looks like during the process of doing but he should also experience how it feels. For this it is necessary that he be given the opportunity to do the work himself. Briefly stated, the following things help in the acquisition of skill :

1. Acting through doing. The method of acting through doing is the most important in learning skill. Hence the trainee must get an opportunity to do it himself. Less time should be devoted to demonstration. He must also be warned about the dangers of the instrument he is using.

2. Selection of movements. Skill means a proper reaction to a specific stimulus. For this reason, the teacher must tell the trainee about the correct movement out of all the movements that he sees or makes. He must also make sure that the student is making the correct movements.

3. Control on guidance. In industrial training, many people lay too much stress on the factor of guidance while in fact beyond a certain limit, guidance becomes more a hindrance than a help. It is true that in the beginning, the teacher may hold the trainee's hand to guide him but the sensations he then experiences will not be the same as when he is performing the function without assistance. Consequently, if the trainee is guided too much, he gets into the habit of working only when assisted. Then he cannot acquire the necessary skill, and for this reason, guidance should not be continued beyond a reasonable time.

4. Emphasis on feeling of correct movement. The true mark of the skilled craftsman is that he can touch a piece of work and point out if it is correct or wrong. The reason of this is that he has knowledge of the correct movement. Once the trainee develops this feeling of correct movement he will find no difficulty.

5. Control of perception. Control of perception plays an important part in the acquisition of skill. If one wants to make use of the telephone directory, it is necessary, first of all, to learn how a name should be seen in order to be recognised. Whether the brush used for painting is a part of the hand or a tool held in the hand, are two different perceptions, and they influence the skill in painting. This fact is also true of other works of manual skill. Accurate perception is necessary for acquiring skill in the different arts. This principle is of particular importance in the teaching of music. A.R. Solem has demonstrated by an experiment that a foreman proved a successful administrator when during a discussion he treated the others not as his subordinates but his equals and his colleagues. In the field of industry, the leaders who treat others as their equals appear to be more kind and cooperative. If the speed in reading is to be improved, it is necessary that the reader must see many words as part of a single group or unit. It is for this reason that it is said that some people read letters, others read words, some read sentences while some read pages.

6. Proper movement in work. Knowing the proper movements required for any work of skill is also important. In teaching these, attention should be paid to individual differences. Different individuals will perform the same work at different speeds. Hence the speed of work should be increased according to the individual qualities of the worker.

7. Control on tension. The skilled craftsman has one peculiarity in as much as he makes use of only those muscles which are necessary for his work. The other muscles are free from tension. An unskilled worker makes many unnecessary movements because he becomes confused and tries many ways of doing it. Consequently, he gets tired rapidly. In training an individual, it should be stressed that he should not get unnecessarily excited. He should also be taught to use only those muscles which are required for performing some specific action and to let the other muscles relax.

8. Provision of incentives for progress. The trainee must be given some incentive for progress if he is to acquire some skill, so that he may be motivated to learn. Roughly speaking, incentives can be financial or non-financial. Financial incentives can take almost innumerable forms such as bonus or additional salary. Non-financial incentives can take the form of improvement in working conditions, praise, social respect, etc. If a study is made of any work curve for any industry, it will be seen that a plateau is reached at one stage or the other if incentives are absent. This plateau can be eliminated by providing incentives, and thus creating motivation.

9. Attention on movements. The trainee must pay attention to his movements if he wants to acquire skill. Wrong movements must be eliminated and the right movements established. It is better to draw attention to the right movements and to stress their repetition rather than to point out the wrong movements because if attention is paid to wrong movements they become habits. In work which is done at speed, attention should be paid to rhythm because once the rhythm is established, the work can be performed without hesitation. In this type of work, the various parts of the work must be tied into a single whole because it is not possible to alter attention and focus it on different aspects at a very high speed. In the same way, the movements of muscles are not to be viewed as separate movements but as part of a single movement. The trainee should also concentrate upon the results of his work because in most kinds of work, the movements are made with a view to attaining a particular objective. In all such work, only the correct result is the criterion of good work. Briefly, it is better to learn works of skill as a whole rather than in parts so that all the various functions are seen as part of the whole operation. Here it is necessary that the entire operation should be so divided into units that maximum production should be possible while each unit should also be complete in itself.

Learning through Understanding

There are some functions in industrial work where insight into the work and understanding are more important than manual skill. In these kinds of functions, the following principles are employed for economy :

1. Organisation of material around principles. In industries, the worker is faced with many new kinds of work every day. If he is to do all this properly, he must not get lost in the variety of the material. He must have clear understanding of the fundamental principles which govern the material involved in that work. For example, the principles of mathematics help immensely in maintaining accounts. Similarly, the principles of distribution and selling play an important role in all sales work. Hence, whenever the salesman is faced with a new customer, he must keep in mind the principles of selling.

2. Encouragement to discussion. Proper training can be imparted only if the trainees are given the freedom to express their opinion and to enter into discussion. Discussion among themselves and the teacher helps to create insight into job and problems can then be solved. Undoubtedly, this is a time consuming process but it helps to focus attention, because it is one method of positive teaching. The intelligent trainer should make use of the correct mode of discussion so that the trainees may develop some insight into their job.

3. Tests of progress. If training is to achieve its objectives, it is necessary that the progress of the trainees should be tested from time to time by correct testing procedures. By doing this, the teacher can establish how far the student has progressed. If he is found to be lagging behind others, then the causes of this retarded progress can be discovered and efforts made to eliminate them.

4. Encouragement to use own words. If the students are to be given an opportunity to develop insight into their work it is necessary that they be allowed to express the problem in their own words.

By doing this they can understand the problem and this helps to improve insight.

METHODS ASSISTING THE TRAINING OF APTITUDES

Sometimes in the course of an industrial training programme, it becomes necessary to pay attention to the trainees' aptitudes because the right aptitude is essential for proper performance of any job. The following means can be employed for this work :

1. Opportunity for discussion. Discussion not only allows a trainee to express his own feelings and attitudes but also provides him with an opportunity of knowing the feelings and attitudes of others. In a group discussion, an individual adopts the attitudes of the group because of social pressure. Hence if the teacher himself takes part in the discussion and guides it correctly then the trainees can develop the correct attitude for the work.

2. Opportunity for expression of frustration. Some trainees cannot develop the correct attitude at times because of their frustration. In such cases it is best to use methods by which these frustrations can be vented and expressed harmlessly. Unless the condition of frustration is cured, the wrong aptitude cannot be eliminated.

3. Method of role playing. One important way of creating correct aptitude is to give the trainee an aptitude to play different roles in different situations. In playing such roles, the trainee gains experience of the problems, aptitudes and feelings implicit in different kinds of work so that he is helped in his understanding of the people who perform this work. For example, if the manager is permitted to work at different posts as foreman, typist, etc., for short times, he will have little difficulty in understanding their problems, aptitudes and viewpoints. Consequently, he will be able to manage the affairs of his organisation much more successfully.

4. Association with pleasant experience. It is a commonly accepted psychological principle that people form positive aptitudes for pleasant experiences and negative aptitudes for painful experience. Hence, the worker should have pleasant experience of the work for which he is to form a positive aptitude. If the conditions of work are such that he experiences pain in performing it, then he will develop a negative aptitude for it. This fact must be well understood by supervisors. If their behaviour towards the employees is kind and pleasant and if the general atmosphere in the factory is one of cooperation and friendship, the workers easily generate a positive aptitude for their work.

27

MOTIVATION, INCENTIVES AND METHODS OF PAYMENT

WHAT IS MOTIVATION?

According to Woodworth, "A motive is a state or set of individuals which disposes him for certain behaviour and for seeking certain goal." In this way one finds goal-oriented behaviour in motivation. The aim of this behaviour is to achieve certain specific goals. By analysing motivation, one can find out why man works. No individual can achieve something solely due to motivation when it is beyond his capacity to achieve it. Hence, the power to do something due to motivation is limited by ability or capacity. Motivation is the method of giving expression to an individual's abilities. The condition of motivation has two aspects — the subjective and the objective. In the subjective aspect, this contains that condition of the individual which is called need, desire or drive. And the objective aspect is the incentive or the goal due to which the individual acts. A situation in which the incentive is one for which some need is experienced, is a motivating situation. For example, an individual gets some salary if he works in some industry. Now, if the money received as salary is a means by which an individual can fulfil his desires then he will work in order to get the salary. Obviously, then motivation changes when the incentive and the need both change. Hence, in order to create motivation in activity, it is desirable that the incentive should be concerned with some or the other need of the worker. If, for example, an individual does not need money, then the incentive of money will not form sufficient motivation by which he will be impelled to work. In such a case, non-financial incentives like social prestige, proper utilization of one's time, etc., may form sufficient motives to induce a man to work.

Motivation in Industry

It is apparent from the above description that both an understanding of human wants and a knowledge of industrial incentives are necessary for understanding the importance of motivation in industry. Broadly, human wants are of two kinds — natural or internal, and acquired. The inner needs include hunger, thirst, maternal instinct, sex needs, sleep, etc. The category of acquired needs includes love, sympathy, social prestige and innumerable others which are products of modern culture. Acquired needs change according to past experience and the individual's own qualities. The most important among them are social needs. And one of the major social needs is the desire to maintain one's respect in society and the desire to be a kingpin among other men. In addition to this, human beings have the need to get something with which they can identify themselves and get satisfaction.

Motivation and the Level of Ambition

Different individuals have their own level of ambition and if these are not achieved, the individuals feel frustrated. People who have a high level of ambition make very great efforts to achieve it. In one of the studies conducted by Coch and French, a production level of 60 units was assumed to be the average. The result was that those who were producing less than this, between 55 and 59 units, immediately increased their production and achieved the average, but those who could not achieve it left their jobs. When the level of ambition is low, the individual does not make any effort to exploit his own capabilities to the fullest extent. On the other hand, a person with a high level of ambition often tries to achieve much that is beyond his capabilities.

Motivation and External Circumstances

External circumstances influence the motivation of an individual only when they have some effect on his internal motivation. This internal motivation has its well spring in the individual's egoistic needs. If a person feels respected in his job, he will be motivated to do well in it. If, on the other hand, he feels neglected, he will not be motivated in work. For this reason, group motivation has very great influence.

Internal Motives in Industry

Considering the importance of various motives in the industrial context, T.W. Harrell[1] has laid stress on three motives which he believes to be most important-sex, self-respect and social prestige. But the motives of remaining active, the desire to work and hunger are also important motives. It is a common fact that the majority

1. Harrell, T.W., *Industrial Psychology.*

of people work to earn their bread. By working, most people can earn enough to satisfy the physical needs of the family and can lead a married life. But some individuals continue to work even after these needs have been fulfilled because work gives them social prestige which satisfies their desire for respect in society. And yet some people continue to work even after both these needs have been satisfied. That is because they want to remain active, because activity is the nature of life. It is difficult to spend life in a completely inactive state. Hence, most work is done without any financial or non-financial incentives. It is done only for the sake of working.

Internal Drive

In connection with internal motives, internal drive is mentioned along with needs. Needs include such physical needs as hunger, thirst, sex desire, excretion, respiration and homeostasis, etc. If these needs are not satisfied then the balance of the body is destroyed with the result that mental adjustment is endangered. Drives pertain to more powerful and intense needs, the non-fulfilment of which leads to anxiety. Conditions of such anxiety can be seen in the case of dissatisfaction of the sex instinct. A similar condition can also be seen when hunger and thirst are not satisfied. If these drives are not satisfied, the individual's balance is upset.

Conflict in Motives

Sometimes many motives in an individual come to conflict. In such a condition, work suffers and production falls. In the sphere of industry, care must be taken to avoid such a situation where motives come into conflict. This must be kept in mind while creating motivation. Conflict always leads to mental conflict and the worker cannot decide what to do. Therefore, only those motives should be created which clearly show him the way. In that case, he does not have to think very much and he can continue to work at peace. Nowadays a variety of methods are used to create motivation among the workers. As far as internal motivation is concerned, it is entirely a matter of the individual worker's mental state. Only external motives can be provided in an industry, and these are called incentives.

THEORY OF INDIVIDUAL MOTIVATION

McGregor's Theory

McGregor propounded two theories of human behaviour in management philosophy on the theme of dual nature of human being best known as theory 'X' and theory 'Y'. McGregor believes that nearly all management actions flow from these two theories and they (actions) reflect their philosophy. As philosophy controls practice, management assumptions about human behaviour influence the personnel practice decision making, operating practices and even organisation design. McGregor observed that people appear to have a capacity for tenderness, sympathy and love, while they also possess tendencies towards cruelty, callousness, hate and malicious aggression. These two different philosophies are based on two different theories of McGregor, Theory 'X' and Theory 'Y'.

Theory 'X' and its Assumptions

It is the traditional theory of management philosophy. 'Power is supreme' is the main theme of the theory where the people at work-level have no authority to suggest or object anything except to carry out the orders of the supervisor. The line of authority or chain of command traditionally goes direct from the top, down through various layers of organisation with some delegation of authority but full and detailed accountability is up the line. People at work-level have no option except to obey the directives or orders of the authority.

Assumptions of Theory 'X'

1. Most people inherently dislike work and always try to shirk their responsibility.
2. Therefore, people must be cursed, controlled, directed and threatened with punishment, rebuffed or rebuked so as to get them to put forth adequate efforts towards the achievement of organisational goals.
3. The average human being prefers to be directed, wishes to avoid responsibility and puts off the work till it is necessary.
4. Most people at work have little ambition as to the improvement of work. They do not work with interest but wait for direction and act according to it.
5. The average human being wants security and safety above all, hence, he tends to work slowly.
6. Most people have little capacity to contribute something towards solving the organisational problems as their importance in the management is always undermined by

the authority and they are treated as an instrument of a machine.

7. Working method of the people is generally traditional and hence, there is little scope for the development and research.
8. People can be motivated at money end. On the basis of financial greed, they can do whatever management wants.

Propositions of Theory 'X'

1. Management is responsible for organising the elements of production — money, material, machine, man and methods — in the interest of economic gain.
2. Management is responsible for directing the efforts of the people, motivating them, controlling their actions and modifying their behaviour to fit the needs of the organisation.
3. People would be passive unless management intervenes. Even they are resistant to organisational needs. They must be persuaded, rewarded punishment and controlled.

Criticism of Theory 'X'

(i) Authoritarian. The theory 'X' is quite unwarranted in the modern times. It supports the authoritarian view which is unwarranted in the present-day economy. The man at work is not a machine, he is a human being. He is not only to execute the orders of the top line executives, but, he should also think over the order on its merits before its execution. Management may get results by coercion, or through pressure tactics only in short run till people respond to pressure and controls partly out of fear of consequences of not following the orders of the top line executives. Himself condemning the theory, McGregor says, "The conventional approach of Theory 'X' is based on mistaken notions of what is cause and what is effect. An organisation built upon theory X notions will be one in which there is clear supervision and control of subordinates and high centralisation of authority. Leadership will tend to be autocratic and workers will have very little to say in decisions affecting them.

(ii) Wrong assumptions of human nature. The assumptions contained in Theory 'X' do not reveal the true nature of human beings. Recent behavioural science research does not support the traditional view. It concludes that the most effective way to get better results in an organisation is to work with people rather than through them.

(iii) Against labour welfare. In modern times, the governments of most of the countries have stressed that the worker should be given an honourable partnership in management. In this way, the theory has now become out of date.

Theory 'Y'

On the basis of the results of many psychological and social researches, McGregor submits an opposing theory — Theory 'Y', as a more realistic assessment of the capabilities of the people. This theory 'Y' presents an alternative management approach which does not involve abdication of managerial responsibility. Management is still responsible for achieving the organisational objectives, but on different assumptions about human behaviour and motivation. The workers are fully aware of the organisational objectives, which is directly related to the satisfaction of employees' needs. McGregor recognised certain needs that Theory 'X' fails to take into account. For example, self-fulfilment, ego satisfaction and social needs of individual workers. Thus, it pleads for a humanistic and supportive approach to managing people. Management tries to provide an atmosphere of peace and discipline within the organisation, without the oppressive measures. Hence, people work with interest and simultaneously enjoy the benefits of congenial relationship.

Assumptions of Theory 'Y'

1. Work is natural. The average human being does not dislike work. Work is as natural as play or rest. Work may be a source of satisfaction of punishment depending upon the controllable conditions.

2. Positive means of motivation. External control and the threat of punishment are not the only means for accomplishing the organisational objectives. Workers are committed to objectives and exercise self-control and self-direction to achieve them. They are fully conscious to their job.

3. Value of responsibility. The average man works under proper conditions, not only to accept but seek responsibilities. Avoidance of responsibility, lack of ambition and emphasis on security are not the inherent qualities of the man but they are all consequences of experience.

4. Reward for work. The reward for the execution of work is that it should be properly recognised. Satisfaction of ego and actualisation needs can be product of efforts directed towards organisational objectives.

5. Co-operation. The capacity to exercise a relatively high degree of imagination, ingenuity and creativity in the solution of organisational problems is widely distributed in the population, *i.e.*, labour co-operates with the management in solving the problems of the organisation.

6. Development of abilities. Human abilities and capabilities are not fully developed till now with reference to modern industrial system. Management has ample scope to develop the intellectual potentialities of the average human being.

7. Democratic theory. The theory is based on democratic principles wherein all persons are given equal chance to develop their skill.

Postulates of Theory

(i) Management is responsible for organising the elements of productive enterprise in the interest of economic and social ends.

(ii) People are not passive but they become so, as a result of experience.

(iii) Motivation, potential for development, capacity for assuming responsibility goal are inherent in the people. It is the responsibility of management to recognise and develop these characteristics.

(iv) The management should arrange for organisational conditions and methods of operations so that workers may achieve their goal through self-direction.

Applicability of Theory 'Y' in India

Thus 'Y' theory establishes co-operation in achieving the objectives of the organisation between the man in authority and the man at work. The fact of interdependence in human organisation is widely recognised. The theory is participative in the sense that supervisors consult their subordinates about proposed course of action before taking any decision. However, management still takes decision for the organisation as a whole.

Development of management in India is slow. Due to the unchanging attitude of employer and employee, relationship of master and servant still persists between them. The development of trade unions is still in its infancy. Organisational behaviour is mainly based on the assumptions of theory 'X'. Recently, some statutory provisions regarding participative management, minimum wages, less hours of work, etc. have been made by the government in order to improve the working conditions and bring about change in the mentality of the employers and the employees. Government has provided training institutes for workers and managers so that they can be conversant with the modern management approaches. Professional Managers have begun to accept the human value for the better management. They repose their faith in workers' participation and profit sharing techniques. But some managements still hesitate to accept the theory is full. Inefficient and uneducated workers are indifferent towards sharing the responsibility. Thus, the assumptions of theory Y have not been fully recognised in India.

Comparison between Theory 'X' and Theory 'Y'

1. Value of work. Theory 'X' assumes that the human beings are inherently distasteful to work, whereas Theory 'Y' assumes that for human beings work is as natural as rest or play. They become distasteful to work only as a result of experience.

2. Ambitions and responsibility. Theory 'X' assumes that people are unambitious and prefer to be directed and they try to avoid responsibilities in jobs. Theory 'Y', on the other hand, assumes that workers are ambitious, and are capable of directing their own behaviour. They are ready to accept responsibilities if proper working conditions are provided.

3. Creativity and change. According to Theory 'X', most people lack capacity for creativity and they always resist change while according to Theory 'Y', the capacity for creativity is widely spread in the population. Most people are creative by nature and they accept every change.

4. Need levels. The motivating factors in Theory 'X' are lower level physiological and safety needs. Theory 'Y', on the other hand, recognises both lower level and higher order needs like social esteem and self-actualisation for motivation. However, emphasis is laid on higher order needs.

5. Control and supervision. Theory 'X' proposes external control and close supervision to achieve organisational objectives. They lack self-motivation, whereas Theory 'Y' proposes self-direction and self-control.

6. Levels of authority. Theory 'X' emphasises scalar chain of command, centralisation of authority and autocratic leadership, whereas theory 'Y' emphasises decentralisation of authority and greater participation in decision-making process.

Criticism of McGregor's Theory

McGregor's theory of motivation helped to crystallise and put into right perspective the findings of the Hawthorne experiments. However, it has been widely criticised on following counts :

(i) Oversimplification. It tends to over-generalise and oversimplify people as being one way or the other. People cannot be put on two extremes. No enterprising man belongs either to Theory 'X' or Theory 'Y'.

(ii) Two extremes. McGregor's theory squeezes managerial styles and philosophies into two extremes of conduct which is devoid of reality.

(iii) Job and motivation. McGregor suggests that job itself is the key to motivation. But all people do not see motivation in the job. The management has to motivate people to work.

(iv) Value of direction and control. People who follow theory 'Y' still find that they have to behave in a very directive and controlling manner.

Most people believe Theory 'Y' to be more appropriate but not in all situations. In some routine and formalised situations, Theory 'X' is more suitable. In underdeveloped countries like India, Theory 'X' is more suitable. Neither theory is best in all situations. An amalgam of both the theories may be more useful than either of the two alone as the best approach to motivation is one which is appropriate to the situation.

MASLOW'S NEEDS PRIORITY MODEL

Propositions about Human Behaviour

1. Man is wanting animal. Wants of man are innumerable and never ending. As soon as one of his wants is satisfied, another appears in its place. This keeps a man engaged on the work. Human needs are multiple, complex and inter-related.

2. A Satisfied need is no more a motivator. As soon as a need is satisfied, it loses its capacity to induce the man to work. Hence only unsatisfied needs or fresh needs can motivate people to work.

3 Needs have hierarchy of importance. Maslow is of the opinion that needs are satisfied in an order. As soon as the lower level needs are satisfied, those on the next higher level emerge and demand satisfaction.

Types of Needs

1. Primary needs. There are two types of needs — basic or primary or innate or physiological needs and secondary or acquired needs. Primary needs are those needs which are very important for the survival and preservation of life. These needs are universal and are felt by everyone in the universe, but their intensity may differ from man to man or from society to society. Food, water, shelter, sex, air to breathe, sleep, clothing are examples of such needs. This theory has also been supported by McGregor and he states, "Man is a wanting animal, as soon as one of his needs is satisfied, another appears in its place. This process is unending."

2. Secondary needs. These are those needs which are related to mind and spirit rather than physiology. These needs develop as one gets maturity or education. These include rivalry, self-esteem, sense of duty, self-assertion, etc. These are acquired needs.

Man has both these types of needs. A.H. Maslow was the pioneer in contributing a systematic approach to this problem. He arranged the needs of a person in order of priority. Maslow's need-priority model was accepted widely. According to this theory, human needs tend to follow the pattern given below, presented in the sequence in which individuals usually become concerned with them.

Hierarchy of Needs

1. Basic physiological needs. The physiological needs include the needs of human body such as food, shelter, clothing, sex, etc. They are basic to preserve human life and are more or less universal. These are at the lowest level in the hierarchy of needs. Therefore, these must be satisfied first of all. These are a powerful motivating force when thwarted. Man lives by bread alone when there is no bread.

2. Safety and security needs. These needs are concerned with the physical and financial security. These include job security, physical security, security of income, old age provision, security from risks, etc. Management can influence these needs by providing security against such uncertainties, *i.e.,* by implementing pension scheme, insurance plans, fear of dismissal, etc.

3. Belongingness, social or love needs. Being a social animal, man is always interested to live in a society or group which loves him most. He wants to give or receive love. These needs include the needs of conversation, sociability, exchange of feelings and grievances, recognition and belongingness.

4. Esteem and status needs. These needs may be : (i) self-esteem or (ii) public esteem. Self-esteem means esteem in the eyes of self, *i.e.*, a feeling that one is doing something worthwhile. Public esteem means esteem or image in the eyes of public such as praise, admiration, public appreciation, etc.

5. Self actualisation or self-realisation needs. These are individual's needs for realising his own potentialities, opportunity for creativity and for continuous development of the individual power and skill. Thus, these are, what a person considers to be his mission in life.

Lower-order and Higher-order Needs

Maslow has further classified the five needs into two categories :

(i) Lower-order needs. Basic physiological and safety and security needs are labelled by Maslow as lower-level needs. These needs are finite. These are to be satisfied in priority to others because they are the first order needs. A man cannot survive without them and he will be ready to do anything to satisfy these needs. A hungry man can do anything to get the bread. His secondary needs of security and safety get priority as soon as he satisfies his basic needs. Hence a man collects grain for further use or tries to save money for his old age.

(ii) Higher-order needs. Belongingness, social or love needs, esteem and status needs and self-actualisation needs are categorised as higher-order needs. They are secondary needs. They relate to the society and are external needs. They are infinite or unlimited. They are satisfied only after lower level needs are satisfied. All the needs under this category should be satisfied in order of priority. Lower-level needs affect the higher order needs and vice versa. Higher order needs are dominant factors in motivating people at higher level in the management.

Appreciation

Maslow's need priority model presenting nature and priority order of needs is a landmark in the field of motivation helping the management in understanding the human behaviour of people at work. It is very simple, direct and practical. Everybody, except few, has some priority of needs, not necessarily in the priority order as described by Maslow. Maslow, himself has admitted that his hierarchy is not rigid.

Criticism

1. Conditional model. If the model may not apply at all times, in all places and in all circumstances, it may not follow the sequence as postulated by Maslow. Following are some examples :

(a) ***More self-esteem than love*** : There are some people in whom self-esteem seems to be more important than love. This reversal in hierarchy is possible where a strong or powerful person seeks self-assertion as a means to love.

(b) ***Absence of ambition and initiative*** : In certain people, the level of aspiration may be permanently dead because of prolonged experience of life at a very low level. Such people lack ambition and initiative.

(c) ***Absence of love needs*** : Some people do not have love needs because they have lost love in their early childhood.

2. Other determinants of behaviour. There are many determinants of behaviour other than needs and desires such as perceptions, expectations, experience, etc. Thus, the behaviour of a man is not a result of his needs or desires only.

3. Neglect of interaction of needs. This approach overlooks the interaction of needs. Motivation is caused by several needs at a time. A person is hardly motivated by a single need.

4. Difference in expectations. People differ in their expectations significantly. The same need does not lead to the same response in all individuals. For example, people who have been satisfying their basic needs throughout their lives, may not be very keen to satisfy higher order needs.

5. General impression only. Maslow's model gives a general impression. Hierarchical order is not very much rigid as Maslow himself accepted.

While designing a plan for people's motivation, the management must keep in mind the above weaknesses of Maslow's need priority model.

Extent of Application in Organisation

1. Environment. The need priority model of Maslow applies to people in general. It does not always apply even to employees working in organisations because people satisfy most of their needs outside their organisations. Needs are conditioned by environment. Importance of different needs is determined by environment or their social system.

2. No general applicability. Maslow's model seems to apply to managers and professionals in developed countries. Several studies have tested the model that show that they meet their physiological and security needs and seek higher order needs. Researches show that in some developed countries like Japan and Continental European countries, the model does not apply even to managers. The order in developed countries too differs because of their culture influences.

3. Applicable in underdeveloped countries. The model seems to apply even in underdeveloped countries like India, where economic conditions of workers do not seem to be satisfactory. They prefer to satisfy their low-order needs, physiological as well as security needs. A survey of 200 factory workers in India in 1960s showed that they gave top priority to lower-order needs, job security, earnings and personal benefits.

4. Applicable in substantive conditions. This model is tightly fit in case of managers and professionals in some of the developed countries and in underdeveloped countries, where men live under substantive conditions. In other cases, the model is unreliable.

HERZBERG'S MOTIVATION — MAINTENANCE MODEL

In the late 1950s, Frederic Herzberg made interesting studies that concentrated heavily on self-esteem and self-actualisation. Out of these studies developed a theory of work-motivation. It has broad implications for management and its efforts towards effective utilisation of human resources. The theory is known as Herzberg Motivation — Maintenance Theory or Motivation Hygiene Theory or Two-Factor Theory of Motivation.

Herzberg's Problem

In his studies, Herzberg tried to understand the motivation problem. He felt that knowledge about human behaviour, nature, motivation and needs could be invaluable to organisations and individuals. In his efforts to uncover the circumstances where a person felt satisfied or dissatisfied with his work, Herzberg conducted a study and interviewed about 200 engineers and accountants from 11 industries in the Pittsburgh area. These engineers and accountants were asked to think of time when they felt especially good about their jobs and the time when they felt particularly bad about it and then to describe the conditions that led to those feelings. Employees named different types of conditions for good and bad feelings. The study revealed that the factors responsible for job satisfaction are different not obverse from the factors that led to dissatisfaction. If a person was satisfied with his job in a particular condition, the absence of such condition would not mean job dissatisfaction but it might be called no job-satisfaction. In this way this theory is based on a two factor hypotheses, *i.e.*, factors leading to job satisfaction and factors leading to job dissatisfaction. These factors were classified into two categories :

(i) Motivational factors and

(ii) Hygienic or Maintenance factors.

1. Motivational Factors. Certain factors are related directly to the job itself. Their presence creates a highly motivating situation, though their absence does not cause dissatisfaction. With the presence of such factors, people always respond positively. Herzberg mentions six such motivational factors : (i) achievement, (ii) recognition, (iii) advancement, (iv) work itself, (v) possibility of growth and (vi) responsibility. While achievement and responsibility are related to job itself, others are secured from it. This set of factors has been designated as motivators or satisfiers. They are job-centred factors related to job contents.

2. Maintenance Factors. There were other factors, the presence of which did not significantly motivate them but the absence of such factors caused serious dissatisfaction. The presence of such factors prevented dissatisfaction and maintained a certain level of motivation, but any reduction in the availability of these factors was likely to affect motivation and bring down the level of performance. For example, an increase of Rs. 10 in the salary of a person does not mean much but a reduction of Rs. 10 from his salary may upset him and is likely to cause dissatisfaction. Maintenance factors are mostly related to environment outside the job. Herzberg called these factors hygiene or maintenance factors or dissatisfiers because they produce nothing to the worker's capacity but they help maintain or prevent losses to the worker's-performance due to work restriction. Herzberg named 10 maintenance factors as : (i) Company policy and administration, (ii) technical supervision, (iii) interpersonal relations with subordinates, (iv) salary, (v) job security, (vi) personal life, (vii) working conditions, (viii) status, (ix) interpersonal relations with supervisors and (x) interpersonal relations with peers.

Intrinsic and Extrinsic Factors

Intrinsic motivations are internal rewards that occur at the time of performance of work. Due to them, there is a direct motivation to perform work because the act of performance is itself rewarding. The employee is self-motivated in this situation. Extrinsic motivators are external rewards which are not directly related to the performance of work. These occur after or away from the work such as retirement plans, leaves, health, insurance, etc.

Prior to Herzberg's research, organisational managers generally paid attention to extrinsic maintenance factors. Now with better understanding, they insist more on intrinsic motivational factors due to their superior possibilities for the worker's society and organisation.

Implications of Herzberg's Research

Herzberg's findings were in sharp contrast to the existing policies. The management used to emphasize hygienic needs because non-satisfaction of these needs means dissatisfaction among workers and the organisation might have faced the resultant consequences. This, in itself, was not wrong but it was based on wrong assumption that prevention would have positive health and the return of increased productivity, lowered absenteeism, turnover, etc. They did not consider that the effect of improved hygiene lasts only for a short time. In fact, man's avoidance needs are recurrent. They will continue to occupy management's attention. Besides, understanding human needs in totally hygienic terms is fundamentally wrong. It has affected the self-concept of the employee very seriously.

Thus, Herzberg reaches a conclusion on the basis of these factors that people felt motivated if the job is challenging and interesting with the possibility of growth in it; authority to use their discretion; and ability to advance in the profession and receive recognition for the task they did.

1. Based on opposite points. Herzberg's model is based on two factor theory of motivation, *i.e.,* factors leading to job dissatisfaction and factors; leading to job satisfaction. It suggests job satisfiers and dissatisfiers as two different qualitative factors. This was objected by others on the ground that job satisfaction and dissatisfaction are two opposite points.

2. Method bound. It is easier to get results favourable to the model by using the Herzberg method, while other methods failed to produce similar results. Thus the model is 'method bound' which limits its applicability for general use.

3. Neglect of pay, status and relations. This model does not lay sufficient emphasis upon the motivation qualities of pay, status and interpersonal relations. While these are important employee-motivators, the model gives credit primarily to their maintenance capabilities.

4. Lack of clarity and distinction. The terminology used in this model is confusing. The difference between motivational and maintenance factors is very thin. Items designated as maintenance factors may serve as motivational factors to some and *vice-versa.* There is no absolute distinction among factors, neither factor is wholly unidimensional in its influence.

5. Limited sample. The theory is based on a small sample of 200 accountants and engineers which cannot be said to be a representative sample. It has not universal application.

In spite of the above criticism, Herzberg's theory is useful in distinguishing factors that motivate people on the job and factors that primarily maintain employees ready to be motivated. The model provides new insights in organisational behaviour.

INCENTIVES IN INDUSTRY

What is Incentive?

Incentives are those goals or objectives which satisfy some needs. For example, food is the incentive of hunger. Water quenches thirst. In the same way, sex activity creates changes in the functioning of internal glands. Curiosity is satisfied by going from one place to another. In this way, incentives are the means of satisfying innate and acquired needs.

Kinds of Incentives

Generally, incentives are divided into two broad classes :

1. Positive incentives. These incentives attract people and when they obtain these incentives, they feel satisfied. For example, increase in wages, promotion or bonus are positive incentives. These incentives motivate an individual to work in a particular way. If, for example, it is said that the worker who works an additional hour every day, will get fifty rupees extra, then this statement is an incentive.

2. Negative incentives. Negative incentives are those which motivate an individual to abstain from doing something. If, for example, a monetary fine is imposed on causing breakages, then this fine is negative incentive which inspires the individual to avoid breaking things. Sometimes, some reform measures are instituted in industries. These reforms constitute negative incentives and although they are beneficial, they are opposed by many workers.

3. Substitute incentives. Sometimes, another class of incentives, the substitute incentives, is also considered. As is evident from the name, this class includes those incentives which are artificial and are replacements of some natural or normal incentives. For example, a worker can be given a rise in pay in lieu of promotion so that he is saved from the frustration of not having been promoted. Evidently, then, the substitute incentive should satisfy the same need which would otherwise have been satisfied by the normal incentive. In the example cited above, the worker satisfies himself with the thought that the actual promotion, too, would only have resulted in a similar improvement of his economic position. It should also be remembered that, in any case, the substitute is not as good or as completely satisfying as the original incentive. To go back to the same example, actual promotion would have resulted not only in an increase in wages but also in the worker getting some additional power and authority. And, in fact, the worker who is satisfied with a rise in salary is only deliberately coming to terms with the situation. He would have been really satisfied only with promotion. And if a worker wants promotion not for economic advantage but for the higher position and the authority accruing with it, he would not be satisfied with an increase in salary. Obviously, then, the substitute incentives cannot satisfy all individuals equally. And the incentive that will satisfy an individual depends upon his individual traits and his condition. For example, a person who does not have a beautiful house will feel satisfied on getting a beautiful house and may even be prepared to give up some post for it, but one who already has such a house will never be willing to give up a post for another good house. Hence, when a substitute motive or incentive is given to a person, it is necessary to keep in mind his individual traits and his needs.

Conflict in Incentives

Sometimes a conflict occurs between incentives. For example, if all the workers in a factory are told that the worker who lives in the quarters provided by the factory will lose are thousand rupees a month while the one who doesn't will get an additional thousand rupees, then there will be a conflict between the incentives of the house and a thousand rupees raise in salary. In such a case, the worker will take sometime to make up his mind. Sometime, positive and negative incentives also come into conflict with each other. There are certain kinds of work, for example, in which the salary is fairly high but the social prestige consequent upon it is not very great. Faced with such a choice, the worker finds it difficult to decide whether he should accept the job with higher pay or the one with greater social prestige. Most industries which take a toll of the worker's health pay more than other industries. The detrimental effect on health is a negative incentive since there is motivation to avoid this kind of work. On the other hand, the higher salary is a positive incentive because it inspires the worker to accept the job. The actual choice made by the worker depends upon his individual needs or his economic condition. Some people would not like to earn money at the expense of their health while others may have such a great need for money, due to their physical or social needs, that they may be willing to endanger their health for the money involved.

Disadvantages of Negative Incentives

In industry, normally positive incentives are offered to motivate the worker to indulge in desirable activity while negative incentives are offered to restrain him from undesirable actions. For example, good work is rewarded with a prize while low production is punished. In certain cases, punishment is given for causing accidents, breakages, destruction of raw materials, etc. There is no doubt that punishment helps as a deterrent and people abstain from such activities, but negative incentives have certain drawbacks, the main ones being the following:

1. Frustration and hostile tendency. If a worker takes some punishment to be unjust or improper then he experiences frustration and hostile tendency. This fact assumes greater importance because punishment is often given only to those workers who in the first place are obstinate and non-cooperative. If such a man is punished, these traits are further intensified.

2. Increase of deceit. When provision is made for punishment on the performance of some activity then the culprits try to avoid being caught rather than avoid doing it altogether. In this way, punishment also leads to an increase in deceit.

3. Negative suggestion. It is believed in psychology that negative suggestion should not be given where it is possible to give a positive suggestion. For example, it is better to say 'Cross this road here' rather than to say 'Do not cross this road here'. In the second case, the pedestrian gets a negative suggestion which does not tell him what to do. The first slogan contains a positive suggestion.

4. Destructive training. Apart from the suggestion, the training implicit in the incentive should be constructive. Punishment is intended to deter a worker from doing something, a destructive training, since it creates an obstruction in the satisfaction of some tendency. On the other hand, constructive training tries to find more legitimate and acceptable means for the expression of this destructive urge.

5. Negative attitude. Punishment leads to a negative attitude towards the work as well as towards the individual giving the punishment. Individuals who are punished in some factory develop a negative attitude not only towards their work but also against the entire organisation, including the management.

6. Creation of fear. The possibility of punishment also creates fear and fear is never a good factor in the working conditions. Hence, instead of creating fear in the worker's mind, it is better to create a positive tendency. Nowadays many experiments are being conducted in industrial conditions to introduce changes through the medium of positive incentives.

Despite all the above shortcomings, the institution of punishment has been part of industry for a long time because no attention has been paid to the consequences of punishment. In fact, punishment is often given in a state of anger, irrespective of the harm done by it. Besides, few, if any, managers and organisers have the patience to suspend punishment and employ more positive measures. In the third place, the negative method is simpler than the positive method, and it is often adopted because it is more expeditious. On the other hand, the adoption of positive incentives involves considerable thinking about the incentives as well as the methods by which they should be introduced.

Nowadays, two kinds of incentives are employed in industries-the financial and the non-financial. The first kind of incentives include all those activities which result in economic benefits. The second category includes all incentives which bestow improvement and benefits other than monetary. Examples of non-financial incentives are praises for work, knowledge of the results of work, encouragement through health competitions, feeling of progress, better work through group motivation, increase in interest in some specific work, reducing boredom, making the job more important, etc.

FINANCIAL INCENTIVES

Money in itself has no value for man but in the context of the existing economic organisation, money has become a means not only of satisfying the physical needs of daily life but also of obtaining social position and power. For this reason, financial incentives have assumed great importance. On getting money man first turns his attention towards the things he needs — food, clothes, house, etc. Then he satisfies the needs of health and education. Once these needs have been satisfied, he tries to obtain more and more luxuries. But some individuals continue to work even after having reached this stage because their social prestige and power increase with their bank balance. Individuals with this lust for money continue their search throughout their life for this search never ends. People who do not feel any specific need for power do not try to earn money once their needs and comforts have been taken care of. In the same way, economic loss has diverse effects. Loss of money deprives the poor man of his bread while the rich man loses his prestige although he does not suffer from hunger. Despite this, the poor man suffers less on account of this loss psychologically because only his body is directly affected. On the other hand, the rich man suffers a blow to his social prestige and his self-respect, which is mental injury. Money has become the means of satisfying many needs because it is the medium of exchange. If social position and power are not based on money in any society, then money will cease to be so powerful an incentive. In communist countries, for example, since the abolition of private property, social respect has been connected with hard work, social service or some other objective, with the result that although there is no possibility of enhancing one's private property, individuals continue to work hard. Money is the most important incentive in a society where a man's success is measured by the money he earns. But where this does not happen money is not a powerful incentive. This analysis will show the importance of financial incentives. Financial incentives are offered in industries in two ways - either in the form of salary increases, or in the form of occasional bonus. Both these financial incentives have the effect of increasing production and inducing the worker to work harder and better.

Method of Wage Payment

The most commonly used financial incentive is the increase in salary. Here we will analyse the advantages and disadvantages of various methods of wage payment to discover the best method which acts as the most powerful motive for the worker to work harder and increase production. Briefly, a description of the methods of wage payment and their respective merits and demerits is given below :

1. Pay according to production. In industry, one of the most common methods of wage payment is the payment of salary according to the production achieved by the worker. In most factories, the work is offered on contract and the rate of payment is predetermined. In this contract, the specific wage for a specific amount of work is clearly indicated. This method of wage payment has the following advantages:

(a) ***Stress on individual differences*** : This method of wage payment lays stress on the individual differences of the workers. If one worker is capable of working faster and better than other workers he earns much more money while the comparatively slower and idle worker suffers a proportionate loss.

(b) ***Importance of skill and production*** : The skill and the capacity for production of an individual are shown to be important in this method. Consequently, the worker tries to improve both these qualities. Since lack of skill and idleness lead to less payment, workers try to overcome these handicaps.

(c) ***Importance to uninteresting functions*** : Because of this method of wage payment, the worker tries to do even uninteresting work with equal zeal because he knows what he stands to benefit by taking interest in it and working more.

Despite the above advantages, this method of payment suffers from the following defects :

(a) *Difference in the standards of life* : Since payment is made according to the goods produced, different workers doing the same kind of work in the same factory will have different incomes which is reflected in the different standards of living the result of varying incomes. The consequence is that individuals with less income have a lower standard of living than the others, whom they begin to hate. This is one reason why at many places even the more skilful workers do not want to work better than the others because of these social reasons. Even trade unions object to this method of payment because it leads to conflict among the workers and their organisation is disrupted.

(b) *Absence of respect for age :* It is a commonly accepted fact that the ability to work decreases as age increases. This fact is particularly true of industrial production. And if wages are paid according to the quantity produced then older people begin to lose their prestige because they earn less. Besides, their entire accumulated experience is also not put to the best use.

(c) *Practical difficulties :* The most valid practical difficulty in this method of payment is that it is difficult to determine the value of different kinds of production. For example, it is difficult to compare the production of an engineer with the production of a labourer. This problem can, at best, be solved only by the trial and error method.

(d) *Undesirable effect on the mobility of workers :* This method of payment has an adverse effect on the mobility of workers. The more skilful and able workers naturally drift towards factories where wages are determined by production while the comparatively unskilful and less capable workers migrate towards factories where wages are paid according to the time.

(e) *Conflicts between workers :* This method of payment creates hatred between the more skilful and the less able workers with the result that the very purpose of giving an incentive is defeated. In fact, since the number of average skilled individuals is far more than the exceptionally skilful individuals in any industry, the better endowed individual is afraid of showing his skill by working better. This fact has been established by many studies.

In spite of the above defects, this method of payment has proved very effective in certain types of work, but generally it is considered better to increase bonus for better work, than to increase wages. Therefore, while evaluating the merits and demerits of this method of payment, it is necessary to keep in mind the economic condition and needs of the worker, etc. It is imperative that the social atmosphere of the factory should not be damaged while the more skilful workers are further encouraged to improve their skill.

2. Payment in terms of time spent. Another common method of wage payment adopted in industry is payment in terms of time spent. In this, the worker is paid wages according to the time he spends in work. In this method, the wages are determined in terms of hours, days or weeks. In every case, the wages are determined by the time spent by the worker, not by the quantity of goods produced by him.

This method of wage payment suffers from the following demerits :

(a) ***Absence of motivation to produce*** : Since, in this method, the amount of wages is not influenced by the quantity of production, the worker is inclined to work only so far as his job security is not endangered. Once this level of production has been achieved, the skilful workers are found wasting their time in roaming around. Therefore, this method does not inspire the worker to increase his production. Wherever no means are employed to measure the minimum production of each individual-worker many workers do nothing more than mark time. As a consequence, in many organisations the more skilled workers have to bear the burden of such incompetent individuals.

(b) ***Absence of any stress on individual differences*** : In this method of wage payment, no importance attaches to the individual capabilities, skill and ability of any individual. Old and young people receive equal wages. For this reason, the more skilled workers do not want to work in any organisation where this method of wage payment prevails.

Despite these two defects, this is the most common method of wage payment because it has many advantages, of which the main ones are :

(a) *Respect for old age* : In this case, the earnings do not fall with increase in age although the individual cannot produce as much. In many cases, wages actually increase with age since promotion comes with age. This gives more respect to the older people and since everyone has to grow old some day, this method of wage payment is liked very much.

(b) *Absence of partial behaviour* : Here the managers cannot be partial in their behaviour towards the workers, for they cannot indiscriminately increase the wages of a worker or reduce those of another. This creates more cordial relations among the workers and it becomes difficult to turn them against each other. For this reason, the trade unions are normally in favour of this method.

It is obvious from the above description of the merits and demerits of this method of wage payment that it should be linked with the method of economic advantage in proportion to the production achieved. Wages should be paid according to the time spent but better and more work should be maintained. The major advantage of this method is that there is no difficulty in determining the wages of a worker since time is measured in terms of minutes and hours. Payment in this manner also induces a sense of security in the worker since he is assured that he will not suffer as he grows older and cannot produce as much as he could when young. Besides, he is always aware of the total emoluments he is going to earn and he can therefore plan his expenditure. This helps him to plan his future and to understand the manner in which he can hope to progress.

The Seniority Method of Pay

Industries which pay more attention to experience use the seniority method of pay so that a worker's wages increase with his age and experience. This method has the following advantages :

1. Importance to experience. In this mode of payment, maximum importance attaches to the experience of the worker with the result that a worker tends to stay at his job with increase in experience. He is not easily tempted to go away.

2. Security. It is advantageous inasmuch as it induces a sense of security in the worker because he does not stand to lose financially with a decline in output despite his advancing age. In fact, he actually gains because his wages increase as he grows older.

This method is common in many industries because of these advantages. But it also has some demerits, as given below :

In this mode of payment, little or no importance is attached to individual differences, abilities, or skills since the wage is determined only by seniority. One consequence of this is that highly skilled young workers are dissatisfied because they are subordinated to older people. On the other hand, they are not motivated to exploit their capacities to the maximum because they know that their salaries will increase only with age. Secondly, it is not scientific to assume that skill and experience increase with age, since beyond a certain level, experience does not increase and skill begins to decrease. Hence, this mode of wage payment is one-sided. It should be implemented along with some other method which encourages workers to work hard. For this hard work, they should be encouraged by promotion or some other method.

Pay According to Needs

In some industries, the method of pay according to needs has been adopted. This method is very useful for determining the minimum wage because a worker must be paid a sufficient sum of money with which to satisfy his own and his family's basic requirements. And, since some workers have a larger family than others they need a large sum of money to maintain a standard of living similar to that of others. If the worker's needs are not satisfied, he will live in a mood of constant anxiety and dissatisfaction, and, if the needs of his family are not satisfied, then, to that extent, society will have so many more individuals whose normal development is retarded. That is why many modern governments believe that the old age security of its workers is the responsibility of the state. It is also the responsibility of the state to provide free education and medical care for their dependants. In many cases, additional salary is given to those with a larger family.

But if the wages in an industry are to be determined according to the size of the family, the number of children, marital state, etc., then there is great chance of injustice being done because the unmarried young workers will be paid less, irrespective of their skill or efficiency. Hence, wages should not be increased or reduced according to the worker's respective needs, but other arrangements should be made to help them to satisfy their needs. Instead of giving additional salary to meet the educational expenses, it is better to provide free education. In the same way, medical care should be provided free of charge. The government may allow a cut in income-tax rates for an individual with a greater number of dependants. All these measures will help the worker to satisfy his needs, and at the same time, there will be no injustice to the other workers.

It is evident from the above discussion of the various modes of wage payment that no single method can be applied to all circumstances. Each method has its merits and demerits and in order to evolve the most useful method, one will have to take into account the merits of each method. It is necessary to provide security for old age and to meet the needs of the worker's growing family, but it is also no less important to give weightage to the skill and efficiency of the worker. In every case, the method of wage payment should be such that each worker is inspired and encouraged to work more and better. At the same time, it must avoid creating hatred and jealousy, and any sense of injustice to one and partiality to another. Economic and old age security are essential for motivation. Besides, wages should increase with increase in the levels of prices.

Among the various methods, the method of wage payment according to production pays special attention to individual differences. It encourages the worker to produce more. Hence, if the aim is to increase production then this method is the best but if increased production is not an important factor then wages can be paid according to the time spent. If linking wages with total production leads to anxiety and unrest among the workers then those who produce less may be compensated in some other way. Sometimes the more efficient worker is not given additional salary but he is allowed to work for a shorter period. Nowadays old age security is provided through life insurance scheme or pension scheme, in most of the progressive countries. In the same way, the needs of the individual with a large family are kept in view by introducing income tax reduction. In determining the method of payment, it is essential to keep in mind certain technical things. For example, the wages to be paid for a particular level of production in some specific sphere is a relative matter and it needs work analysis. This analysis becomes even more complex in the case of non-productive work, for example, the work of the engineer. Finally, the satisfaction of the worker is also a criterion for the correct method of wage payment. Therefore, the workers and the management should determine the correct level of payment through discussion. It is also necessary in this case to take the views of the trade unions. Putting it briefly, no one method is the best since different methods will meet the requirements in different sets of circumstances.

Non-Financial Incentives

In addition to the financial method of providing motivation, industries make use of many non-financial incentives also. These methods include all those which do not involve the payment of money to the worker. Since work in the industrial sphere is no joke and it must also inevitably lead to boredom at some stage, motivation must be provided. But, this should not be taken to mean that motivation exists only in financial gain. Many people continue to do some work because it is made more pleasant and enjoyable. Hence, many different methods are used to provide motivation, the main ones being the following :

1. Making work pleasant. The reason why people enjoy playing but easily become bored with work is that playing is enjoyable, although that does not make it comfortable. Something being enjoyable means simply that it is an outlet for natural instincts.

This is possible in the case of work also. Hence, work can also be made enjoyable and pleasant if it is so designed that it allows the worker to express his natural instincts.

2. Use of praise. Often children are praised so that they may do some work. This love of praise or the use of praise as an incentive is successful not only in children but also in adults. Human beings in general are amenable to praise and want to do that work which will win them praise. If praise is given then they are inspired to do the work with even greater application. A common mistake made by many employers is that they do not praise good work although they severely criticise all mistakes, a psychologically unsound principle. Studies indicate that praise is a better incentive than criticism. Whether criticism is offered privately or in public, it invariably has some consequences. In the same way, abuse or blunt language is harmful. Very positive results can be obtained, on the other hand, by offering praise in public. Criticism has had consequences because it injures the worker's self-respect. So do abuse and blunt language. Criticism in public is even more harmful than criticism in private because in the former case, the worker also feels insulted and humiliated. Hence, offering criticism in public is the worst method of giving an incentive. Briefly, a worker will be inspired to work better if he is praised in public while the other workers will also be encouraged to work better to win similar acclaim.

3. Knowledge of results. Knowledge of results implies simply that the worker is aware of how much work remains to be done, or the consequences of what he has done. Both interest and motivation are influenced by a knowledge of results. No individual likes to play in the dark because then he cannot gauge the results of his play. The value of results has also been established by some experiments. The experiments of S.J. Macpherson, V. Dees and G.C. Grindley[2] have shown that approximately 25 per cent progress in work is seen with a knowledge of results. At the same time the interest in the work is maintained. D.B. Lindsley[3] has demonstrated by his experiments that skill in work deteriorates when there is ignorance about mistakes and progress. In an experiment conducted

2. S.J. Macpherson, V. Dees and G.C. Grindley, "The Effect of Knowledge of Results on Learning and Performance".
3. D.B. Lindsley, Radar Operator Training: Results of Study of CSR 270-271 Operators at Drew Field.

by W.F. Book and L. Norvelle[4] two groups of students were given mental tasks of reality and the use of speed. One group was asked to put in the maximum effort of which it was capable while the other group was kept informed of the results and asked to improve upon them. A total of 20 experiments were conducted on these two groups. Finally, it was discovered that the group which was kept informed of results did 16.5 per cent better work than the other group. G.F. Arps[5] conducted an experiment in which the students were asked to raise a weight with one finger and to continue to do so until completely exhausted. This experiment was repeated 11 times with an interval of 48 hours between every two experiments. These students invariably achieved better performance when they were aware of results than when they were kept in the dark about their achievements. In this experiment, self-competition was noticed because each individual wanted to improve upon the grades achieved by him in the earlier experiments. Knowledge of results not only helps to make improvements in the methods of working but also provides inspiration to work harder. The importance of knowing the results in learning has already been established. N.R.F. Maier[6] has given an example to prove the effect of knowledge of results upon motivation. In one telephone industry, the mechanics suggested that they should be sent out to attend to complaints about an instrument rectified by them in the first place. They suggested this because in that case they would be able to gauge how well they had done their work earlier. They argued that just as a doctor wants to find out how far his medicine has helped the patient, in the same way they also wanted to know how well they had worked, and that their plan should be adopted. No such plan had been adopted by the company before this suggestion. And once it was adopted it was seen that cases of repeated complaints fell from 70 per cent to only 4 per cent.

4. Competition. Another non-financial means of providing incentive is to organise competitions between different individuals or different group. Sometimes one particular individual may make an effort to improve his earlier performance, which should be an example of self competition. Even if competition does not lead to

---

4. W.F. Book and L. Norvelle, *An Experimental Study of Learning Incentives.*
5. G.F. Arps, "Work with knowledge of Results *versus* Work without Knowledge of Results".
6. N.R.F. Maier, *Principles of Human Relations*, pp. 225-28.

any economic gain, it has the advantage of giving self-satisfaction to the winner. Hence there should be some advantage attached to the winning of a competition, the advantage, for example, of increased social prestige, winning praise from others, appearing to be ahead of others, etc. But while organising competition among workers, attention must also be paid to the losers because they often suffer from frustration and they may at times also have to face humiliation. Therefore, a competition must be designed in such a way that it should not result in loss of cooperation and lowering of morale. There is normally a healthy competition in games because it is considered unsporting to raise the question of insult or humiliation on losing the competition. If the same spirit can be introduced into industrial context, then competitions can be put to good use. In order to increase the scope of the competition, it is sometimes divided into zones. Prize has a very great importance in competitions and it should normally be clear and obvious. Promotion of sales is done by giving prizes to the best salesmen and competitions are organised for the selection of good salesmen. Competitions have also been organised sometimes to reduce the incidence of accidents. In such a competition, the group involved in the least number of accidents is adjudged to be the best. Because of such a contest, the members of a group prevent each other from causing accidents while themselves taking care to avoid them. But if, as a result of such a competition, the groups try to conceal accidents or if a worker continues to work despite injuries, then these are harmful effects of such contests.

Some industrial trade unions have objected to the use of the competition method as a means of giving incentive since, according to them, this is a means of exploitation used by the employers who follow the policy of divide and rule. Hence in encouraging a spirit of competition, it is necessary to see that the workers are willing to cooperate and that they also understand the objective of such a measure. Competition is rarely introduced artificially because at times it naturally appears among the workers. It may be a competition in doing more and better work or in avoiding work. It also has a favourable impact upon the decision of the group. Factors like regular attendance, punctuality, the quantity and quality of work, safety, avoidance of waste and damage, etc., are amenable to competition and the results can be measured. Yet care must be taken to prevent competition from becoming a burden because in that case, it becomes more frustrating than pleasure giving.

As a result of research, it has been seen that competition between individuals is more effective than between groups because in the latter case ego satisfaction is less since the responsibility is shared. This fact has been established by the experiments of V.M. Sims.[7] In one of his experiments, some college students were given a test of reading. After taking the test, 45 students were divided into three groups having equal ability. They were then tested again. One group was not asked to compete but in comparison to the first test it showed a progress of 8.7 per cent. This was the result of practice. The other two groups were divided into two equal parts and made to compete, and an improvement of 14.5 per cent was observed. Obviously 8.7 per cent progress was the result of practice while 5.8 per cent was the result of competition. Members of the third group were motivated to individually produce better results than other competitors. This group showed a progress of 34.7 per cent of which 28 per cent was the result of competition alone. Hence it is obvious that individual competition is more productive than group competition. But it is also possible that group competition may be able to raise to a very high level. Team spirit has the effect of putting social pressure so that each member feels more responsible.

5. Experience of progress. In many kinds of games, constant notice is taken of the progress achieved. For example, the progress in a foot-ball match is measured by the number of goals scored by a particular team. On the other hand, progress in a card game is measured by the points scored by each individual player. In some other games, progress is measured in more ways than one. In the sphere of industry also, the worker is inspired to work better if he has knowledge of the progress he is making. In that case he works better but the difficulty lies in making an accurate measurement of the progress achieved. This job is done in different ways in different industries. It is measured by the quantity of production, the quality of production, or even by the satisfaction given to the customer. In all these ways, the performance of the worker can be evaluated. As has been pointed out, each individual and each group wants to know how much work it has done. Actually, progress itself is the prize of work since it indicates that the workers' skill is improving. Therefore, each worker wants to feel that he is progressing but as skill continues to increase it becomes more

7. Sims, V.M., "The Relative Influence of two types of Motivation on Improvement".

difficult to see this progress clearly. For example, even if safety is increased to extreme limits, accidents can be prevented only up to a certain extent just as the quantity and quality of production can be improved within limits. Describing some experiments on the experience of progress, Viteles has pointed out that motivation improves with a knowledge of results and experience of progress and for this reason, the worker should be told of his progress from time to time. One good way of doing this is to interview him. During this interview, the weekly or terminal report of the worker's performance can be determined by fixing a limit to the work to be done during a day because if he feels that he has completed the day's work, he realizes that he is progressing towards his objective.

6. Social motives. In addition to the above-mentioned kinds of non-financial incentives, there are certain motives which act as incentives. Factors which increase social facilities are among the main social motives. Social facilitation implies an increase in a feeling of co-operation and group formation. Learn spirit is of particular importance in this connection. In an industry, the worker should have the feeling that as a member of a group, he is performing some task of vital importance. Group decision also plays a vital role. Motives which prove an obstacle in progress should be continuously eliminated, examples of which are mutual hatred and jealousy, conflict, unhealthy competition, etc. In order to give motivation, the goal should be made to create a group decision in favour of it. Once the group decision is favourable, the task becomes easier because no individual wants to lag behind the group and become a laughing stock while some individuals want to work more than the others in order to reach a position of command and leadership. The workers should also have the freedom to discuss various aspects of their job because this increases a sense of participation and responsibility, thus leading to more self-satisfaction. For this purpose various committees or groups should be created which can, discuss ways and means of increasing production and of finding new ways of doing the tasks more efficiently.

7. Increasing interest in the work. Increase in interest leads to an increase in motivation. Hence, efforts should be made to increase the worker's interest in his job. Human beings naturally take an interest in games because they are chosen by the individual himself and because they provide him with a means of expressing his natural instincts. If the job is also chosen by the worker himself and it also gives him the opportunity of manifesting his natural talents, he will take interest in the job. But sometimes he is compelled to take up a job not preferred by him because of the possibilities of choice, the salaries available in different jobs, his educational ability, etc. Consequently, he finds it difficult to take interest in his job.

In order to create interest, the worker should be made aware of the importance and value of his work because if he feels that he is doing something worthwhile and making a useful contribution to this entire effort, then he will take interest in what he is doing. As F.R. Wickert[8] has demonstrated, a worker's motivation for some work diminishes very rapidly if he does not know why he is doing something or if he does not know the value of his work in relation to the entire work. Hence it is better to explain to the worker the various kinds of work done in the organisation and the part he himself is playing in its success. Motion pictures and meetings can help in doing this, thus increasing the worker's self-respect. In moments of emergency, the level of motivation improves even more because then the worker is aware of his contribution in tiding over a difficult time. It has been seen that in times of emergency in a country, the workers are motivated to work.

Another way of improving interest is to reduce the monotony involved in the work. For this, all those psychological measures can be adopted which are suggested for removing monotony. Monotony itself is the result of low motivation. Therefore, if it is removed, motivation improves. Variety of work and a sense of having completed some task tend to reduce monotony.

8. Consideration of the demands of industrial unions. Nowadays it is impossible to do anything by neglecting the industrial unions. These unions take up the task of propagating and ventilating the demands and grievances of the workers. Efforts should be made to increase motivation by keeping these demands in view. It is true that at times these demands are contrary to the well-being of the organisation because these unions promote class-consciousness when they are influenced by political parties. But the industrial unions are the actual representatives of the workers' dissatisfaction and their demands should not be neglected. If these demands can be satisfied, the level of motivation improves automatically.

---

8. Wickert, F.R., "Turnover and Employees Feelings of Ego Involvement in the Day to Day Operation of a Company".

9. Study of the worker's need. Finally, the next important way of improving motivation is to make a detailed study of the demands of the workers. At the same time, his order of preferences out of all the demands should be found out, if he is given the choice to prefer one demand to another. Studies of this kind can help in deciding upon the conditions which must be created for the improvement of morale and motivation. If, for example, the worker places the greatest emphasis upon security of job, the motivation can be improved by making his job secure. If, on the other hand, he grants priority to social prestige then his motivation can be increased by giving him respect. In certain industries, demands for wages or bonus head the list, in which case serious thought should be devoted to increasing them. Therefore, psychologists nowadays pay much attention to the study of the demands.

It is evident from the foregoing account of the financial and non-financial incentives in industry that both kinds of incentives should be used. For effective use of these incentives, there must be cooperation by the employers, workers, trade unions and the government.

QUESTIONS FOR EXERCISE

1. Define motivation and discuss briefly the non-financial methods of motivating workers in industry.
2. Discuss the relating importance of financial and non-financial incentives in industry, giving appropriate examples.
3. Make a critical estimate of the methods commonly used for studying the motivation of industrial workers, and discuss the incentives that generally operate for them. Cite relevant studies.
4. What types of incentives are generally used in industry? Discuss their merits and limitations.
5. Discuss the problem of effective incentives in industry.
6. Discuss the measures that can be adopted to motivate the workers for better work.
7. Discuss the role of financial and non-financial incentives for the promotion of productivity in our country.
8. Comment on the view that an incentive plan to be really effective, must be anchored to the cultural values of the employees.
9. Studies of incentives have borne out the fact that factors other than high pay loom large in the worker's life. Examine.

10. Is it possible to draw up a comprehensive incentive programme by including only the monetary incentives? What are the non-monetary incentives which, according to you, should be considered important?
11. Do you believe that a comprehensive incentive programme in industry could be drawn up based only on monetary incentives? If not, describe in detail the non-monetary incentives which you believe are conducive to individual output.
12. Discuss the problem of inadequancy of financial incentives in industry.
13. Discuss the problem of effective incentives in industry in the light of recent findings.
14. Distinguish between financial and non-financial incentives.
15. How will you distinguish between motive and incentive?
16. Critically examine the merits and demerits of different wage payment.
17. Write a short note on method of payment of wages and their psychological effects.
18. Explain the utility of wage incentive system clarifying the relation of incentive and work.

28

Executive Development

TRAINING AND EDUCATION

Concerned with imparting specific skills for particular purposes, training is the act of increasing the knowledge and skill of an employee for doing a particular job. Education is concerned with increasing general knowledge and understanding of the employee's total environment. For example, teaching a person how to assemble two objects and tighten a nut, means training him to do a specific job but giving him a course in engineering, is education. The distinction between the training and education is like the distinction between pure and applied sciences.

Examples

(a) *Education* : A course in management or human relations is education because no one specific technique or procedure is taught but certain fundamentals common to all business situations are emphasised. A football coach who knows the theory of the game but who is utterly useless as a player is educated, but, not trained.

(b) *Training* : A clerk who an compute the loan value of any insurance policy quickly and accurately is no doubt trained but not necessarily educated because he may be unaware of the actuarial principles upon which the values are determined. A mechanic who repairs an automobile better than an engineer is only trained and not educated for he does not know engineering education and principles.

Distinctions between Training and Education

1. Content and scope. The content and scope of training are always specific, narrow and job-related; the content and scope of education are always broad and general.

2. Application and theory. Training is always applied and practical; education is usually pure and theoretical.

3. Duration. Training is mostly of short duration; education is of long duration.

4. Speed. Training gives quick and apparent results; the results of education are not so quick and apparent.

TRAINING AND DEVELOPMENT

The term 'development' includes both training and education. It seeks to improve the overall personality of an individual. It is mostly used in the context of executives. Following are some important distinctions between training and development :

1. Personnel using. Training is meant for operatives, while development is meant for executives.

2. Aim. While the aim of training is to develop some specific skill in an individual, the aim of development is to develop the total personality of the individual.

3. Periods. Training is a one-shot affair, while development is a continuous process.

4. Initiative. The initiative for training comes from management while the initiative for development comes from the individual himself. Training is mostly the result of some outside motivation, while development is the result of internal motivation.

5. Process. Training is a reactive process, preparation to meet an individual's present needs. Development is a proactive process, a preparation to meet individual's future needs.

PRINCIPLES OF EXECUTIVE TRAINING

1. Knowledge of results. Seeking to know what is expected of him and how well he is doing, every employee in a learning situation seeks information, appraisal and guidance about his progress. He is made uneasy by the possibility that he may be making some serious error in his behaviour and not knowing that he is doing so. Knowledge of results provides the trainee the basis for correcting his error. Knowledge of results is mandatory for learning in some tasks as that of a crane operation. It produces motivational effect on the trainee. Once he comes to know what is right, his tendency to repeat it, is strengthened.

2. Feedback. Researches on feedback have shown that : (i) Positive feedback *i.e.*, telling the trainee what is appropriate has a better effect than negative feedbacks, *i.e.*, telling him that he is not correct. (ii) Delay in feedback is detrimental to learning. (iii) Trainee should not be overburdened with feedback.

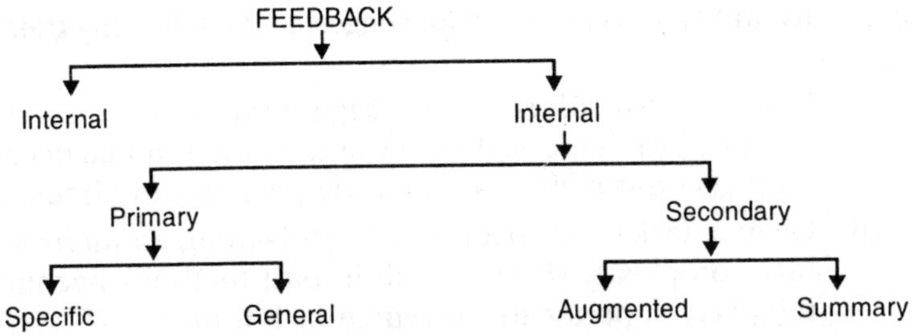

When feedback comes from cues internal to the organism, it is called internal feedback. When it comes from cues external to the organism, it is called external feedback. For example, in target shooting, the feeling that one has shot accurately may either come from cues in the body such as contraction of muscles, etc. or from cues outside the body such as the hole made by the bullet in the target. In the first case, it is internal feedback, in the second it is external feedback. External feedback can be either primary or secondary. It is secondary if someone else has collected it. In our example of target shooting if the learner himself determines his success or failure in hitting the target it is primary feedback. But if he is given feedback by the trainer or someone else, it is secondary feedback. Specific primary feedback pinpoints the error. General feedback does not do so. Secondary feedback can be augmented if it is given simultaneously with the performance, *e.g.*, the trainer exclaiming 'fine' simultaneously with the shooting. It may be summary if it is given some time after the performance.

3. Motivation. Until the worker has become convinced of the need of training and of the worthwhileness of the returns, the level of motivation will be low and learning will be perfunctory and slow.

4. Reinforcement. In order to acquire modified and sustained behaviour, it must be rewarded (reinforced). Reward should be distributed cautiously or discreetly as praising an inefficient and poor learner may disappoint the good trainees.

5. Supporting climate and practice. Practice makes a man perfect. In order not to revert back to the old behaviour, it is essential that the trainee practises the new learning daily. When the internal environment of many organisations is hostile to this, the trainee is not able to implement in his workplace what he has learned during the training session.

6. Part *versus* whole learning. In a comprehensive literature review, Naylor found that the tasks were seen to differ in complexity and organisation. Naylor suggested the following training principles :

(i) Given a task of relatively high organisation, as task complexity is increased, whole task training should become relatively more efficient than the part task methods.

(ii) Given a task of relatively low organisation, an increase in task complexity should result in part methods becoming relatively superior to the whole task training.

7. Transfer of learning. Transfer of learning from the training situation to the job depends upon the extent to which there are identical elements in the two. This means that the trained employee by virtue of his training would display superior "physical fidelity" if the devices and facilities used in training are similar to the devices and facilities used on the job and psychological fidelity where the human elements involved in the training performance on the job. If the physical and psychological fidelities are wanting there would be negative transfer of learning and the trained employee would display inferior performance on the job. Although one can easily ensure physical fidelity in a training programme it is not always easy to ensure psychological fidelity. For example, an employee on return from the training programme to the factory may find that his supervisor is a very different kind of person from the encouraging, understanding training director. The impact of such differences can be controlled to some extent by taking the following steps :

(i) Transfer at least 2 trainees to the same section. The support they can give each other is vital to their morale.

(ii) Let the production supervisor be involved with the training programme and have good relations with the training director.

(iii) On the day of transfer, let the trainer accompany the trainees to their, new section, stay with them a little while and check them at regular intervals for some time subsequently.

EXECUTIVE DEVELOPMENT METHODS

1. Methods for improving the decision-making skills of executives;
2. Methods for improving the inter-personal skills of executives and
3. Methods for improving the executives' knowledge.

1. Methods for Improving the Decision-making Skills of Executives

(i) Case study method. A case is a written account seeking to describe an actual situation. A good case brings chunk of reality into the classroom to be discussed over by the class and the instructor. Pioneered by the Harvard Business School, the case study method aims at compelling the student to think actively, to analyse and sift evidence, to see beyond the confines of his speciality and to communicate coherently. The student has the benefit of listening to his companions arriving at different situations using the same data. He learns about himself, his assumptions, talents and limitations. He comes to see that there are many possible good answers to a problem.

There are two types of case study methods — directed and non-directed.

(a) *The directed case study* : In it the students are presented with the case and given a number of questions to answer or decisions to make.

(b) *Non-directed case study* : In this the student is simply presented with the material and is expected to explore the possible outcomes.

(ii) Incident method. Developed at the Massachusetts Institute of Technology, it is an outgrowth of dissatisfaction with the case method felt by Paul and Pigors. In the usual case method, the entire problem is presented to the student, whereas in the incident method, only a brief incident is presented to provoke discussion in the class. The group puts questions to the instructor to draw out of him the salient facts and additional information needed to arrive at a reasonable solution or resolution of the case. The method draws the participants into discussion with greater emotional involvement. Its unique advantage over the case method is the procedure of obtaining information by questions, which must take place in actual business situations.

(iii) In-basket method. It consists of letters, notes, documents and reports designed to simulate on-the-job reality of the manager's in-basket. The trainee deals with the in-basket materials as he would in his job. Feedback is provided so that he can appraise his results. The advantages of this method are realism, high involvement, and built-in motivation, similar to those of the case method.

(iv) Management games. A management game is a dynamic training exercise simulating a real business situation. The participants are divided into various teams placed in competition with each other in resolving some problem, information about which is supplied to all teams. The game tests player's ability to absorb information quickly and make decisions under fire. With the introduction of video and audio, business games are getting more and more into live 'emulations' and away from traditional 'simulations'.

2. Methods for Improving the Inter-personal Skills of Executives

(i) Sensitivity training (or laboratory training). It involves the use of a training-group, in which ten to fifteen persons are put into a face-to-face situation. As the group has no agenda, no established roles, no established norms of performance, it creates tension and anxiety. Group members attempt to relieve it by withdrawing from active participation or by attempting to provide the missing structural elements, assuming leadership, establishing goals, setting up an agenda. These attempts may not meet with unanimous approval but they do reveal the needs of individuals and some of their habitual reactions to stress. Members of the group are told that from continuous observation and analysis of experiences in the group, they can learn much about their own behaviour and that of others and about group behaviour. The trainer does not act as a discussion leader; he helps group members to find ways of utilising their experiences for learning.

A laboratory should develop situations which will induce the individual to examine his incongruities and discrepancies and endeavour to integrate his behaviour, values, need, knowledge and feelings, constituting his inner world with the expectations of his social environment. Thus, the laboratory programme aims at achieving behavioural effectiveness in transactions with one's environment. Conditions for success : (a) There should be exploration of each other's feelings. Without bringing forth one's own feelings and thoughts, and knowing the reactions of others, the individual may not recognise needed changes in his behaviour, (b) In a competitive or hostile atmosphere, exposure of self can lead towards rejection, loss of reputation or ridicule. By encouraging trust among members, laboratory conditions reduce the threats inherent in self-exposure.

(ii) Role playing. In the area of "interpersonal relations" discussion of case studies generally remains at an unemotional intellectual level of role-playing has been developed to correct this deficiency. In this method, the instructor assigns parts taken from case materials to group members. Working without a script or memorised lines and improvising as they play the parts, the role players attempt to act their parts as they would behave in a real life situation. The very act of arguing for another view, even if it is purely an exercise, exposes the person to some of its virtues which he had previously denied. A supervisor might play the role of a subordinate, a sales-person the role of a customer and a nurse's aide the role of a hospital patient. The role playing lasts 20-30 minutes, after which data are collected about the performance of each role-play and a discussion takes place. Role playing tends to be enjoyed by participants. It develops empathy and sensitivity in them. It allows for their emotional release in a fairly harmless manner. It promotes insight. It emphasises the importance of acceptability in decision making.

(iii) Transactional analysis. A transaction is a social intercourse between two or more people who encounter each other. In every social intercourse, there is a *stimulus* provided by one individual and a response to that stimulus given by another individual. This stimulus-response relationship between two individuals is a transaction. Introduced over two decades ago by Berne and further popularised by Haris and Jongewald, Transactional Analysis (TA) provides an individual with a practical and useful method for analysis and understanding of human behaviour. It is a method of analysing a transaction.

Berne says that every normal individual functions from three ego states — parent, adult and child. An ego state is a system of feelings accompanied by a related set of behaviour patterns. Each ego state can be described as under.

(a) *Parent* : The parent ego is a huge collection of recordings in the brain of an individual of attitudes and behaviours imposed on him in his early years (roughly first five years) from various external sources, primarily his parents. The characteristics of this ego are to be owner protective, officious, distant, dogmatic, etc. Verbal clues that a person is operating from the parent ego state are his use of such words as 'always', 'never', 'should', 'ought', etc. He uses language of threat or tries to resolve conflict by force. There are physical clues also like raised *eyebrows, pointing an accusing finger at* somebody, and so on.

(b) *Child* : The child ego is a collection of recordings of attitudes, behaviours and impulses in the brain of an individual which come to him naturally from his own seeing, hearing, feeling and understanding as a child. Characteristics of a person acting in the child state include being curious, impulsive, sensuous, affectionate, dependent, fearful and depressed. Verbal clues about operating from the child ego state are the use of words like "I wish", "I guess', 'I do not care", and so on. There are physical clues also like temper tantrums, attention seeking, giggling, coyness, silent compliance, etc. The child in us is likely to lead us to behave as dependants, as competitive and to approach conflict resolution through avoidance or smoothing.

(c) *Adult* : Adult ego state includes reality testing, rational behaviour and decision-making or problem-solving analysis. In this state processes, an individual verifies and updates the data which he receives from the other two states. Thus, this state is a shift from the "taught and felt concept" to "tested concepts". Adult data are gathered by the individual's ability to find out for himself the difference between life as it was taught and demonstrated to him (parent), life as he felt, wished or fantasied (child) and life as he figures out by testing now (adult). The adult-ego state does not do away with parent and child data. It examines these data and tries to update them in the reality of the external world. In an individual, the adult shows itself in a variety of ways. The indicators of the adults-ego state in an individual are phrases like "I see", I think", "It is my opinion", words with an emphasis on data collection, *e.g.*, why, where, when, who, how, what, and an emphasis on data processing and problem-solving.

Types of Transactions

When we evoke behaviour from one ego state responded to by the other individual from any one of these three ego states, it gives rise to three types of transactions : complementary, crossed and ulterior.

(a) ***Complementary transactions*** : It is one in which the stimulus and response ego states are complementary to each other; the

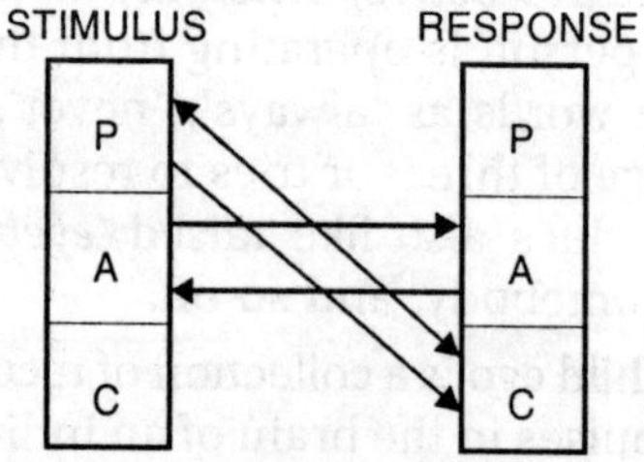

Fig. 28.1. Complementary Transaction

communication between any two individuals runs along parallel lines between them (Fig. 28.1). Thus, the parent in one individual is responded to by the child in the other as shown and the adult in one is responded to by the adult in the other. Both parties feel satisfied in this type of transaction.

Examples

1.	Workers	:	I cannot do this job myself. Please help me. Will you? (Child-Parent).
	Foreman	:	Sure, I am coming just now. (Parent-Child).
2.	Foreman	:	Have you finished the job? (Adult-Adult).
	Worker	:	Yes, I finished it long back and it has already been delivered to the assembly line. (Adult-Adult).

(b) ***Crossed transactions*** : When communication runs along crossed lines between individuals, the transactions are crossed. Further transactions stop, in this communication.

Examples

Foreman to Worker	:	How many pieces have you made by now? (A-A).
Worker to Foreman	:	Do not disturb me. When I complete the whole work I will let you know. (P-C).

(c) ***Ulterior transaction*** : This type of transaction has double meaning. On the surface level, it is a clear adult message though it also carries a hidden message. For example, husband while sitting on the dining table may find the table dirty. If he writes on the table "I love you" to be read by his wife, he is on the surface using his child ego state but his ulterior motive is to hint her that she has not cleaned the table. Thus, his message is proceeding from the parent state. His wife must respond to it form her child state by cleaning the table.

Thus transaction analysis give an insight into the fundamentals of human psychology and helps to improve interpersonal relations.

(d) ***The Johari window*** : It is a conceptual model developed by Joseph Left and Harry Ingham; the name Johari combines their first names. It is for increasing personal effectiveness. As shown in Figure 28.2, this model divides an individual's personality into four parts "Arena". The part known to the individual but not to others is called closed. "Blind" is the part which is known to others but not to the individual. The part not known both to the individual and to others is called "Dark".

	Know of self	Not know of self
Know to others	Arena	Blind
Not Know to others	Closed	Dark

Fig. 28.2. Johari Window

In order to make oneself effective in interpersonal relations, one should expand one's arena. One must try to reduce the other three areas. "Blind" can be reduced by "receiving feedback from others" "Closed area" can be reduced by self-disclosure.

3. Methods for Improving the Executive's Knowledge

(i) Conferences. Mutual problems are the subject of discussion in a conference. In attempting to arrive at improved methods of dealing with these problems, participants pool their ideas and experience for joint exploration.

(ii) Buzz session. When a conference group is broken up in several small groups of four-five participants, it is called buzz session. Members of the group come together to teach each other and to learn together. This method is most appropriate for the purpose of presenting new and sometimes complicated material.

(iii) Autonomy training. "Autonomy training" is aimed at developing the individual's ability to manage his own training. It leaves the trainee almost on his own. He has first to work out what he would like to learn and then teach himself. This method rests on the concept that with the tremendous speed at which new knowledge is replacing the old one, it is impossible for standardised course to cater for individual training needs. Therefore, the managers must be trained to teach themselves new skills as they go along the situation is kept unstructured. In this training also, as in the sensitivity training, the trainer refuses to direct the programme or give lectures. He merely indicates a vast array of resources such as books, films, articles, management games, psychological tests, etc., from which the participant may choose to build his own programme. Consultants are available for discussion or counselling but only if the participant seeks them out. Participants can also consult with each other.

FACTORS FOR SELECTION OF A TRAINING AND DEVELOPMENT METHOD

1. Training objective. It is far more difficult to define the objectives at the managerial level than at the blue-collar level. Experts agree on the form and content of training to be given to a machinist or electrician but they differ widely in case of a junior executive because they do not know why some senior executives are more effective than others or what does a successful manager know better than his less successful colleagues.

From an opinion survey of 200 training directors of large American companies, post training work, it is revealed that :

(i) For acquisition of knowledge, programmed instruction is the best, lectures are the worst.

(ii) For changing trainee's attitudes, sensitivity training is the best, television lectures are the worst.

(iii) For increasing trainees' problem-solving skills, case method is the best, lectures are the worst.

(iv) For increasing trainees' interpersonal skills, sensitivity training is the best, television lectures are the worst.

(v) For increasing trainees' acceptance of the training method, conference (discussion) is the best, television lectures are the worst.

(vi) For trainee's retention of knowledge, programmed instruction is the best, television lectures are the worst.

2. Level of trainees in the organisation's hierarchy. At different levels in the organizational hierarchy, training needs of employees differ in the degree to which emphasis is placed on various training inputs. This difference makes certain techniques better for one class of employees than for the other.

3. Method's ability to hold and arouse the interest of trainees during the training period.

4. Availability of competent trainers.

5. Availability of finance.

6. Availability of time.

DIMENSIONS OF EVALUATION

1. Evaluation of contextual factors. It involves evaluation of the pre-training and post-training :

(i) ***Pre-training work*** : It includes proper identification of training needs, developing criteria of who should be sent for training, how many at a time and in what sequence, helping people to volunteer for training, building expectations of prospective participants from training, etc.

(ii) ***Post-training work*** : It includes helping the concerned managers to plan to utilise the participants' training and provide the needed support to them, building linkages between the training section and the line departments and so on.

2. Evaluation of training inputs. It involves the evaluation of training curriculum and its sequencing.

3. Evaluation of training process. Some of the important elements of the training process which also need to be evaluated are the climate of the training organisation, the relationship between participants and trainers, the general attitudes and approaches of the trainers, training methods, etc.

4. Evaluation of training outcomes. The main task of evaluation is measuring the carry home value of a training programme in terms of what has been active and how much. This is a complex technical and professional task. Benefits of a training programme are not always obvious nor are they readily measurable. Pay-offs from training are intangible and slow to become apparent. A central problem is the absence of objective criteria and specific definitions of relevant variables by which to measure the effectiveness either of specific programmes or of results in terms of general employee development or changes in employee behaviour. However, good personnel managers do make an effort to systematically appraise the benefits and result of their programmes.

(i) ***Evaluation in job-related training.*** Here the objective is to train people for specific job skills so that their productivity may increase, hence evaluation can be done either according to the direct criterion of increase in output or according to the indirect criteria of decrease in cost, breakage or rejects. Even more indirect are measures that point out changes in absenteeism or turnover.

(ii) ***Evaluation of human relations skills training.*** This is given to the supervisors and middle-level managers. Supervisory and managerial training programmes are less amenable to objective review procedures. Since exact standards and criteria are hard to devise, much subjectivity enters into evaluations.

Methods of Evaluation

2. Reaction evaluation. Opinion surveys of participants or of people who have seen the participants in action are reaction evaluations. There are following variations of this method :

(i) ***Questionnaire*** : It is given to the participant at the end of the programme which asks him to rate in terms of his personal perceptions what he liked best, what he liked least and any other comments he might have about the programme.

(ii) ***Scalar ratings*** : There are given against every question and the trainee is required to check off the degree of satisfaction which he found in each answer.

(iii) ***Daily ratings*** : Participants are required to give daily ratings for each segment of this programme. It provides an immediate feedback to the manager of the training programme who can use it for the adjustment and improvement of the following day's programme.

(iv) ***In panel questioning*** : Dropping around during a coffee break a management representative may put questions to one or two participants and informally collect information about the success of the training programme The results may not be always accurate such samplings are not scientifically designed.

(v) ***Follow-up opinions*** : Sometimes on returning to their organisations, the participants may be asked to send their opinions by mail. It is so because opinions given immediately at the conclusion of the course cannot possibly have the objectivity which is desired in the appraisal of the programme.

2. Outcome evaluation. Outcome evaluation may be done at immediate, intermediate and ultimate levels :

(i) ***Immediate*** : To find out the extent to which positive transfer of learning has taken place from the training to the job situation, this form of evaluation measures, analyses and interprets changes in the knowledge, skills and attitudes of trainees soon after they have returned to their jobs. This evaluation may be done by using behaviourally anchored rating scales or self-reports supplemented by reports of subordinates, peers and supervisors or critical incidents, etc.

(ii) ***Intermediate*** : Intermediate evaluation measure, analyses and interprets changes in the performance of trainees when they have returned to their jobs. It is based on the assumption that effective training should be reflected in the trainee's increased job proficiency. For example, a training given to salesmen is successful to the extent it increases sales. A training given in cost reduction is successful to the extent it helps people in reducing costs. A training in work simplification is successful to the extent people simplify their jobs. If the trainee is in a supervisory capacity, evaluation may have to be based upon the performance of his subordinates because no objective criteria are available for supervisory personnel. Group standards of performance, group efficiency and group behaviour may become the focal point of study, where the training programme is to be evaluated for its impact on co-operation between the small groups, interpersonal relationships, etc.

There are three basic techniques followed under this method :

(a) Controlled experimentation. It requires the use of two groups of employees, namely, "training" group and a "control" group. Performance is measured of both the groups *before* training is started. The training group is then given the training, while the control group is not. After the first group is trained, performance of both the groups is again measured. A subsequent comparison is made of the improvement in both groups to determine if the training group improves significantly more than the control group. It involves the use of a single training group with performance being measured *before and after* the training.

(b) "Before-and-after" comparison.

(c) After the training study. It involves a single training group but with performance being measured after the training.

Of these controlled experimentation is the most scientific technique that really provides a solid basis for evaluation of the training. Before and after company technique does not provide the basis for knowing how much improvement would have occurred without training. The third technique does not provide any basis for knowing how much improvement actually occurred during training.

Routine appraisal of employees may be used to evaluate the effectiveness and impact of training. For example, if on his annual appraisal, an individual is reported by his boss to be somewhat deficient in human relations, he might be enrolled in a course to correct these defects. It will be appropriate to ask at the conclusion of this course, what his next appraisal showed. If his behaviour did change and the appraisal is better, this is an evidence to show that the training programme had an effect.

(iii) ***Ultimate*** : Ultimate evaluation measures and analyses changes in the ultimate results achieved by trainees. Sometimes, in the evaluation of management training, instead of attempting atomistics measurements of improvement in an individual, an overall look is taken at the aggregate growth of people in the total organisation. The indexes of productivity, labour turnover, etc., studies of organisational climate and human resources accounting are taken as the ultimate results achieved by trainees.

Principles of Effective Evaluation

1. Planned. What is to be evaluated, when, by what means, and by whom, must be determined in advance.

2. Objective. It should not be a mere eyewash — an attempt by the trainer to vindicate the programme instead of to verify it.

3. Verifiable. Results can be confirmed by the same or different means.

4. Co-operative. It must involve all those who are a part of or affected by the training and development programme. It is not a contest between the evaluator and the subject of evaluation.

5. Continuous.

6. Specific. It should tell about specific strengths and weaknesses and should not make vague generalisations.

7. Quantitative.

8. Feasible. It must be administratively manageable.

9. Cost Effective. The results must be commensurate with the costs incurred.

QUESTIONS FOR EXERCISE

1. Distinguish between :
   (i) Executive Training and Education.
   (ii) Executive Training and Development.
2. Describe the principles of Executive Training.
3. Describe Executive Development methods.
4. How will you select a training and development method? Explain developing of evaluation of training and development.

29

Job Evaluation

WHAT IS JOB EVALUATION?

1. Kimball and Kimbal. "Job evaluation represents an effort to determine the relative value of every job in a plant and to determine what the fair basic wages for such a job should be."

2. A. Shubin. "Job evaluation is a systematic procedure for measuring the relative value and importance of occupation on the basis of their common factor (skill, training effort) for the purpose of determining wage and salary differentials."

3. Bethel, Atwaker, and Smith etc. "Job evaluation as a personnel term has both a specific and generic meaning. Specially it means the entire field of wages and salary administration along modern lines."

4. Alford and Beauty. "Job evaluation is the application of the job analysis technique to the qualitative measurement of relative job worth, for the purpose of establishing consistent wage rate differentials by objective means. It measures the differences between jobs based on the job requirements and establishes the differential numerically (job rating) so that it can be converted to wage rates after the wage level is determined".

5. Dale Yoder. "Job evaluation is a practice which seeks to provide a degree of objectivity in measuring the comparative value of jobs within an organisation and among similar organisations. It is essentially a job rating process, not like the rating of employers."

6. I.L.O. "Job evaluation may be designed as an attempt to determine and compare the demands which the normal performance of particular job makes on normal workers, without taking account of the individual abilities or performance of the workers concerned."

7. Edwin B. Fillippo. "The systematic and orderly process of measuring the worth of job within an organisation is called job evaluation."

8. Maurice B. Cuming. "Job evaluation is a technique of assessing the worth of each job in comparison with all others throughout an organisation."

9. Wendell L. French. Job evaluation is "a process of determining the relative worth of various jobs within the organisation, so that differential wages may be paid to jobs of different worth."

10. Langriser, A and H.G. Zollitsch. Job evaluation is "the overall activity of involving an orderly, systematic method and procedure of ranking, grading and weighing of jobs to determine the value of specific job in relation to other jobs."

11. British Institute of Management. Job evaluation is "the process of analysing and assessing the content of jobs, in order to place them in an acceptable rank order, which can then be used as a basis for a remuneration system. Job evaluation, therefore, is simply a technique, designed to assist in development of new pay structures by defining relativities between jobs on a consistent and systematic basis."

Thus, job evaluation is a process of determining the relative worth of jobs, ranking and grading them by comparing the duties, responsibilities, requirements like skill, knowledge of a job with other jobs in order to fix compensation payable to the concerned job holder.

OBJECTIVES OF JOB EVALUATION

1. Gathering data. To gather data and information relating to job description, job specification and employee specifications of various jobs in an organisation.

2. Comparison. To compare the duties, responsibilities and demands of a job with that of other jobs.

3. Determine hierarchy. To determine the hierarchy and place of various jobs in an organisation.

4. Determine ranks and grades. To determine the ranks or grades of various jobs.

5. Ensure wages. To ensure fair and equitable wages on the basis of relative worth or value of jobs. Equal wages are fixed to the jobs of equal worth or value.

6. Minimise discrimination. To minimise wage discrimination based on sex, age, caste, region, religion, etc.

Steps in Preparing the Ground for Job Evaluation

1. Appointing job evaluation committee. As it is very difficult for a single man to study, review and evaluate all jobs, appointment of a job evaluation committee consisting of technical and non-technical people is more appropriate.

2. Analysing the jobs. Analysing the job, job knowledge can be obtained from the job description and job specification records. It can be gathered and collected through interviews, observations, activity sampling, questionnaires, critical incidents, diaries, etc.

3. Identification of compensatory factors. This refers to knowledge in respect of education, experience, skill, etc. This ground work is more useful for systematic job evaluation.

Essentials for the Success of Job Evaluation Programme

1. Representative factors. Compensable factors should represent all of the major aspects of job content. Compensable factors selected should (a) avoid excessive overlapping or duplication; (b) be definable and measurable; (c) be easily understood by employees and administrators; (d) not cause excessive installation or administrative cost; and (e) be selected with legal considerations in mind.

2. Training. Operating managers should be trained in the techniques and programme of job evaluation and fixing and revising the wages based on job evaluation.

3. Information. All the employees should be provided with complete information about job evaluation techniques and programme.

4. Coverage. All groups and grades of employees should be covered by the job evaluation programme.

5. Facilitation. The programme and techniques selected for job evaluation should be easy to understand by all the employees.

6. Unions' support. Trade unions' acceptance and support to the programme should be obtained.

JOB EVALUATION METHODS/TECHNIQUES

Jobs are evaluated on the basis of conventional and non-conventional techniques :

(a) ***Conventional techniques*** : These are divided into (i) quantitative and (ii) non-quantitative techniques. Non-quantitative techniques include : (i) simple ranking (ii) paired comparison ranking, (iii) job classification and (iv) grading method. Quantitative techniques include points rating and (v) factor comparison method.

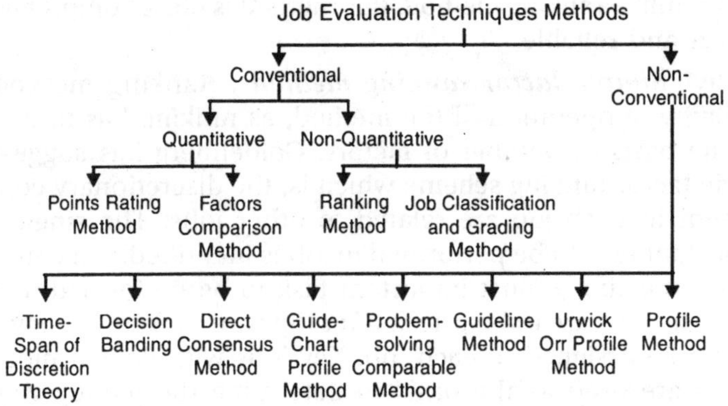

Chart 29.1. Types of Job Evaluation Techniques Methods

(b) ***Non-conventional methods*** : These consist of (1) time-span of discretion theory, (2) decision-banding, (3) direct consensus method, (4) guide-chart profile method, (5) problem-solving compensable factor, (6) guideline method, (7) Urwick Orr profile method and (8) profile method.

[A] Conventional Techniques/Methods

Non-quantitative conventionally, non-quantitative simple and crude techniques are developed. They are ranking and job classification methods :

1. Ranking Method

(i) *Simple ranking* : This is the simplest and administratively easiest technique. The evaluator compares one job with other jobs about duties, responsibilities and demands made by them on the job incumbent and the degree of importance of the job to the organisation. He ranks all the jobs from the most to the least important. He has to appraise and rank the jobs but not the job incumbents.

(ii) *Ranking the key jobs* : Ranking all the jobs at a stretch under. In order to minimise difficulty, the evaluator identifies the key or representative jobs at the first stage; ranks the key jobs at the second stage; identifies and ranks all other jobs at the third stage.

(iii) *Paired comparison* : As each job cannot be compared with all other jobs for the purpose of ranking, the method of paired comparison is adopted to minimise this problem. Under this method, the evaluator ranks each job against all other jobs to be appraised, so that a series of paired rankings is produced. Compared to the simple ranking method, this method is more comprehensive, logical and reliable.

(iv) *Simple factor ranking method* : Ranking method has difficulty of operation of the method, as ranking has to be done on the basis of number of factors. Goldenberg has suggested a single factor ranking scheme which is, the discretionary contents present in each job are related to other jobs. The single most important task to be performed in job is identified and compared within the single most important task to be performed in other jobs. The jobs are to be priced after they are ranked. Money value should be assigned to each job. Key jobs with known monetary values are used as the basis to determine the money value of other jobs. Generally, there is agreement about the rates of key jobs.

Advantages of Ranking

(i) It is the simplest, quickest and least costly from the viewpoint of time and money.

(ii) It is most appropriate in small organisations.

(iii) It is appropriate for ranking the top managerial personnel in large organisations.

(iv) It is useful as a first and basic step of job evaluation.

2. Job classification and grading methods. A grade is a group of different jobs of similar difficulty or requiring similar knowledge and skill to perform, while class is a subdivision of a given occupation. In the occupation of Accountant, Assistant Accountant,Senior Accountant and Chief Accountant are the classes. While the jobs within a class have fairly similar tasks to be performed, the jobs within a grade may have more different tasks. As classes and grades are designed for the similar jobs, they receive similar pay. For example, while a grade may consist of jobs like Financial Accountants, Cost Accountants and Management Accountants, a class may consist of Assistant Financial Accountant, Financial Accountant, Senior Financial Accountant and Chief Financial Accountant.

Under grading method, jobs at different levels in the organisational hierarchy are divided into various grades, with a clear-cut definition of each grade. Grades are formulated on the basis of nature of tasks, requirements of skill, knowledge, responsibilities and authority of various jobs.

Steps in Grading Method

(i) Determining the shape and size of organisational structure such as tall or flat organisation, geographical or functional organisation, etc.

(ii) Preparing job descriptions.

(iii Preparing grade descriptions based on various components.

(iv) Establishing a number of job grades and division of the organisation into various grades like Grade-I, Grade-II... Grade VI, as shown in Chart 29.2.

(v) Discussing and negotiating with trade union representatives regarding the number of grades, grade descriptions, getting their consent, finalising the number of grades and grade description and recording them.

(vi) Selecting key jobs and grading them.

(vii) Grading the entire jobs.

(viii) Classifying the jobs of each grade.

(ix) Assigning the money value to the key grades first and then to all other grades.

Advantages of Grading

(i) It is simple and easy to understand and operate.

(ii) It provides an opportunity for a systematic organisation structure.

(iii) Pay grades are better and appropriate for comparison with those of other organisations.

(iv) It is more elaborate than ranking method.

Limitations of Grading Method

(i) It sometimes seems to be arbitrary, though it takes the views of the representatives of the trade unions.

(ii) Writing grade descriptions is not easy in this method.

[B] Conventional Quantitative Techniques

Under conventional quantitative techniques, there are two methods *viz.*, points rating and factor comparison system :

1. Points rating method. Introduced by Merill R. Lott, it was one of the earliest approaches for evaluating jobs based on quantitative values. It is analytical in the sense that jobs are broken

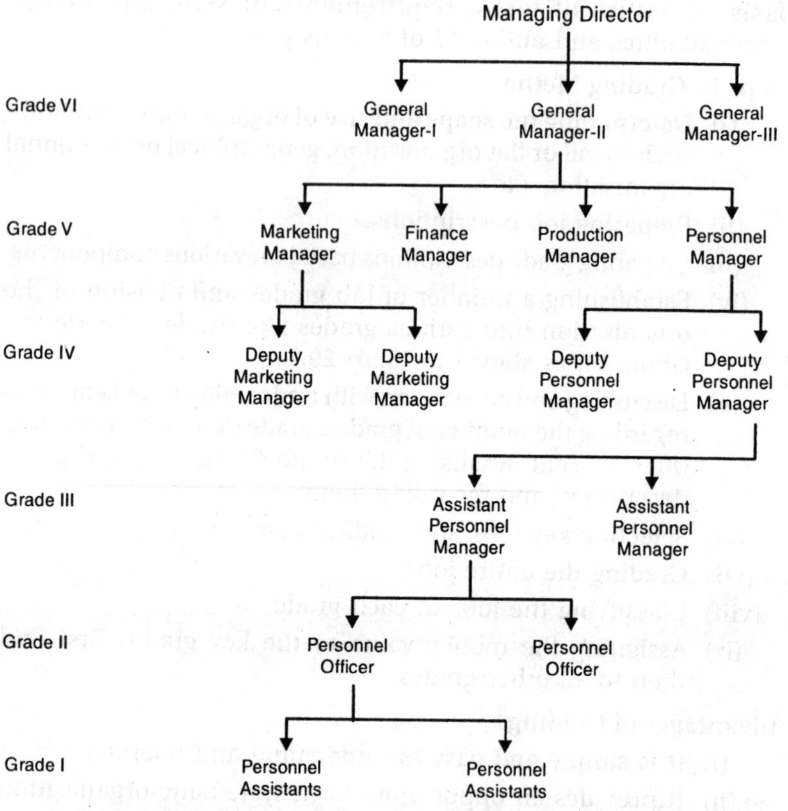

Chart 29.2. Grading the Jobs

into components for purposes of comparison. It is quantitative as each component of the job is assigned a numerical value. The characteristics having a bearing on all jobs in the programme like skill, knowledge, responsibility, working conditions, etc., are selected under this method. Each factor is divided into degrees or levels. Point value is assigned to each level. The total of point values assigned to each factor gives the total point values for each job.

In order to avoid the anomalies, this method of job evaluation should be developed systematically and applied methodically.

Steps in Points Rating Method

(i) ***Committee*** : Constituting a representative committee of members from various departments for job evaluation.

(ii) ***Sample*** : Selecting a sample of jobs and preparing job descriptions, job specifications and employee specifications.

(iii) *Factors* : Selecting and defining factors related to all jobs and considered to be most critical in determining the relative degrees of difficulty and responsibility between jobs. Following factors are most desirable :

(a) *Skill* : Education, training, judgement, analysis, mental complexity, mental dexterity, adaptability, etc.

(b) *Effort* : Physical demand, visual effort, concentration, mental effort, alertness etc.

(c) *Responsibility* : For preventing monetary loss, machines, materials, safety policy, etc.

(d) *Job Conditions* : Working conditions, hazards, etc.

(iv) *Weightage* : Determining the weightage of each factor according to its relative importance. Assigning the percentage value to each factor. The total percentage of all factors is 100.

(v) *Scope* : Defining each factor, specifying the scope and elements of each factor.

(vi) *Value* : Determining relative value of each level within factors. Factors can be divided into point values by arithmetic or geometric progression.

(vii) *Testing the mechanism* : Get the total points with the help of above discussed method for a few sample jobs and compare them with the results obtained through other methods. Proceed further, if the system produces acceptable results.

(viii) *Appraisal* : Appraise all the jobs and arrive at a composite numerical value for each job.

(ix) *Pricing* : Price the points in order to arrive at the wage level.

(x) *Wage structure* : Establish a wage structure with the help of organisational hierarchy of jobs and salary policy.

Job Factors	Weights	Degrees				
		1	2	3	4	5
1. Skill	20	4	8	12	16	20
2. Kowledge	15	5	10	15	20	25
3. Training	10	3	6	9	12	15
4. Experience	20	2	4	8	16	32
5. Complexity of duties	10	3	6	9	12	15
6. Contact with others	25	5	10	15	20	25
	Total : 100					

Factor	Experience
1st degree	up to 6 months
2nd degree	6 months to 1 year
3rd degree	1 year to 2 years
4th degree	2 years — 3 years
5th degree	Above 3 years

Chart 29.3. Example of Mechanism of Points Rating Method — Job : Marketing Manager

Regarding factors, sub-factors assigning the weightages, deciding upon degrees and values, there are no hard and fast rules.

Points Rating Method is only a preliminary step is arriving at an equitable pay structure. There are no scientific techniques to guide about assigning money value to the points. But, influence of trade unions, pay structure in comparable industries, financial position of the company, living cost affect the pay level. However, this method may help in arriving at an equitable pay structure. It was important for conversion of point scores into monetary values by assigning a standard unit of money to each point. Money value of various scores can be attained by plotting a graph with points ratings on the X-axis and money value on the Y-axis. There are certain alternatives regarding plotting money on the Y-axis, such as showing current salary rates on Y-axis and the score of the job concerned on X-axis. Trend line through a scatter of points is seen

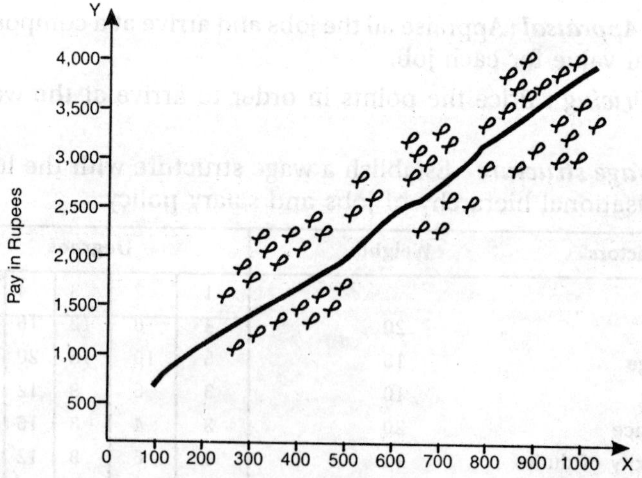

Fig. 29.1. Trend Line through a Scatter of Points

in Fig. 29.1. If point score is divided among various grades of jobs in an organisation, the pay level can be related to the grades as shown in Chart 29.4. While the minimum and maximum pay of each grade are shown in the figures the pay scale of various jobs will be fixed within the minimum and maximum limits of the pay.

Advantages of Point Rating Method

(i) *Same pay scale* : As agreement among rates on the same is very close, almost the same pay scale can be arrived at for the same jobs.

(ii) *Applied definitions* : Definitions are written in terms applicable to jobs.

(iii) *Assigning monetary values is very easy.*

(iv) *Prejudice, bias and error of human judgement are minimised.*

(v) *Point score or monetary values* : There cannot be manipulated easily.

(vi) *Assignment of point score or money values* : It is consistent and accurate.

(vii) *The Score* : Assigned to a particular job, it is long standing.

(viii) *Wage differentials* : They are systematic and according to the content of the job under this method.

Disadvantages of Point Rating Method

(i) *Determination* : Factor levels and assigned point values are difficult to determine.

(ii) *Explanation* : It is difficult to explain the mechanism and operation of this method to employees, supervisors and trade union leaders.

(iii) *Operation* : It involves heavy expenditure, spending of much time and clerical work.

However, this technique is superior to the conventional non-quantitative techniques in several respects.

2. The Point factor or factor-comparison method. Based both on the principles of points rating and principle of ranking, this method is analytical. Jobs are broken into sub-factors and components. First the components or sub-factors are ranked under various factor headings. Next step is assigned for the monetary values to the components or sub-factors of each job. Thus, each job is ranked a number of times.

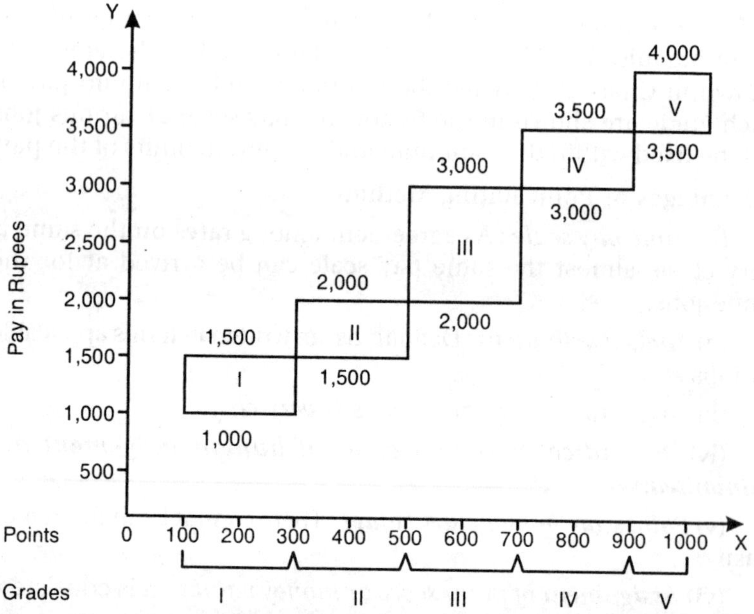

Chart 29.4. Relationship between Pay Level and Job Grades

Points Range	Grade	Pay at the Minimum		Pay at the Maximum
	Grade I Pay Scale	1,000	to	1,500
	Grade II Pay Scale	1,500	to	2,000
	Grade III Pay Scale	2,000	to	3,000
	Grade IV Pay Scale	3,000	to	3,500
	Grade V Pay Scale	3,500	to	4,000

Steps in Factor Comparison Method

1. Development. Developing job descriptions, job specifications or job requirements, covering physical requirements, mental requirements, skill requirements, training and experience, responsibility and authority, working conditions, etc.

2. Selection. Selecting a number of key jobs is more critical and useful from the point of final evaluation as the other jobs are assigned monetary values based on the fixed wage rates arrived for the key jobs on the basis of negotiations. A key job must be clearly divisible into sub-factors and components. This step also involves dividing the job into sub-factors and components.

3. Ranking. In ranking of key jobs, the sub-factors of each key job are given relative ranks, based on their individual contribution to the total job. Chart 29.5 shows ranking of sub-factors of two key jobs *viz.*, Welder and Mechanical Engineer.

Factor Rank Order	Welder	Mechanical Engineer
1	Physical requirements	Skill requirement
2	Working conditions	Mental requirement
3	Skill requirements	Responsibility
4	Responsibility	Working conditions
5	Mental requirements	Physical requirements

Chart 29.5. Factor Ranking of Two Key Jobs

Competitive picture of the ranking of Welder and Mechanical Engineer is shown in a matrix of factor rankings as shown in chart 29.6 :

Rank Order	Skill Require-ments	Mental Require-ments	Physical Require-ments	Responsibility	Working Conditions
1.	Mechanical Engineer (25)		Welder (15)		
2.		Mechanical Engineer (20)			Welder (5)
3.	Welder (10)			Mechanical Engineer (15)	
4.				Welder (4)	Mechanical Engineer (10)
5.	Welder (5)	Mechanical Engineer (8)			

Chart 29.6. Matrix of Factor Ranking of Welder and Mechanical Engineer

Valuation. This involves valuing the sub-factors of each of key jobs. It is also known as factor evaluation. In order to know the total money value (or salary) of each of the key jobs, money worth of each sub-factor of the key jobs in ascertained. Following Chart 29.7 shows factor evaluation or monetary value (per day) of each of the key jobs.

Sub-Factors	Welder (Rs.)	Mechanical Engineer (Rs.)
Mental Requirements	5	20
Skill Requirements	10	25
Physical Requirements	15	8
Responsibility	4	15
Working conditions	5	10
Total	39	10

Chart 29.7. Factor Evaluation or Monetary Value of Key Jobs (per day)

5. Integration. This is integrating the monetary value of sub-factors arrived through factors evaluation with those of ranking of factors to find out whether the difference among factors as per the ranking and factor evaluation is one and the same. Cross checking is provided through Chart 29.6 where the money value of each sub-factor is given in brackets.

6. Comparison. It is comparing all the jobs (factor by factor) of the same grade or level with the related key job and establishing monetary value to the sub-factors of various jobs based on the monetary value of sub-factors or key jobs.

Advantages of Factor Comparison Method

(i) ***Analytical and Quantitative***

(ii) ***Combination*** : It is a combination of two techniques i.e., ranking and factor comparison.

(iii) ***Easy*** : Its modes operandi is relatively easy to understand. Hence it can be operated and explained to supervisor, employee and trade union leaders.

(iv) ***Reliable*** : It is more reliable and valid, compared to other techniques, as each job is compared with all other jobs from two respects *i.e.*, factor rank order and factor comparison.

(v) ***Objective*** : It assigns money value more or less fairly and objectively. As there is cross checking of money value with rank order.

Limitations of Factor Comparison

(i) ***Costly*** : It is costly and somewhat difficult to operate compared to the conventional non-quantitative techniques.

(ii) ***Less objective*** : Factor evaluation in this method is not that much objective as that of point-rating technique.

(iii) ***Less coverage*** : It does not consider all the sub-factors as the operation of the system would be difficult if it considers all the factors.

Non-Conventional Techniques of Job Evaluation

These include : (1) Time-span of discretion theory, (2) Decision-banding, (3) Direct consensus method, (4) Guide-chart profile method, (5) Problem-solving compensable factor, (6) Guideline method and (7) Urwick or profile method, (8) Profile method.

1. Time-span of discretion theory. Based on his investigation into organisational structure, roles relationships at Glacier Metal Company in England, Proferssor Elliott Jaques constructed a different system for determining rates of pay based on psycho-economic considerations. He criticised the conventional techniques of salary determination on the grounds that they are based on relative strengths of the bargaining parties and fixation of salary on subjective judgements and assumptions. The laws of wage fixation are the laws of the jungle. Jaques suggests a technique giving social, psychological and economic satisfaction to the employee. It has an objective and scientific procedure from political and negotiating strengths.

According to Jaques, an employee would be in a state of equilibrium when his capacity to do certain volume of work (C) matches with the actual level of work turned out by the employee in his present role based on job demands (W) for which correct payment is made (P), *i.e.*, C.W.P. Employee feels (i) inequitable treatment when capacity matches work and payment is below par *i.e.*, $C = W < P$, (ii) frustration when capacity matches, with pay and work is below the capacity, *i.e.*, $C = P < W$, (iii) stress when pay is greater than work demanded and it is greater than capacity, *i.e.*, $P < W < C$. Thus according to Jaques, employees "whose capacities are well adjusted to the level of work they do, and where work provides them with a subjectively felt equitable level of payment are said to be in a state of 'psycho-economic' equilibrium." Jaques uses three systems *viz.*, (a) time-span of discretion, (b) equitable work payment scale and (c) Standard Earning-progression :

(a) ***Time-span discretion*** : The time-span of discretion is "the longest period of time which can elapse in a role before a superior can be sure that his subordinate has not been exercising marginally standard discretion continuously in balancing the pace and quality of his work." Thus, the time-span is the time in hours (or days) from which an error, for example, wrong discussion or too much material left or too rough a finish by one operator goes until it is detected by the next operator in sequence of work or by the inspector or supervisor :

General and universal pay structure can be introduced and practised when the level of work (W) is measured by 'time-span'. The work is divided into prescribed and discretionary activities. The discretionary activities are those aspects of a work role, about which a subordinate must exercise his own discretion. Prescribed activities are carried out by following the laid down rules and procedures.

(b) ***Equitable work payment scale*** : Jaques relates 'equity payment theory' with the time-span of discretion. He says, "Equitable payment is the common norm, which people in roles of the same time-span, when asked in confidence, indicate, they would consider to be fair pay." Feeling of inequity of pay or dissatisfaction with pay are due not only to comparisons but also from maladjustments in C-W-P relations.

(c) ***Standard earning profession*** : Standard payment and progression method involves determining the time-span bracket for each job holder and assigning the equitable salary bracket. A person's actual earnings progression over the past years to date are plotted graphically. Based upon his work performance and history Sugesiot makes a potential assessment for the man. Pay adjustments are made in accordance with movements in the countrywide salary index. The immediate superior assesses the performance of the employee and adjusts the pay from time to time. Thus the wages can be fixed on scientific basis of time, span discretion. However, a number of studies conducted during 1960s and 1970s did not confirm this contention. Further, it is difficult to understand and explain the mechanism of this method to workers and union leaders.

2. Decision-Banding. According to Paterson, the major weakness of the conventional techniques is subjective measure. This weakness is more apparent when organisations compare dissimilar jobs. Paterson proposed a scheme which uses a single factor, *i.e.*, decision-making. Based on the kind of decisions to be made in performing the job, jobs differ from each other.

Paterson's approach to job evaluation involves four main stages, *viz.* : (i) establishment of job hands according to decision type and structure; (ii) job analysis; (iii) job-grading, sub-grading and ranking of jobs and (iv) job-assessment and assigning money values.

The quality of decision made the significant difference among jobs. Every known job can be compared against the following six basic levels of decision-makings.

(i) ***Band E*** : Policy-making decisions — made at the top level.

(ii) ***Band D*** : Programming decisions — made in the execution of the policy.

(iii) ***Band C*** : Interpretive decisions — made in interpreting the programme.

(iv) ***Band B*** : Routine decisions — made in execution of interpreted policy.

(v) ***Band A*** : Automatic decisions — made on the operational aspects of the process such as when, how, where, etc.

(vi) ***Band O*** : Defined decisions — decisions permitting very limited discretion.

Each band except 'O' is divided into Upper and Lower Levels.

3. Direct consensus method. Developed by Associated Industrial Consultants Ltd., this method can be applied to all types and levels of jobs. The key criteria against which jobs are to be assessed is determined in advance. Key criteria common and relevant to some jobs, are determined by cross-sampling of opinion and statistical analysis. The next step is preparing job descriptions from a representative sample of jobs in the survey. The number of jobs chosen should be 11 and 79. A committee of assessors is to be selected, the number of members must be geared to the number of jobs to be evaluated (for technical reasons) so that assessors ranks an equal percentage of total. The number of paired comparisons number of jobs in the sample. Jobs are ranked on the basis of paired comparisons. If is the number of jobs, the number of comparisons is $N\left[\frac{N-1}{2}\right]$. Assigning money value is based on the company policy, negotiation and market rates.

4. Guide chart profile method. Developed by a firm of management consultants Hay-MSL Ltd., it is modification of point method. The concept of accountability of manager's job is a common factor for evaluation. Other important factors necessary for job performance are know-how, problem-solving skill. These three aspects are key elements in any managerial job. Points scales are allocated for know-how and accountability. Problem solving is a percentage of the know-how deployed. Each job is rated under each criterion. Jobs can be plotted on charts to show up the job structures in quantitative terms. Common score is calculated for all the three factors of all the jobs. In order to arrive at the salary figure, money values are assigned to the scores.

5. Problem-solving compensable factor. According to A.W. Charles, problem solving skill is a single universal compensable factor. Jobs can be evaluated from the lowest to highest on the basis of degree of the problem solving skill required to perform a job. Wages should be proportional to the responsibility required by the problem solving activities of a job. Wages should be high to those jobs whose responsibility requirements for problem skills are high and vice versa. Charles developed a matrix which permits the measurement of amount of responsibility required of problem solving of a job in comparison with those of other jobs. Charles is confident that this technique overcomes the weakness of point, rating method.

6. Guideline method. Richard C. Smith and Matthew J. Murphy used this method consisting of four elements, *viz.*, (i) a guideline scale, (ii) scope data, (iii) market pricing and (iv) horizontal guideline display.

(i) ***The guideline scale*** : A standard scale of salary range indicating minimum, maximum and mid-point, it contends that 5 per cent difference in mid-points between pay grades is ideal. It allows flexibility of moving job up and down.

(ii) ***Scope data*** : In order to identify the salaries paid to these jobs in comparable industries, it helps in identifying, defining and describing key jobs.

(iii) ***Market pricing*** : To find out wages for similar jobs in comparable industries, it involves conducting market survey.

(iv) ***Horizontal guideline displays*** : It involves development of horizontal guideline displays. Its process involves two or more vertical guideline displays for ensuring equitable relationships.

7. Urwick or profile method. Developed by management consultants Urwick Orr and Partners Ltd. in 1960, it is more akin to direct consensus method, although it is a combination of points rating and ranking methods at the root level. Because of its adaptability and its participative approach, it is highly accepted in large -scale industries. It involves the following steps :

(i) ***Selecting*** : Key jobs from jobs under consideration.

(ii) ***Rating*** : The jobs based on six sub-factors, *viz.*, responsibility, knowledge, mental demands, social demands, physical demands and work environment. Each sub-factor is scored on a four-point scale, *i.e.*, basic, moderate, high and exceptional. Minor differences in sub-factors are ignored.

(iii) ***Ranking*** : The key jobs according to total score values of sub-factors.

(iv) ***Re-ranking*** : The jobs on a 'Whole' job basis.

(v) ***Comparing and reconciling*** : The ranks based on sub-factors and whole job basis.

(vi) ***Removing discrepancies*** : If any, by reconsidering the weights of sub-factors until a workable and acceptable framework is reached.

(vii) ***Presenting*** : The jobs are a profile and point scores.

Representatives of workers, their unions and management have overall control on the mechanism of this technique.

8. Profile method. Similar to guide chart profile method and points system, this method considers smaller number of factors *viz.*, the amount of knowledge of job calls for as shown on the vertical line of Chart 29.8, the experience rating for jobs shown on the horizontal line of Chart 29.8. Degrees are to be assigned to both the factors. A point score for that overall factor is determined on the basis of the points of these two factors where the degrees of these two factors meet. Money values are assigned to the overall points.

Most of these non-conventional techniques have been developed by management consultants for helping their client companies. Based on the variations of the points methods, there techniques are quantitative. To be successful, any scheme should aim at a high degree of reliability and validity. Apart from various theoretical concepts, the adaptability and usage of the job evaluation are increasing. It contributes to the rational wage payment, to building up rational wage structure and helps to stabilise, control and forecast cost of human resources. It is a part of pay fixation machinery along with other concepts like wage theories, seniority, performance, career progression, wage survey and other factors influencing wage determination.

Experience Knowledge	1-2 Year	2-4 Years	4-S Years	8-12 Years	Over 12 Years
1. Good basic education without specialisation.	10	20	40	80	160
2. Proficiency in a technical subject without a professional qualification.	20	40	80	160	320
3. Professional qualification in a single science or business field.	40	80	160	320	640
4. Highest professional qualification, Expert recognised knowledge in one or more scientific or specialised managerial fields.	80	160	320	640	1280
5. Complete professional knowledge of scientific and/or management function.					
Recognised authority on L.S. subjects.	160	320	640	1280	2560

Chart 29.8. Profile Method Know-how

Source : G. McBeath and D.N. Rands, *Salary Administration*, Business Books Ltd., London, p. 66.

ADVANTAGES OF JOB EVALUATION

1. Logical and objective. It is a logical and to a certain extent an objective method of ranking and grading the jobs.

2. Fitting. It helps to fit the newly created jobs in the existing structure.

3. Less hrievances. Employee grievances, doubts and complaints would be at the lower ebb, as it is a systematic and objective method of wage fixation.

4. Eliminates undesirable factors. It eliminates some undesirable factors like it. Equalities in bargaining capacities of employees and employers fluctuations in market rates, etc.

5. Principles. It satisfies the principles of fair wage, wage equity, uniformity in wages, etc.

6. Redesigns. It helps to redesign the jobs for minimising wide wage level and wage equity.

7. Employee satisfaction. It ensures employee satisfaction about wage level and wage equity.

8. Reallocation. It also helps to redesign the jobs by reallocating the easy and difficult tasks equally among various jobs.

Limitations of Job Evaluation

1. Less scientific. Job evaluation is not exactly scientific.

2. Difficult method. *Modus operandi* of most of the techniques is difficult to understand even to the supervisors.

3. Not exhaustive. The factors taken by the programme are not exhaustive.

4. Fluctuations. There may be wide fluctuations in compensable factors in view of changes in technology, values and aspirations of employers, etc.

5. Different perceptions. Employees, trade union leaders, management, and the programme operators may perceive differently in selecting the compensable factors, in giving weightages or degrees, etc.

6. Unreliable. The results of job evaluation may not exactly coincide with social evaluations, which, in turn, result in employee dissatisfaction.

7. Only one factor. Job evaluation is only one among several factors in determining wage level. Sometimes other factors like government policy may dominate the job evaluation.

QUESTIONS FOR EXERCISE

1. What is Job Evaluation? Explain the objectives of job evaluation. How do you prepare the ground for evaluating jobs?
2. What are the conventional and non-conventional techniques of job evaluation? What types of technique do you adopt to evaluate the jobs of maintenance, operation marketing and chief engineer in a large machine tools industry?
3. Explain the advantages and limitations of job evaluation as a basis for fixing and removing wages and salaries.

30

Quality of Work Life and Quality Circles

WHAT IS QUALITY OF WORK LIFE?

The term 'Quality of Work Life' (QWL) appeared in research journals and the press in USA in 1970s. It refers to the favourableness or unfavourableness of a job environment for people.

Definitions of QWL

1. **Grey Densler Lloy.** "QWL means different things to different" people.

2. **J. Richard and Lloy.** QWL as, "the degree to which members of a work organization able to satisfy important personal needs through their experience in the organization."

3. **Lee M. Ozley and Judith S. Ball.** Quality of work life improvements are defined as "Any activity which takes place at every level of an organisation, which seeks greater organisational effectiveness through the enhancement of human dignity and growth...a process through which the stakeholders in the organisation — management, unions and employees — learn how to work together better...to determine for themselves what actions, changes and improvements are desirable and workable, in order to achieve the twin and simultaneous goals of an improved quality of life at work for all members of the organisation and greater effectiveness for both the company and unions."

4. **Richard E. Walton.** He explains quality of work life in terms of eight broad conditions of employment that constitute desirable quality of work life (QWL). He proposed the same criteria for measuring QWL.

CRITERIA OF QWL

1. **Adequate and fair compensation.** The Committee on Fair Wages defined fair wage as "...the wage which is above the minimum wage but below the living age."

2. Safe and healthy working conditions. Most of the organisations provide safe and healthy working conditions as humanitarian and/or legal requirements. These conditions are a matter of enlightened self-interest.

3. Opportunity to use and develop human capacities. QWL is improved "...to the extent that the worker can exercise more control over his or her work, and the degree to which the job embraces an entire meaningful task...." QWL provides opportunities like autonomy in work and participation in planning in order to develop human capabilities.

4. Opportunity for career growth. Either due to educational barriers or due to limited openings at the higher level. Opportunities for promotions are limited in case of all categories of employees. By expanding one's capabilities, knowledge and qualification, QWL provides future opportunity for continued growth and security.

5. Social integration in the work force. Social integration in the workforce can be established by creating freedom from prejudice, supporting primary work groups, a sense of community and interpersonal openness, egalitarianism and upward mobility.

6. Constitutionalism in the work organisation. QWL provides constitutional protection to the employees only to the level of desirability. It hampers workers' satisfaction of doing the job beyond that level. The management's action is challenged in every action and bureaucratic procedures need to be followed at that level. Constitutional protection is provided to employees on such matters as privacy, free speech, equity and due process.

7. Work and quality of life. QWL provides for the balanced relationship among work, non-work and family aspects of life. Family life and social life should not be strained by working hours including overtime work, during inconvenient hours, business travel, transfers, vacations, etc.

8. Social relevance of work. QWL is concerned about the establishment of social relevance to work in a socially beneficial manner. The workers' self-esteem would be high if his work is useful to the society and *vice versa* is also true.

SPECIFIC ISSUES IN QWL

Klott, Mundick and Schuster suggested 11 major QWL issues as follow :

1. Pay and stability of employment. Good pay dominates most of the other factors in employee satisfaction. In view of increase in the cost of living index, increase in levels and rates of income-tax and professional tax, various alternative means for providing wages should be developed. Stability of employment is guaranteed to a certain extent in India. However, stability can be provided by enhancing the facilities for human resources development.

2. Occupational stress. According to Keith Davis, stress is a condition of strain on one's emotions, thought process and physical condition determined by the nature of work, working conditions, working hours, pause in the work schedule, worker's abilities and nature and match with the job requirements. Stress is caused due to irritability, hyperxatation or depression, unstable behaviour, fatigue, stuttering, trembling, psychosomatic pains, heavy smoking and drug abuse. It adversely affects employee productivity. In order to minimise the stress, the P.H.R. Manager has to identify, prevent and tackle the problem. He may arrange for the treatment of the problem with the health unit of the company.

3. Organisational health programmes. They aim at educating employees about health problems, means of maintaining and improving of health, etc. They cover drinking and smoking cessation, hypertension control, other forms of cardiovascular risk reduction, family planning, etc. Effective implementation of these programmes results in reduction in absenteeism, hospitalisation, disability, excessive job turnover and premature death. This programme should also cover relaxation, physical exercise, diet control, etc.

4. Alternative work schedules. As the work schedule offers the individual the leisure time, flexible hours of work are preferred. Alternative work schedules including work at home, flexible working hours, staggered hours, reduced work week, part-time employment may be introduced for the convenience and comfort of the workers.

5. Participative management and control of work. Trade unions and workers believe that workers' participation in management and decision-making improve. QWL. Workers feel that they have control over their work. They use their skills and make a real contribution to the job if they are allowed to participate in creative and decision-making process.

6. Recognition. Recognising the employee as a human being rather than as a labourer increases the QWL. Some means to recognise the employees are participative management, awarding and rewarding systems, congratulating the employees for their achievement, job enrichment, offering prestigious designations to the jobs, providing well furnished and decent workplaces, offering membership in clubs or associations, providing vehicles, offering vacation trips.

7. Cogenial worker-supervisor relations. Harmonious supervisor, worker relations provide the worker a sense of social association, belongingness, achievement of work results, etc. This, in turn, leads to better QWL.

8. Grievance procedure. Workers have a sense of fair treatment when the company gives them the opportunity to ventilate their grievances and represent their case succinctly rather than settling the problems arbitrarily.

9. Adequacy of resources. Resources should match with stated objectives, otherwise, employees will not be able to attain the objectives. This results in employees, dissatisfaction and lower QWL.

10. Seniority and merit in promotions. In case of operating employees, seniority is generally taken as the basis for promotion. For managerial people, merit should be considered as the basis for advancement. Seniority-cum-merit is preferred for promotion of ministerial employees. In order to ensure higher QWL, the promotional policies and activities should be fair and just.

11. Employment on permanent basis. While employment of workers on casual, temporary, probationary basis gives them a sense of insecurity, employment on permanent basis gives them security and leads to higher order QWL.

IMPACT ON QWL

1. Fringe benefits. P/HR manager has to build and maintain QWL by providing a wide range of fringe benefits. These benefits include medical and health benefits, safety measures, legal and financial services, consumer services, retirement benefits, conveyance, canteen facilities, recreational services, career counselling, employee information reports, etc. They result in improvement in productivity, reduction in absenteeism, turnover, sick leave, alienation, etc.

2. Productivity. Improvement over the existing salary, working conditions and benefits cost much but the rate of increase in productivity is higher than that of cost of QWL. Increase in QWL results in increase in productivity. However, continual increase in QWL eventually leads to reduction in productivity due to increase in cost of output because the worker's output does not increase proportionately after a certain level even though QWL increases.

3. Performance. Performance is not only physical output but also the behaviour of the worker in helping his colleagues in solving job related problems, accepting orders with enthusiasm, promoting a positive team spirit and accepting temporary unfavourable work conditions without complaint. Improved QWL leads to improved performance.

4. Personnel/human resource management. All personnel related activities affect quality of work life. This is as follows :

(i) ***Job analysis*** : Analyse the job in such a way that human needs like freedom, challenging work, autonomy can be satisfied.

(ii) ***Selection*** : Select the right man and place him in the right position. This satisfies his needs for reward, interesting work, etc.

(iii) ***Job enrichment*** : It satisfies higher order needs like pride, ego.

(iv) ***Job evaluation*** : It leads to equitable wages.

STRATEGIES FOR IMPROVEMENT IN QWL

1. Self-managed work teams. Also called autonomous work groups or integrated work teams, these are formed with 10 to 20 employees who plan, co-ordinate and control the activities of the team, with the help of a team leader, who is one among them. Each team performs all activities including selecting their people. Each team has authority to make decisions and regulate the activities. Group, as a whole, is accountable for the success or failure. Salaries are fixed both on the basis of individual and group achievement.

2. Job redesign and enrichment. Narrow jobs can be combined into larger units of accomplishment. Jobs are redesigned to enrich them to satisfy higher order human needs.

3. Effective leadership and supervisory behaviour. '9-9' style of managerial gird is suitable for effective leadership and supervisory behaviour.

4. Career development. Provision should be made for career planning, communicating and counselling the employees about the career opportunities, career path. Education and development and for sound careers.

5. Alternative work schedules. Provision should be made for flexible working hours, part-time employments, job sharing and reduced work week.

6. Job security. As it tops the employee's list of priorities, it should be adequately taken care of.

7. Administrative or organisational justice. The principles of justice, fair play and equity should be taken care of in disciplinary procedure, grievance procedure, promotions, transfers, demotions, work assignment, leave, etc.

8. Participative management. Employees should be allowed to participate in management. The most sophisticated participative management is quality circle.

QUALITY CIRCLE (QC)

History of Quality Circles

The credit of developing the concept quality circles has gone to the Union of Japanese Scientists and Engineers along with Kaoru Ishikawa of Tokyo University. Historically 'Gun Mandal' (Quality Circles) have been used in different social, religious, and political settings since the dawn of Indian civilisation to enhance '*Satvic* qualities' *i.e.*, urge for excellence and knowledge, concern for others' interest, trust and confidence, self-actualisation, etc., minimise *rejasic* qualities such as urge for economic resources, authority and power, concern for personal interest, restlessness and tension, craze for ego inflation, etc., and *tamasic* qualities such as prone to err, indolence and wickedness, urge to exploit and damage others, distrust, loss of self-identity, etc. Non-application of the science of Bhagavatgita and Vedas to industrial and business organisations is one of the reasons for dependence of Indian organisations on the techniques developed in foreign countries.

Definition of Quality Circle

According to Edwin B. Flippo, a quality circle is a "self-governing group of workers with or without their supervisors who voluntarily meet regularly to identify, analyse and solve problems of their work field".

Quality circle *Vs.* Task force. Quality circle and task force are not one and the same. Quality circle is not a task force. It is broader than the task force. A task force is a group of most skilled employees selected and appointed by management, engaged in various functions, with an orientation to problem-solving. The QC is a voluntary association of workers engaged in similar work with an orientation of human relations. QCs are formed to attain specific objectives.

Objectives of Quality Circles

1. To develop, enhance and utilise human resources effectively.
2. To improve quality of products/services, productivity and reduce cost of production per unit of output.
3. To satisfy the workers' psychological needs for self-urge, participation, recognition, etc., with a view to motivate them. This will ensure enhancement of employee morale and commitment.
4. To improve various supervisory skills like leadership, problem solving, interpersonal and conflict resolution.
5. To utilise individual imaginative, creative and innovative skills through participation, creating and developing work interest, inculcating problem solving techniques, etc. This requires the use of certain techniques.

Techniques for Quality Circles

Following are the three main techniques used in discussing various problems for quality circles :

1. Brain storming processes. This technique is useful to generate as many ideas as possible. Under this technique, completely free environment is created to stimulate creativity. As employees' ideas are free from criticism, they voice all their worthy as well as stupid ideas. These ideas are recorded seriously. Later, the plus and minus points of each idea are discussed, before taking a final decision.

2. Cause and effect. Members are asked to find out the causes for the identified problem. They identify one important effect of this cause on the problem. Then they identify other causes and their effects. As charting out of those causes and effects resembles fish-bone diagram, this technique is also called 'fishpond diagram'.

3. Sampling and charting methods. Members of the quality circles observe the events and their consequences in the form of positive or negative results. They chart out all their observations either in sequence or in some other relationship, which give clear idea of the problem.

Requirements of Quality Circles

1. Participative management. Both employees and management are jointly involved in decision-making process on matters of mutual interest in participative management. The participative management produces better solutions to the problems which benefit all concerned. Participative managers consult their followers and involve them in decision-making so that their group acts as a social unit in work performance. Participating managers are not autocratic or free-rein managers. They are responsible and accountable for the success or failure of their departments.

Participative management satisfies economic, psychological and social needs of employees. It gives them a sense of significance, pride and accomplishment, freedom and opportunity for expression, a feeling of belongingness to the place of work and a sense of creativeness to the employees. It aims at : (i) improving organisational efficiency, (ii) developing social education for effective solidarity among workers, (iii) attaining industrial peace, (iv) treating the workers as human beings and (v) developing self-management teams in industry. It results in effective management.

2. Group interaction. A group is two or more interacting and interdependent individuals who come together to achieve particular objectives. Groups may be formal or informal. Formal groups are defined by organisation structure with clear-cut assignment, responsibility, accountability, rules and norms. Informal groups are the natural formations in the work environment in response to the need for social contact. Both these groups are not structured and determined by the organisation. They satisfy the social needs of their members. The important aspects of group interaction are group goals, participation, leadership norms and cohesiveness.

(i) ***Goals*** : Group has two types of goals *viz.*, task goal and maintaining the group itself. Task goal is related to the main function for which the group is formed. The other goal is related to dealing with interpersonal conflict, resolving it and maintaining interpersonal relations. Group members' trusting behaviour contributes to increased originality, greater emotional stability, less defensive and improved self-control.

(ii) *Type of participation in group* : Participation in a group may be voluntary, invited or assigned. Members voluntarily join the group.

(a) *Voluntary* : In significant numbers if the group activity is effective. Experts and specialists are invited to join the group as members or advisors. Group as a whole and other members of the group are benefited by the interaction of those special members.

(b) *Assigned* : Participation in group is also assigned. The management forms various groups and assigns the membership including the tasks and responsibilities to various individuals. For example, to suggest measures to minimise absenteeism the personnel manager may form a group with three assistant personnel managers. He assigns three different aspects of the problem like absenteeism among unskilled workers, technical personnel and managerial personnel to the three assistant personnel managers of the group.

(iii) ***Leader*** : The leader is a must to co-ordinate and control the members as well as activities whether it is a formal group or an informal group. Groups may have two types of leaders *viz.*, tasks leader and unofficial social leader. They achieve two basic objectives, *i.e.*, performing the main task and satisfying members' social needs.

(iv) ***Norms*** : Group norm is expected behaviour of group members. Norms are normally unwritten in the informal groups. The norm of quality circles is openness which helps to solve the problems better.

(v) ***Cohesiveness*** : It is the degree of attraction that the group has for its members. It may be in the form of loyalty, sense of belongingness, friendliness, feeling of responsibility for group tasks. It can be increased through stability of membership, similar values of members, providing free communication opportunities, physical isolation from the formal control, small size.

Organisational Structure

Organisational structure of QC consists of four levels, *viz.*, (1) Steering Committee (2) Facilitator, (3) QC Leader (4) QC member.

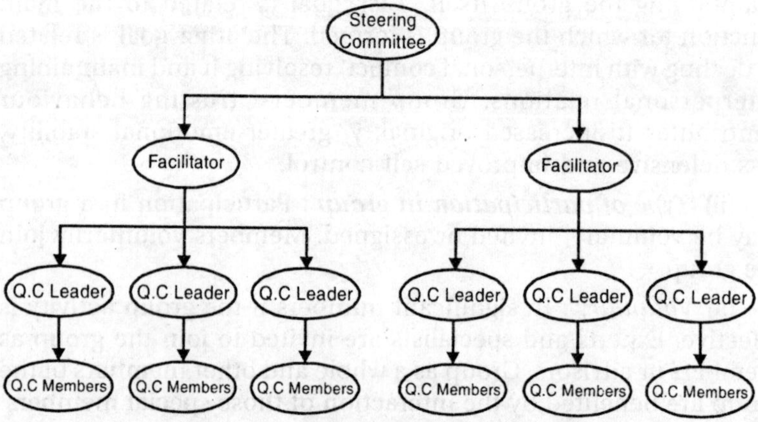

Fig. 30.1. Organisational Structure of Quality Circles

1. Steering committee. It consists of representatives of management from different departments at top level and top level representatives of recognised unions/federations of employees.

Functions of Steering Committee **(i)** Sponsoring QC programme in the entire organisation : This is done by defining overall objectives and operating guidelines relating to the identification of the department where the circles are to be formed, provision of training to leaders and members of QCs, identification of the problems to be discussed, receiving, discussing and finalising the suggestions, action plans, budget, etc.

(ii) Selecting and training the facilitators.

(iii) Providing the resources and moral support to the facilitators.

2. Facilitator. An important person between the quality circle and the steering committee, Facilitator (i) acts as a consultant and guide to the QC leaders; (ii) initiates the setting up of QCs by persuading the supervisor, by teaching and training the QC leaders and members; (iii) provides feedback to the steering committee about the proceedings and results of the QCs and (iv) acts as an evaluator and reviewer of QC operations and programmes.

The facilitator maintains sound interpersonal relations in order to function as a social leader. He has to prove himself successful in acting as a co-ordinator, coach, promoter, teacher and innovator. He should be an excellent resource person for training the managers at higher level.

3. QC leader. Activities of each circle are co-ordinated and streamlined by its leader who is an elected member of the circle. Manager/supervisor of that particular department/section where the QC is set up, may act as the leader. The leader must have skills in discussion, initiation and promotion of active participation. He should be a trained one in group dynamics, human behaviour and participative leadership styles. The activities of a QC leader are :

Conducting : the meetings, initiating the discussion and motivate the members to participate actively; (i) acting as a link between the members and facilitator; and (ii) training the members in problem identification, discussion and problem-solving techniques.

4. QC members. Members of a single work group form a quality circle, joining voluntarily or on invitation. They are free to withdraw from membership. Their activities include : attending meetings, participating actively in problem-identification, contributing ideas in developing solutions to the identified problems and the like.

QC Process

In order to attain the objectives effectively, QCs should follow systematic process. In addition to the sound organisational structure, size of each QC may vary between 6 and 12. QC members and leader are given instructions regarding problem-solving techniques. The QC Members should acquaint themselves about the objectives and role of QCs.

1. Session. Each working session of a QC may be for one hour. There should be at least one working session every week, preferably during working hours and in the company premises. If the working session is conducted after the working hours, the members may be paid honorarium for attending the meeting.

2. Problem. The members of QC select the problem from the operational problems suggested by management or by the members of the QC. After selecting the problem, the members analyse it by using the various problem-solving techniques. Sometimes the QC leader invites experts to analyse the problem and their effects. The members develop alternative solutions, their effect and consequences on organisation and members, cost-benefit analysis and merits and demerits of each solution.

3. Selection of solution. Now, the members select the best solution from among the alternative solutions. Some of then present the selected solution to the management. Management reviews the solution and may or may not accept it but in most cases managers accept the solution.

4. Implementation. After the solution is accepted, the members either by themselves and/or with the help of others, implement the solution. Management has to provide of all types of support, including finance, to implement such solutions.

Concepts to make QC Process Effective

According to Edwin B. Floppso, the following concepts make the QC process effective :

1. Acceptance by all, particularly the leader, that there is more than one way to solve a problem successfully.
2. Encouragement of all members to clarify and build on each other's ideas.
3. Periodic summarising of the activities by the leader, or a member to ensure common understanding.

4. Avoidance of heated arguments in favour of one particular position. Vigorous eloquence should not be a substitute for clarity and logic.
5. Avoidance of such techniques as majority vote and conflicting to obtain group agreement.
6. Promotion of constructive disagreements in place of dodging arguments in search of an artificial state of harmony.

QUESTIONS FOR EXERCISE

1. What is quality of work life? Discuss its criteria and items.
2. Explain the impact of fringe benefits, productivity and good human resource management on QWL. Suggest strategies for improvement of QWL.
3. Trace the history of Quality Circle. Give its definitions and objectives and techniques.
4. What are the essential requirements of Quality Circle?
5. Analyse organisational structure of Quality Circle. What concepts make its process effective?

31

EMPLOYEE STRESS

WHAT IS EMPLOYEE STRESS?

Employee stress is a dynamic condition in which an individual is confronted with an opportunity, constraint or demand related to what he or she desires in his working conditions and for which the outcome is perceived to be both uncertain and important.

Typical Symptoms of Stress Employee

1. Adverse strain. Employee stress can cause adverse strain on one's emotions, thought processes and physical conditions. When it becomes excessive, employees develop various symptoms of stress that can harm their job performance and health, and even threaten their ability to cope with the environment. Stress is not

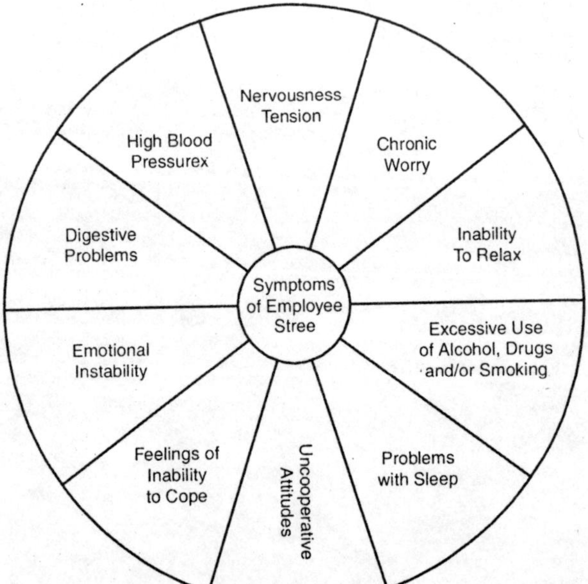

Fig. 31.1. Symptoms of Employee Stress

necessarily bad in and of itself. While stress is typically discussed in negative context, it also has positive value. It is an opportunity when it offers potential gains. Many individuals often use stress positively to rise to the occasion and perform at or near their maximum.

2. Psychological symptoms. The individual may become nervous and develop chronic worry. They are easily provoked to anger and are unable to relax. They may be uncooperative or use alcohol or drugs excessively. These conditions are common symptoms of stress.

3. Physical disorders. Employee's stress also leads to physical disorders, as the internal body system changes to cope with stress. Some physical disorders are short range such as an upset stomach. Others are long range such as a stomach ulcer. Stress over a prolonged time also leads to degenerative disease of the heart, kidneys, blood vessels, and other parts of the body. Therefore, stress, both on and off the job, should be kept at a level low for most people to tolerate without disorders.

4. Constraints and demands. More typically stress is associated with constraints and demands. The constraints prevent employees from doing what they desire; the demand refers to the loss of something desired.

For potential stress to become actual stress, there must be uncertainty about the outcome and the outcome must be important. Regardless of the conditions, it is only when there is doubt or uncertainty about whether the opportunity will be seized, the constraint removed, or the loss avoided that there is stress. Stress is highest in those individuals who perceive that it is uncertain whether they will win or lose. It is lowest in those individuals who think that winning or losing is an unimportant outcome. If keeping our job or earning promotion doesn't hold any importance for us, we have no reason to feel stress over having to undergo a performance review.

THE POTENTIAL SOURCES OF STRESS

(1) Environmental factors. These are as follows :

(i) *Environmental uncertainty* : It influences the design of the organisation's structure, which influences stress levels among employees in that organisation.

(ii) *Changes in the business cycle* : These create *economic uncertainties.* When the economy is contracting, people become increasingly anxious about their security.

(iii) ***Political uncertainty*** : It is also a probable sources of stress. New innovations can make an employee's skill and experience obsolete in a very short period of time.

(iv) ***Technological uncertainty*** : It is a factor which causes stress.

2. Organisational forces. Pressure to avoid errors or complete task in limited time period, work overload, a demanding and insensitive superior and unpleasant co-workers are few examples of organisational forces causing stress.

(i) ***Task demands*** : These are factors related to a person's job. They include the design of the individual's job (autonomy, task variety, degree of automation), working conditions and the physical work layout. Assembly lines can put pressure on people when their speed is perceived as excessive. Increase in interdependence between a person's tasks and the tasks of others, increase potential

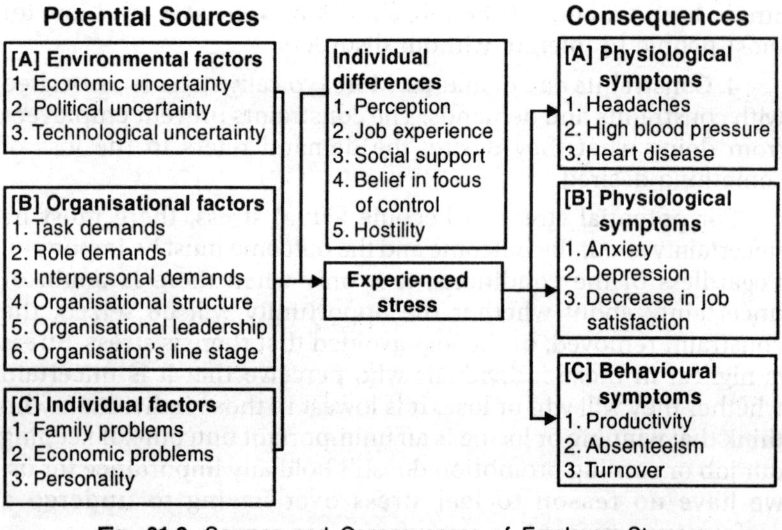

Fig. 31.2. Sources and Consequences of Employee Stress

stress. On the other hand, autonomy tends to decrease stress. Jobs where temperatures, noise, or other working conditions are dangerous or undesirable can increase anxiety. Working in an overcrowded room or in a visible location where interruptions are constant increases stress.

(ii) ***Role demands*** : These relate to pressures placed on a person as a function of the particular role he or she plays in the organisation.

(a) *Role conflicts* : These create expectations that may be hard to reconcile or satisfy.

(b) *Role overload* : It is experienced when the employee is expected to do more than time permits.

(c) *Role ambiguity* : It is created when role expectations are not clearly understood and the employee is not sure what he or she is to do.

(iii) *Interpersonal demands* : There are pressures created by other employees. Lack of social support from colleagues and poor interpersonal relationships may cause considerable stress, especially among employees with a high social need.

(iv) *Organisation structure* : It defines the level of differentiation in the organisation, the degree of rules and regulations, and where decisions are made. Excessive rules and lack of participation in decisions that affect an employee are examples of structural variables that might be potential sources of stress.

(v) *Organisational leadership* : It represents the managerial style of the organisation's senior executives. Some chief executive officers create a culture characterised by tension, fear, and anxiety. They create unrealistic pressures to perform in the short run; they impose excessively light controls. They routinely fire employees.

3. Individual factors. These factors include family issues. Personal economic problems and inherent personality characteristics :

(i) *Family issues* : The marital difficulties, the breaking off a relationship and discipline troubles with children create stress for employees and that are not left at the front door when they arrive at work.

(ii) *Economic problems* : Created by individuals by over-extending their financial resources, these can create stress for employees and distract their attention from their work.

(iii) *Inherent personality characteristics* : Some people have an inherent tendency to accentuate negative aspects of the world in general. A significant individual factor influencing stress is a person's basic dispositional nature. Stress symptoms expressed on the job may actually originate in the person's personality.

STRESS THRESHOLD

People have different tolerance for stressful situations. This helps to explain variations in employee performance across similar jobs. Stress threshold is the level of stress that one can tolerate before negative feelings of stress occur and performance is adversely affected. Some people are easily upset by the slightest change or disruption in their work routines. Others are cool, calm and collected under the same conditions, because they have confidence in their ability to cope. They have a much higher stress threshold. Their performance does not suffer unless a stress is major or prolonged.

Type A and Type B People (Behaviour)

Type A and Type B persons show different reactions to stress conditions.

1. Type A behaviour. It is characterized by feeling a chronic sense of time urgency and by an excessive competitive drive. Type A people are aggressively involved in a chronic incessant struggle to achieve more and more in less time, and against the opposing efforts of other things or other persons. Type A people are :

(i) Always moving, walking and eating rapidly.
(ii) Impatient with the rate at which most events take place.
(iii) Thinking or doing two or more things simultaneously.
(iv) Not coping with leisure time.
(v) Obsessed with numbers, measuring their success in terms of how much of everything they acquire.
(vi) Are more likely to experience stress on or off the job.
(vii) They are at higher risk for heart disease.
(viii) They are chronically angry, suspicious and mistrustful persons.

2. Type B behaviour. It is the opposite of Type A. Type B are rarely hurried by the desire to obtain a widely increasing number of things or participate in the endless growing series of events in an ever decreasing amount of time. The Type B people :

(i) Never suffer from a sense of time urgency with its accompanying impatience;
(ii) Feel no need to display or discuss their achievements or accomplishments unless such exposure is demanded by the situation;
(iii) Play for fun and relaxation rather than to exhibit their superiority at any cost and
(iv) Can relax without guilt.

STRESS MANAGEMENT STRATEGIES

Some organisations' managements may not be concerned when employees experience low to moderate level of stress, because such levels of stress can be functional and lead to higher employee performance. But high or low levels of stress, sustained over long period of time may lead to reduce employee's performance and this requires stress by management.

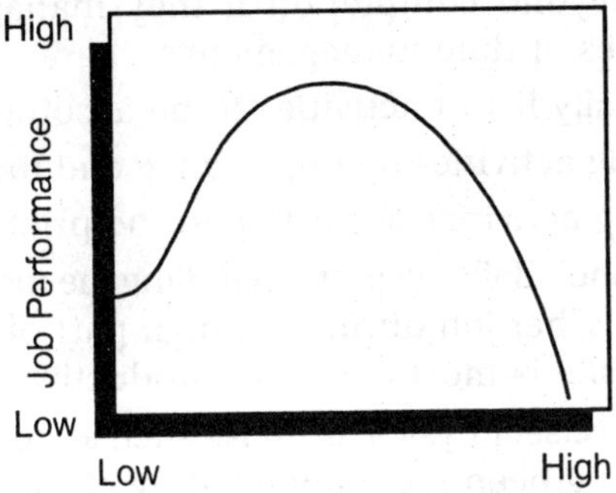

Fig. 31.3. Relation between Stress and Performance

When there is no stress, job challenges are absent and performance tends to be low. As stress increases, performance tends to increase, because stress helps a person call up resources to meet job requirements. Stress is a healthy stimulus that encourages employees to respond to challenges. It reaches a plateau that corresponds approximately with a person's day-to-day performance capability. At this point, additional stress tends to produce no more improvement.

However, if stress becomes too great, performance begins to decline because stress interferes with it. The employee loses ability to cope, becomes unable to make decisions, and is erratic in behaviour. If stress increases to a breaking point, performance becomes zero. The employee has a breakdown; he becomes too ill to work. He is fired, quits, or refuses to come to work to face the stress.

STRESS MANAGEMENT

[A] Individual Approaches to Stress Management

Employees and management have different notions of what constitutes an acceptable level of stress on the job. From the individual's standpoint, even low levels of stress are likely to be perceived as undesirable.

Individual approaches. An employee may take personal

responsibility for reducing his or her stress level. Through individuals strategies proven effective are :

1. Time management. Some people manage the time poorly, though the things they have to accomplish in any given day are not necessarily beyond completion if they manage their time properly. Principles of time management :

(i) Making daily list of activities to be accomplished;

(ii) prioritizing activities by importance and urgency;

(iii) scheduling activities according to the priorities set and

(iv) knowing one's daily cycle and handling the most demanding parts of his/her job during the high part of his/her cycle when he/she is most alert and productive.

2. Physical exercise. Physical exercise such as aerobic, jogging, swimming have long been recommended by physicians as a way to deal with excessive stress levels.

3. Relaxation training. To reach a state of *deep relaxation,* individuals can teach themselves to relax through techniques such as meditation, hypnosis and biofeedback. When one feels physically relaxed, he is somewhat detached from the body sensations. Deep relaxation of fifteen to twenty minutes a day releases tension and provides a person with a pronounced sense of peacefulness.

(4) Social support. Talking to friends, family or work colleagues provide an outlet when stress levels become excessive. Thus, a social support network can considerably reduce the tension.

[B] Organisational Approaches

Management strategies are as follows to control stress :

1. Selection and placement. While certain jobs are more stressful than others, individuals also differ in their response to stress situations. The individuals with little experience or an external locus of control are more stress prone. While management cannot have only experienced individuals selection and placement decisions to consider individuals who may adapt to high stress jobs and perform them more effectively.

2. Job redesigning. Redesigning jobs to give employees more responsibility, more meaningful work, more autonomy and increased feedback reduces stress, because these factors provide greater control over work activities and lesser dependence on others. As all employees do not want enriched jobs, the right job design for employees with a low need for growth should have less responsibility and increased division of labour.

3. Goal setting. Having specific and challenging goals and receiving feedback on how well they are progressing toward these goals, individuals perform better. Thus, goal selling can reduce stress and provide motivation. Specific goals perceived as attainable clarify performance expectations. Goal feedback reduces uncertainties about actual job performance. This reduces employee frustration, role ambiguity and stress.

4. Organisational communication. By lessening role ambiguity and role conflict, increased formal communication with employees reduce uncertainty. Management can use effective communication as a means to shape employee perceptions.

5. Participative decision-making. By role stress, employees feel uncertain about goals, expectations, how they will be evaluated and the like. The management can increase employee control and reduce role stress by giving these employees a voice in those decisions that directly affect their job performance.

QUESTIONS FOR EXERCISE

1. What is employee stress? What are its symptoms? Explain its potential sources.
2. What is stress threshold? Analyse A and B behaviour types. How does stress affect job performance?
3. Explain industrial and organisational approaches to stress management strategies.

32

Consumer Psychology

ROLE OF NEEDS, GOALS AND SELF-IMAGE

1. Needs. Every individual has some innate and acquired needs :

(i) ***Innate needs*** : Innate needs are physiological (*i.e.* biogenic). They include the needs for food, for water, for air, for clothing, for shelter and for sex. As they are needed to sustain biological life, the biogenic needs are considered primary needs or motives.

(ii) ***Acquired needs.*** These needs we earn in response to our culture or environment. These may include needs for self-esteem, for prestige, for affection, for power, and for learning. Acquired needs are generally psychological or psychogenic. They are secondary needs or motives. They result from the individual's subjective psychological state and from relationships with others. For example, as all individuals need shelter from the elements, finding a place to live fulfils an important primary need. However, the kind of residence one rents or buys may be the result of secondary needs. He may seek a place in which he and his wife can entertain large groups of people and fulfil social needs. They may want to live in an exclusive community in order to impress their friends and family and fulfil ego needs. Thus, the house an individual ultimately purchases may serve to fulfil both primary and secondary needs.

2. Goals. Goals are the sought-after results of motivated behaviour. All behaviour is goal-oriented. Goals are of many types :

(i) ***Generic goals*** : These are the general classes or categories of goals that consumers select to fulfill their needs. Marketers are even more concerned with consumers.

(ii) ***Product-specific goals*** : These are the specifically branded or labelled products the individual select to fulfil their needs. For example, Thomas J. Lipton Company want consumers to view iced tea as a good way to quench summer thirst (*i.e.* as a generic goal). Marketers recognize the importance of promoting both types of goals.

The Selection of Goals

There are many different and appropriate goals for any given need. The goals selected by individuals depend on their personal experiences, physical capacity, prevailing cultural norms and values, and the goal's accessibility in the physical and social environment. For example, an individual may have a strong hunger need. If he is a young college athlete, he may envy a thick sirloin steak as his goal object; if his doctor has advised him to avoid red meat, he may settle for a thick tuna steak instead. If he has a toothache, he may not be able to chew a steak; he may have to select hamburger. If he has never tasted steak, if it is outside his realm of personal experience, he probably would not even think of steak, but instead would select a food that has previously satisfied his hunger.

Finally, the goal object has to be both socially acceptable and physically accessible. If our college athlete was having dinner with his mother, she might frown on his consuming red meat, and insist he eats fish or chicken instead. If he were shipwrecked on an island with no food provisions or living animals, he could not realistically select steak as his goal-object, though he might fantasize about it. If he were in India, where cows are considered sacred, he would not be able to consume steak but select a substitute goal more appropriate to the social environment.

3. Self-Image. An individual's own perception of himself or herself serves to influence the specific goals selected. The products a person owns, would like to own, or would not like to own are often perceived in terms of how closely they reflect his self-image. A product that is perceived as matching an individual's self-image has a greater probability of being selected than one that is not. Thus, a man who perceives himself as young and "with it" may drive a Porsche. A woman who perceives herself as rich and conservative may drive a Mercedes. The types of houses people live, the cars they drive, the clothes they wear, the very foods they eat, these specific goal objects are chosen because they symbolically reflect the individual's self-image while they satisfy specific needs.

Interdependence of Needs and Goals

Needs and goals are interdependent; neither exists without the other. However, people are as aware of their needs as they are of their goals. For example, a teenager may not consciously be aware of his social needs but may join a photography club to meet new friends. A local politician may not consciously be aware of a power need but may regularly run for public office.

Among needs, individuals are usually more aware of their physiological needs than of their psychological needs. Most people know when they are hungry or thirsty or cold, and they take appropriate steps to satisfy these needs. They may not be aware of their needs for acceptance, for self-esteem, for status though they may subconsciously engage in behaviour that satisfies these psychological needs.

CONSUMER MOTIVATION

Motivation can be positive or negative. One may feel a driving force towards some object or condition; he may feel a driving force away from some object or condition. For example, a person may be impelled towards a restaurant to fulfil a hunger need and away from motorcycle transportation to fulfil a safety need.

Psychologists refer to positive drives as needs, wants, or desires, and to negative drives as fears or accretions. Thus negative and positive motivational forces seem to differ dramatically in terms of physical and sometimes emotional activity. However, they are basically similar in that both serve to initiate and sustain human behaviour. Therefore, researchers refer to both kinds of drives or motives, needs, wants, and desires. Some theorists distinguish wants from needs, by defining wants as product-specific needs. A person may experience thirst, a need in which she may want Lipton's iced tea as means to alleviate her thirst.

Positive and Negative Goals

A positive goal is one towards which behaviour is directed. It is often referred to as an approach object. A negative goal is one from which behaviour is directed away. It is sometimes referred to as an avoidance object. As both approach and avoidance goals can be considered objects of motivated behaviour, most researchers refer to both simply as goals. A middle-aged woman may have a positive goal of fitness and so join a health club to work out regularly. The house-wife joins a health club to help her achieve her positive goal — health and fitness. Her husband may have a negative goal of getting rid of fat-and so he joins a road runners club to maintain his shape. The husband's action is designed to avoid a negative goal — a bloated figure.

Psychological Reactance

Some people become motivationally aroused by a threat to or elimination of a behavioural freedom such as the freedom to make a product choice without undue influence from a retailer. This motivational state is called psychological reactance. It is usually manifested by a negative consumer response. When the Coca-Cola company changed its traditional formula and introduced "New Coke", many people reacted negatively to the fact that their "freedom to choose" had been taken away. They refused to buy the New Coke. Coca-Cola management responded to this unexpected psychological reaction by reintroducing the original formula as "Classic Coke."

Rational *versus* Emotional Motives

Consumer researchers who subscribe to the positivist perspective tend to view all consumer behaviours as rationally motivated. They try to isolate the causes of such behaviour so that they can predict, and thus influence, future behaviour. Experimentalists are interested in studying the hedonistic pleasures that consumption behaviour requires such as fun, or fantasy, or sensuality. They study consumer behaviour in order to gain insights and understanding of the consumer in his or her unique circumstances. Thus, consumer behaviourists distinguish between so-called rational motives and emotional or non-rational motives. They use the term rationality in the traditional economic sense. It assumes that consumers behave rationally when they carefully consider all alternatives and choose those that give them the greatest utility. In a marketing context, the term rationality implies that consumers select goals based on totally objective criteria, such as size, weight, price, or subjective criteria, *e.g.*, the desire for individuality, pride, fear, affection, status.

The assumption underlying this dissection is that subjective or emotional criteria do not maximize utility or satisfaction. However, it is reasonable to assume that consumers always attempt to select alternatives that, in their view, serve to maximize satisfaction. The assessment of satisfaction is a very personal process. It is based on the individual's own need structure as well as on past behavioural and social or learned experiences. What may appear irrational to an outside observer may be perfectly rational in the context of the consumer's own psychological field. For example, a product purchased to enhance self-image is a perfectly rational form of consumer behaviour. If behaviour does not appear rational to the person at the time it is undertaken, he or she would not do it. Thus the dissection between rational and emotional consumption motives is not always warranted.

THE DYNAMIC NATURE OF MOTIVATION

Constantly Changing Needs and Goals

Motivation is a highly dynamic construct that is constantly changing in reaction to life experiences. Needs and goals are constantly growing and changing in response to an individual's physical condition, environment, interaction with others and experiences. As individuals attain their goals, they develop new ones. If they do not attain their goals, they continue to strive for old goals, or they develop substitute goals.

Reasons of Dynamic Nature

Following are the reasons of the dynamic nature of motivation :

1. Full satisfaction of needs. Most human needs are never fully or permanently satisfied. For example, people experience hunger needs at regular intervals. Most people regularly seek companionship and approval from others to satisfy their social needs. Even more complex psychological needs are rarely satisfied, *e.g.*, temporary goal achievement does not fully satisfy the need for power, and the individual keeps striving to satisfy the need more fully. For example, a person may partially or temporarily satisfy a power need by working as assistant to the CEO of a Fortune 500 company, but this small taste of power may not sufficiently satisfy her need, and so she may strive for her own decision-making position in the company.

2. Emergence of new needs. Some motivational theorists believe that a hierarchy of needs exists, and that new, higher-order needs emerge as lower-order needs are fulfilled. For example, a man who has largely satisfied his basic psychological needs may turn his efforts to achieving acceptance among his new neighbours by joining their political clubs and supporting their candidates. After achieving acceptance, he may seek recognition by giving lavish parties or making large charitable contributions.

Marketers have to be attuned to changing needs. Car manufacturers stressing the prestige value of their automobiles fail to recognise that many consumers now satisfy needs for prestige eles where — such as through charitable gift-giving or public service. Manufacturers of prestige cars might do better if they stressed other need satisfactions such as family enjoyment or safety as reasons for buying a new model.

Expectations of success or failure in reaching certain goals often influence the nature and persistence of an individual's behaviour. Expectations are often based on past experience. A person who takes good snapshots with an inexpensive camera may be motivated to buy a more sophisticated camera that will enable him to take even better photographs. He may eventually upgrade his camera by several hundred dollars. On the other hand, a person who has not been able to take good photographs is likely to keep the same camera or may even lose all interest in photography.

Effects of success and failure on goal selection have strategy implications for the marketer. Goal should be reasonable. Advertisements should not promise more than the product will deliver. Even a good product will not be approached if it fails to live up to expectations. A consumer is likely to regard a disappointing product with even less satisfaction than its objective performance warrants. Advertisers who create unrealistic expectations for their products may cause dissatisfaction among consumers. The frustration and disappointment resulting from consumer dissatisfaction are the driving force behind consumerism.

3. Substitute Goals. When an individual attains a specific goal or the goal that will satisfy certain needs, behaviour may be directed to a substitute goal which may not be satisfactory as the primary goal but is sufficient to dispel uncomfortable tension. Continued deprivation of a primary goal may result in the substitute goal assuming primary-goal status. A man who has stopped drinking whole milk because he is dieting may actually begin to prefer skimmed milk.

4. Frustration. Failure to achieve a goal results in feelings of frustration. Everyone has sometimes experienced the frustration that comes from the inability to attain a goal. The barrier that prevents attainment of a goal may be personal to the individual such as physical or financial limitations. It may be an obstacle in the frustrating situations. Some people are adaptive and manage to cope by finding their way around the obstacle or by selecting a substitute goal. An example of adaptive behaviour would be that of the college student who would prefer to own a sports car, but settles for a second-hand sedan. Others are less adaptive and may regard their inability to achieve a goal as a personal failure and experience feelings of anxiety.

5. Defence mechanisms. People failing to cope with frustration mentally redesign the frustrating situation to protect their self-image and defend their self-esteem. For example, a young woman may yearn for a mink coat she cannot afford. The coping individual may select a less expensive fur, such as suskrat, or a cloth coat with a fur colour. The person who cannot cope may react with anger towards her boss for not paying her enough money to buy a fur. Alternatively, she may decide that wearing the fur of animals is a barbaric custom in which she will not participate. These last two possibilities are examples respectively of aggression and rationalization. Other defence mechanisms includes regression, withdrawal, projection, autism, identification and repression. People adopt defence mechanisms to protect their egos from feelings of failure when they do not attain their goals :

(i) ***Aggression*** : Individuals who experience frustration may resort to aggressive behaviour. In attempting to protect their self-esteem being disappointed at their poor showing in a sailing competition, two British Yachtsmen burned their boat and swam ashore. Frustrated consumers have boycotted manufacturers in efforts to improve product quality and boycotted retailers in efforts to have prices lowered.

(ii) ***Rationalization*** : In rationalization, individuals redefine a frustrating situation by inventing plausible reasons for being unable to attain their goals. They may decide that the goal really is not worth pursuing. Rationalizations are not deliberate lies, as the individual is not fully aware of the cognitive distortion that occurs as a result of the frustrating situation. Consumers who cannot quit smoking may convince themselves that they are smoking less if they switch to low-tar cigarettes.

(iii) ***Regression*** : Some people react to frustrating situations with childish or immature behaviour. A shopper attending a bargain sale may fight over merchandise and resort to tearing a garment rather than allow the other person to have it.

(iv) ***Withdrawal*** : In withdrawal, frustration is often resolved by simply withdrawing from the situation. A person who has officer status in an organization may simply quit it. He may rationalize his resignation by deciding that the organization is not true to its stated ideals and the other members are somewhat shallow. He may decide to use his time more constructively in other activities.

(v) ***Projection*** : By projecting blame for his or her own failures and inabilities on the other objects or persons, an individual may redesign a frustrating situation. For example, the golfer who misses a stroke may blame the caddie or her golf clubs. The driver who has an automobile accident may blame the other driver or the condition of the road.

(vi) *Autism* : Autism means autistic thinking. It refers to thinking that is almost completely dominated by needs and emotions, with little effort made to relate to reality. A person who is shy and lonely, may daydream about a romantic love affair. Daydreaming fantasizing enables the individual to attain imaginary gratification of unfulfilled needs.

(vii) *Identification* : Some people resolve their feelings of frustration by subconsciously identifying with other persons or situations they consider relevant. Marketers have recognized the importance of this defence mechanism and used it as the basis for advertising appeals. Hence slice-of-life commercials and advertisements are so popular. Such advertisements usually portray a stereotypical situation in which an individual experiences a frustration and then overcomes it by using the advertised product. If the viewer can identify with the frustrating situation, he or she may very likely adopt the proposed solution and buy the product advertised. A fellow who has difficulty in attracting dates may decide to use the same mouthwash, shampoo, or clothing that "worked" for the man in the commercial. Use of the product may increase his self-confidence sufficiently to enable him to achieve his goal.

(viii) ***Repression*** : Individuals avoid the tension arising from frustration by repressing the unsatisfied need. Thus, they may "forget" a need. They force the need out of their conscious awareness. Sometimes these repressed needs manifest themselves indirectly. A couple who cannot have children may surround themselves with plants or pets.

(ix) ***Sublimation*** : The manifestation of repressed needs in a socially acceptable form is called sublimation. It is another type of defence mechanism.

(x) ***Other defence mechanisms*** : People have virtually limitless ways of redefining situations by which they protect their self-esteem from the anxieties resulting from the failure. Based on their early experiences, they tend to develop their own characteristic ways of handling frustration. In their selection of advertising appeals, marketers often consider this fact. A flour manufacturer may try to convince consumers that previous baking failures were caused by the ingredients they used, rather than the ineptness of their efforts.

6. Multiplicity of needs. A consumer's behaviour often fulfils more than one need. Specific goals may be selected because they fulfil several needs. We buy clothing for protection and for modesty. Clothing also fulfils an enormous range of personal and social needs. However, there is one overriding need that initiates behaviour. For example, a man may stop smoking because he wants to rid himself of a chronic cough or he may be concerned with cancer or his girlfriend may be "turned off" by the smell of cigarette smoke. If the cumulative amount of the pain produced by each of these reasons is sufficiently strong, he will stop smoking. However, just one of the reasons may also serve as the triggering mechanism. It would be the pre-potent need.

7. Variety of motives. One cannot always infer motives from behaviour. People with different needs may seek fulfilment through selection of the same goals. On the contrary, people with the same needs may seek fulfilment through different goals. Five people who are active in a consumer advocacy organization may each belong for a different reason. The first may be genuinely concerned with protecting consumer interests. The second may be concerned about an increase in counterfeit merchandise. The third may seek social contacts from organizational meetings. The fourth may enjoy the status provided by membership in a powerful organization.

Again, five people may be driven by the same need to seek fulfilment indifferent ways. The first may seek advancement and recognition through a professional career. The second may become active in the League of Women voters. The third may join a health club. The fourth may take professional dance lessons. The fifth may seek attention by monopolizing classroom discussions.

AROUSAL OF MOTIVES

Most of the individual's specific needs are dormant much of the time. The arousal of any particular set of needs at a specific point in time may be due to internal stimuli found in the individual's physiological condition, emotional or cognitive processes, or by stimuli in the outside environment. These are as follows :

1. Physiological arousal. Physical needs are rooted in an individual's physiological condition at that moment. A drop in blood sugar level or stomach contractions may trigger awareness of a hunger need. Secretion of sex hormones may awaken the sex need. A decrease of body temperature may include shivering. Most of these physiological tensions continue until they are satisfied. A shivering man may turn up the heat in his home to relieve his discomfort; he also may make a mental note to buy flannel pajamas. Television programmes often generate physiological arousal that affects the impact of ensuing commercials.

2. Emotional arousal. Thinking or daydreaming may result in the emotional arousal of latent needs. People who are bored or frustrated in attempts to achieve their goals often engage in daydreaming in which they imagine themselves in all sorts of desirable situations. These thoughts tend to arouse dormant needs. These may produce uncomfortable tensions that "push" them into goal-oriented behaviour. A young woman who dreams of becoming a business tycoon may enrol in business school. A young man who dreams of being a writer may sign up for a mail-order writing course.

3. Cognitive arousal. Random thoughts or personal achievements may lead to a cognitive awareness of needs. An advertisement that provides reminders of home might trigger instant recognition of the need to speak with one's parents.

4. Environmental arousal. The set of needs activated at a particular time are often determined by specific cues in the environment. For example, the six o' clock news, the sight or smell of bakery goods, fast-food commercials on television, the end of the school day — all these may arouse the "need" for food. Thus, modification of the environment may be necessary to reduce the arousal of hunger. A most potent form of situational cue is the goal object itself. A couple may experience an overwhelming need for a new dishwasher when they see their neighbour's new dishwasher. A person may suddenly experience a need for a new car when passing a dealer's display window. Sometimes environmental cue produces a psychological imbalance in the viewer's mind. For example, a man who prides himself on his gardening may see an advertisement for a tractor mower that apparently works more efficiently than his own rotary mower. The ad may make him so unhappy with his old mower that he experiences severe tension until he buys himself a new tractor model.

People living in a complex and highly varied environment experience many opportunities for need arousal. Conversely, fewer needs are activated when their environment is poor or deprived.

Therefore, television has such a mixed effect on the lives of the ghetto poor. It exposes them to various lifestyles and expensive products that they would not otherwise see. It awakens wants and desires for which they have little opportunity or even hope of attaining. Thus, while it enriches some lives, it also serves to frustrate people and sometimes results in the adoption of antisocial defence mechanisms such as aggression.

Explanation of Arousal of Motives

There are following two opposing explanations about the arousal of human motives :

1. The behaviourist. It considers motivation to be a mechanical process. Behaviour is seen as the response to a stimulus. Elements of conscious thoughts are ignored. An extreme example of this stimulus-response theory of motivation is the impulsive buyer who reacts largely to external stimuli in the buying situation. The consumer's cognitive control is limited or she does not act, but reacts to stimuli in the market-place.

2. The congestive school. It believes that all behaviours are directed at goal achievement. Needs and past experiences are reasoned, categorized and transformed into attitudes and beliefs that act as predispositions to behaviour. Aimed at helping an individual to satisfy needs, these predispositions determine the direction that he or she takes to achieve this satisfaction.

TYPES AND SYSTEMS OF NEEDS

1. Views of Daniel Starch. Most lists of human needs tend to be diverse in content as well as in length. While there is little disagreement about specific physiological needs, there is considerable disagreement about specific psychological or psychogenic needs.

Table 32.1 presents a list of 44 human motives compiled in 1923 by Professor Daniel Starch of the Hayward Business School for use as copy appeals.

2. Views of Henry Murray. In 1938, the psychologist Henry Murray prepared a detailed list of 28 psychogenic needs that have served as the basic constructs for a number of widely used personality tests such as the Edwards Personal Preference Schedule. Murray believed that everyone has the same basic set of needs, but individuals differ in their priority ranking of these needs. Murray's basic needs include many motives such as acquisition, achievement, recognition and exhibition that are assumed to play

Table 32.1

MOTIVES IN MALE AND FEMALE ADULTS

Appetite — hunger	Respect for deity
Love of opposing	Sympathy for others
Health	Protection of others
Sex attraction	Domesticity
Parental affection	Social distinction
Ambition	Devotion to others
Pleasure	Hospitality
Bodily comfort	Warmth
Possession	Limitation
Approval of others	Courtesy
Gregariousness	Play-sport
Taste	Managing others
Personal appearance	Coolness
Safety	Fear — caution
Cleanliness	Physical activity
Rest — sleep	Manipulation
Home comfort	Construction
Economy	Style
Curiosity	Humour
Efficiency	Amusement
Competition	Shyness
Co-operation	Teasing

an important role in consumer behaving. These are given in table 32.2.

Table 32.2

MURRAY'S LIST OF PSYCHOGENIC NEEDS

1. **Needs associated with Inanimate Objects**
   Acquisition
   Conservancy
   Order
   Retention
   Constriction
2. **Needs that Reflect Ambition, Power, Accomplishment, and Prestige**
   Superiority
   Achievement

Recognition
Exhibition
Inviolate (inviolate attitude)
In avoidance (to avoid shame, failure, humiliation, ridicule)
Definance (defensive attitude)
Contraction (constructive attitude)

3. **Needs concerned with Human Power**
Dominance
Deference
Similance (suggestible attitude)
Autonomy
Contravene (to act differently from others)

4. **Sado-Masochistic Needs**
Aggression
Abasement

5. **Needs concerned with Affection between People**
Affiliation
Rejection
Nurturance (to nourish, aid, or protect the helpless)
Succourance (to seek aid, protection, or sympathy) play

6. **Needs concerned with Social Intercourse (the Needs to ask and tell)**
Cognizance (inquiring attitude)
Exposition (expositive attitude)

THEORY OF HIERARCHY OF NEEDS

Dr. Abraham Maslow, a clinical psychologist, formulated a widely accepted theory of human motivation. It is based on the notion of a universal hierarchy of human needs. It postulates five basic levels of human needs, which rank in order of importance from lower-level (biogenic) needs to higher-level (psychogenic) needs. It suggests that individuals seek to satisfy lower-level needs before higher-level needs emerge. The lowest level of chronically unsatisfied need that an individual experiences serves to motivate his or her behaviour. A new (and higher) need emerges when that need is fairly well satisfied. When this need is satisfied, a new and still higher need emerges, and so on. However, if a lower-level need experiences some renewed deprivation, it may temporarily become dominant again.

Figure 32.1 presents Maslow's hierarchy of needs in diagrammatic form. According to the theory, there is some overlap between each level, as no need is ever completely satisfied. Though

Fig. 32.1. Maslow's Hierarchy of Human Needs

all levels of need below the dominant level continue to motivate behaviour to some extent, the prime motivator — the major driving force within the individual — is the lowest level of need that remains largely unsatisfied.

1. Physiological needs. In the hierarchy-of-needs theory, the first and most basic level of needs is physiological. These needs are required to sustain biological life. These include all the biogenic needs — food, water, air, shelter, clothing, sex.

According to Maslow, physiological needs are dominant when they are chronically unsatisfied. He says, For the man who is extremely and dangerously deprived of food, he thinks about food, he emotes only about food, he perceives only food, and he wants only food." Though the biogenic needs are generally satisfied and the higher-level needs are dominant, yet the lives of a large and growing population of major cities are focused almost entirely on biogenic needs: the needs for food, for clothing, for shelter from the elements in freezing weather.

2. Safety needs. Safety and security needs become the driving force behind an individual's behaviour after the first level of needs is satisfied. These needs are concerned with much more than physical safety. They include order, stability, routine, familiarity, control over one's life and environment, and certainty. For example, health is also a safety concern.

3. Social needs. These include needs of affection, friendship and belonging.

4. Egoistic needs. When the social needs are more or less satisfied, the fourth level of Maslow's hierarchy becomes operative. It is concerned with egoistic needs which can take either an inward or an outward orientation, or both.

(i) ***Inwardly-directed ego needs*** : These reflect an individual's need for self-acceptance, for self-esteem, for success, for independence, for personal satisfaction with a job well done.

(ii) ***Outwardly-directed ego needs*** : These include the needs for prestige, reputation, status and recognition from others.

The ego need is sometimes fulfilled in dysfunctional ways. Poverty-stricken youngsters may value expensive sneakers as symbols of status, and steal in order to acquire them. The incredible increase in gun possession among teenagers in inner city schools (in western countries) has been attributed to the need for status and "respect" from their peers. They believe that the bigger the gun, the more respect they command.

5. Need for self-actualization. Most people do not satisfy their ego needs sufficiently to ever move to the fifth level — the need for self-actualization (self-fulfilment). This need refers to an individual's desire to fulfil his or her potential to become everything he or she is capable of becoming. In Maslow's words, "What a man can be, he must be." This need is expressed in different ways by different people. A young man may desire to be an Olympic star and work single-mindedly for years to become the best in his sport. An artist may need to express herself on canvas. A research scientist may strive to find a new drug to eradicate disease. The self-actualization need is not necessarily a creative urge. However, in people with some capacity for creativity, it is likely to take that form. Advertisements for art lessons, for banking services, and even for military recruitment often try to appeal to the self-actualization need.

Limitations of the Need Hierarchy Theory

The need hierarchy has received wide acceptance in many social disciplines. It appears to reflect the assumed or inferred motivations of many people. The five levels of need postulated by the hierarchy are sufficiently generic to encompass most lists of individual needs. Some critics, however, maintain that Maslow's concepts are too general. The major problem with the theory is that it cannot be tested empirically; there is no way to measure precisely how satisfied one need must be before the next higher need becomes operative The need hierarchy also appears to be very closely bound to contemporary American culture.

Advantages of Maslow's Theory

1. Tools for understanding consumer behaviour. Despite these criticisms, Maslow's hierarchy is a useful tool for understanding consumer motivations. It is readily adaptable for marketing strategy, because consumer goods often serve to satisfy each of the need levels. For example, individuals buy houses, food and clothing to satisfy physiological needs. They buy insurance and radial tires and vocational training to satisfy safety and security needs. Almost all personal care products like cosmetics, mouthwash, shaving cream are bought to satisfy social needs. Luxury products such as furs, or jewels, or big cars are often bought to fulfil ego needs. College training and banking services are sold as ways to achieve self-fulfilment. Maslow's need hierarchy has been called an "emotional trigger" that enables marketers to communicate with their target audiences on a personal, meaningful level that goes beyond product benefits.

The hierarchy theory offers a useful, comprehensive framework for marketers trying to develop appropriate advertising appeals for their products. It enables marketers to focus their advertising appeals on a need level that is likely to be shared by a large segment of the prospective audience. It facilitates product positioning or requisitioning

2. Segmentation applications. The need hierarchy is often used as the basis for market segmentation. Specific advertising appeals are directed to individuals on one or more need levels. For example, soft-drink ads are directed to teenagers stressing a social appeal by showing a group of young people sharing good times as well as the advertised product. Research sponsored by the National Spa and Pool Institute found that men and women had different motivations concerning these products. Women saw the purchase of a pool as an enhancement of family life (the social need), but were concerned about the safety of their small children (the safety need.) Thus, pool advertisement tend to stress the supervision of children, health and family enjoyment. These are targeted primarily to women. As the study found that men were more interested in spas than pools, spa commercials stress a more intimate message relaxation, privacy, time together.

3. Positioning applications. The need hierarchy is used for positioning products — that is, deciding how the product should be perceived by prospective consumers. The key to positioning is to find a niche that is not occupied by a competing product or brand. This application of the need hierarchy relies on the notion that no need is ever fully satisfied. It always, continues to be somewhat motivating. Safety, for example, is a continuing need.

Most manufacturers of luxury cars use status appeals ("Impress your friends"), self-actualizing appeals ("You deserve the very best"), or even social appeals ('The whole family can ride in luxurious comfort"). Some automobile companies have used a safety appeal in advertisements directed to well-to-do executives, for example "When your wife is driving the two children home on a dark and stormy night, you can relax if she's driving the Mercedes."

4. Versatility. The need hierarchy is useful in designing promotional programmes. Workable appeals for a single product can be developed from each level. For example, the potential promotional appeals for home Nautilus equipment. An appeal to physiological needs would show how the home exercise unit can improve body tone and health; a social appeal might show how much fun it can be to exercise with a friend, or even how a streamlined figure would encourage social encounters. Self-esteem is easily demonstrated through a narcissistic appeal such as "Be proud of your body." Finally, an appeal to self-actualization may suggest to career couples that they deserve the convenience and the luxury of home exercise after a long and challenging work-day.

BUYING MOTIVES

Buying motives induce an ultimate consumer, industrial consumer or user, organisational consumer or merchant buyer to purchase a product. These are controlled by the socio-economic, psychological and other factors. Some of these operate from outside and some from within a person. These imply/stimulate him to realise his need or want; choose a product or service that will satisfy it; select the place from where to purchase it; and decide upon the price he will be willing to pay; and also decide upon the time when he may actually purchase it.

Buying motives range from satisfying hunger to seeking protection against clemencies of weather and attack of wild animals, to gratification of sex urge or that for love, curiosity, prestige, social status, personal advancement, and convenience, etc. Some of these motives may be instinctive, while others are acquired from environment, education, social status, age, etc.

An individual consumer buys goods or services to satisfy his personal or household wants. He is the most important class of buyer and among it, the principal customer is the family. He is located in villages, towns and cities. He purchases product for three important reasons : (i) desire which needs to be satisfied; (ii) urge which induces him to purchase and (iii) reasoning. He is motivated to buy by external and internal forces : external and internal motive.

Fig. 32.2. A Model of the Buying Organisation Behaviour

1. External motives. These are outside oneself. A consumer is the product of his environment. His attitudes and behaviour influence his culture and various factors like income, occupation, religion, culture, family and social environment act as motives to buying behaviour.

2. Internal motives. These originate in the minds of the people and are both physical and psychological in nature. They are broadly classified into two classes : (i) *Rational* : These are based on logical reasoning or thinking. (ii) *Emotional* : These are based on personal feelings.

Classification of Buying Motives

The simplest classification is based on primary, selective and patronage motives :

1. Primary buying motives. These relate to the reasons why consumers buy one class of goods rather than another. These result directly from the needs and wants. They include the desire to achieve recognition, physical well-being, preservation of self-image, relaxation, beauty creation, knowledge, money gain, etc. The seller must discover the customer's primary motives and then direct his appeal as effectively as possible.

2. Selective buying motives. These relate to causes that induce a consumer to purchase certain class or quality goods. Selection is based on such selectives as the desire for both economy and convenience. Some of the most common selective buying motives include desire for convenience, versatility, economy, dependability and durability.

3. Patronage buying motives. These cause a customer to buy products from a particular manufacturer or retailer. These are those concerned with fashion, exclusiveness, dependable repairing service, convenience of location, quality, large selections, price, friendship for or reliability of the seller, punctuality in delivery, variety of selection, etc.

David Schwartz's View

Prof. David Schwartz classifies motives according to factors that affect consumer behaviour in following categories :

1. Ego-related motives. These include self-interest, desire for a better self-image, desire for status among one's peers.

2. Rational motives. Based on a man's reasoning, logic and ability and a consideration of economic consequences, rational motives include the immediate monetary cost, and long-range cost affecting the buyer such as durability, depreciation, length of usage, degree of labour needed and ultimate benefit achieved. Prof. Copeland enumerates following rational motives: handiness; dependability in quality and use; durability; happiness; healthfulness; efficiency in operation and use; reliability of auxiliary service; economy in purchase and use; enhancement of earnings; and enhancing productivity of property.

(i) ***The desire for economy*** : The purchases that buyers make enable them to gain monetary gain or personal benefits or to acquire better product at a comparatively low cost. Some examples of appeals made are :

"Buy now — only 10 per cent above cost."

"A bumper sale at 15 per cent above cost."

"Shop at ours, get the choicest product at the cheapest price."

(ii) *Efficiency for doing a task* : It provides motive for use of mechanical devices which reduce the physical or mental tiresomeness in completing a task such as electric can-openers, knife sharpeners, blenders, mixers, razors, crushers and grinders in the kitchen and automatic bottlers, sealers, stammers, packaging machines, etc., and in offices, electric typewriters, copiers, pencil sharpeners, and long-distance communication devices. Examples of appeals made are :

"Fabric that never needs ironing."

"Fabrics that never shrink if they have sanforized mark."

"Push button control."

(iii) *Dependability motive* : It compels an individual to buy to satisfy his desire to obtain "quality" goods of "reliable" and durable nature. Examples of appeals made are :

"The Firestone tyre rolls at least 3,000 miles".

"This mixer is guaranteed for 2 years".

"It is most dependable for nutrition and purity".

3. Emotional movies. Based on personal feelings, emotional buying motives cover a wide range of irrational motives including impulses, instincts, habits and drives and are varied in nature. According to Prof. Copeland, these include : emulation, pride and ambition, economic emulation, social achievement, happy selection of gifts, maintaining and preserving health, satisfaction of appetite, proficiency, expression of artistic taste, ambition, romantic instinct, securing personal comfort, security from danger, securing comfort and obtaining greater leisure, distinctiveness, desire for recreation and entertainment, cleanliness, pride of personal appearance, satisfaction of physical and emotional appetites, alleviation of laborious task; and pleasing sense of taste.

(i) *Attraction for opposite sex* : It works in both young and old and involves pleasing or flattering the opposite sex, or appearing attractive before the other. Men dress in their best to appeal to women; and women put attractive hairdos, jewellery, pleasing perfumes and make-up in a modern style to appeal to men. Appeals to this motive are made in marketing of almost everything-perfumery, cosmetics, lipsticks, deodorants, shampoos, shaving lotions, toiletries, corsets, imitation or real jewellery, birthday presents, sexy books, clothing, automobiles, soft drinks and even cigarettes. The appeals are usually indirect, implying that if you buy a particular product you will be more popular with the opposite sex. Some examples of such appeals are :

"Every woman has a right to look younger than she is".
"Bold, defiant — the male scent".
"It gives your face a sex appeal".

(ii) ***Love and affection for others*** : It includes a sense of duty, love for family members and society and a desire to see justice done to oneself and others. Baby food, readymade baby suits, toys, children's books and insurance for children; labour saving kitchen appliances, beautiful birthday or marriage anniversary presents of costly jewellery, beauty preparations, fashion goods, perfumes, romantic and sexy novels, costly fruitier and prize bonds for wife are generally purchased to satisfy buyer's affection motive. Examples of its appeals are :

"Don't leave your family helpless".
"Because you love them, protect them".
"Wise parents give their children good education and breeding".
"Wise mothers give their family a nourishing breakfast".

(iii) ***Social acceptance motive*** : Every individual wants to have respect and information from the group to which he belongs and to escape rejection and loneliness. Taking advantage of this motive, the marketers issue appeals such as the following :

"Your neighbours shop here — you should too".
"It makes you nice to be near all day".
"It's the 'in' thing to do".

(iv) ***Recreation and relaxation motive*** : Vacations, sports and leisure time activities such as indoor games or going to cinema shows, music concerts, mushairas and Kavi sammelans are activities of the good life desired by most people. Hence people purchase sports and games materials, indoor games, tickets for cinema shows or horse racing, boxing; they buy bathing suits, radios, television sets, record players, light books and magazines. Examples of appeals :

"Quiet heaven for you to spend your holidays-come and stay at Shalimar".

"Relieves all pains and brings safe and restful sleep".

"Enjoy the beauty of nature, warm sunshine, cool breezes on the beach — come and visit once and again".

(v) ***Conquering fear motive*** : Due to fear, physical or psychological people are induced to buy seat belt, burglar alarms, door locks, lockers in banks, life insurance or general assurance policy, home fire extinguisher, pistol, exercising machines, woollen clothings, medicines and tonics, etc. Example of appeals are :

"Save now for the rainy day".

"Drive slowly, someone is waiting for you at home".

"Safety first, speed next".

(vi) ***Curiosity motive*** : Adolescent boys and girls and even adults are curious about certain things — such as curios, old paintings, old coins, blue films, cabaret dances, or sex literature. Examples of appeals are :

"For Adults Only".

"Something New has been Added — come and see."

"Be in the know of the Eighth Wonder of the World."

"Everything about Sex and Love Life — Read and enjoy".

(vii) ***Satisfaction of pride and vanity motive*** : People like to feel important in the society, among friends, in associations and clubs, to achieve status symbols which feed their vanity. Hence, ladies purchase costly costumes, jewellery or join expensive clubs; go to theatres and purchase products of arts; have improvements and expensive home decoration objects. Men purchase television, refrigerators, costly furniture, coolers, scooters and cars, fancy ties, after-shave lotions, perfumes and other variety goods. Appeals are made as the following :

"Be the first to own one".

"Designed exclusively with you in mind".

"It is a limited edition, so buy yours now".

(viii) ***Emulate motive*** : Some people are motivated to buy what is reported to be used by persons whose opinions matter. Hence, a new company may hire highly respected leaders as corporate directors to entrap the investors to buy its shares. Five-star hotels may say that film artists patronise them. Popular entertainers, athletes, film actors/actresses may give testimonials about the use of a product which are utilised for creating demand for that product.

(ix) ***Comfort and convenience motive*** : It plays an important part in the sale of luxury articles, labour saving devices, gas cylinders and gas oven; stoves, pressure cookers, electric irons, lounge chairs, sofa set, soft bed, good nourishing and tasty food, some type of conveyance, air conditioners, washing machines, etc. Mortimer gives ten kinds of convenience to be reckoned with in marketing:

(a) *Form* : Products must be available in a wide variety of form. The drug products, for example, may come in liquid, paste, syrup, powder, pill or inhalant form.

(b) *Quantity or units* : Goods must be offered in all sizes, quantities or units desired by the consumer.

(c) *Time* : Products must be available at the time the consumer wants them.

(d) *Place* : Sellers must offer opportunities to consumers for shopping in the most convenient locations possible.

(e) *Packaging* : Packages must be easy to find, open, use and store.

(f) *Combination or "Packaging" convenience* : It is found in service industries.

(g) *Automation* : Many consumers dream of push-button home.

(h) *Credit* : Instalment and credit purchases of furniture, appliances, radios, and other time, saving devices, where products are purchased now and paid in future.

(i) *Selection* : A seller must offer his products at convenient prices and in an assortment of colours, materials or flavours.

(j) *Readiness* : Everything one purchases must be ready and easy to use.

4. Patronage motives. Patronage motives explain why a consumer purchases a product only from one seller rather than another. Following are the key patronage motives :

(i) ***Price*** : As the budget is limited, an individual would like to purchase cheap or at discount. Hence, following "price appeals" attract him :

"Price slashed by 50%".

"Old price Rs. 135/- Today's price Rs. 50/- only. Rush and make a choice before the stock runs short".

"Price right for quick sale".

(ii) ***Location*** : Nearness to one's residence induces people to buy from a particular store which may say :

"Five conveniently located cooperative stores waiting to serve you.

"Come and be satisfied".

"Location in the heart of the city, accessible from all sides".

(iii) ***Quality consciousness*** : It appeals some customers to buy standard quality goods, even if costly. The usual appeals are :

"Our products are priced a bit higher because quality is so much better".

"We guarantee price back, if quality is found inferior".

'The quality goes in before the name goes on".

"We guarantee every product we sell".

(iv) ***Services*** : Services like credit, home delivery, good gift, attractive wrapping, easy returns, guarantees, and free installations, maintenance and technical assistance help in attracting and holding a clientele. Examples of appeals are :

"All this at no extra cost".

"We service what we sell".

"Free home delivery within the town".

(v) ***Integrity of the merchant*** : It attracts buyers, especially of the product as an intangible such as insurance, security or pest control or when post-sale service is likely to be needed as in the case of automobiles.

(vi) ***Variety of goods at one place*** : It saves time and energy in marketing. Hence, appeals like these attract buyers :

"We have the largest selection in town".

"See our complete line of latest fashions in maxis, bikinis and bras".

(vii) ***Likeable and competent personnel*** : Sympathetic and helpful salesmen and clerks do attract customers. Marketers stress that services of trained experts are available. They assure the buyers by saying.

"You are never a stranger when you shop with us".

"The friendliest place in town to shop for you — visit once and be convinced".

According to Carter, buying motives include : money, vanity, acquisitiveness, rivalry, comfort, adornment, cleanliness, companionship, collecting, amusement, sensual gratification, construction, aggrandisement, mental culture, affection, social achievements, ambition, inhibitiveness, reverence, romance, aesthetic tastes, sex, imitation, curiosity, self-preservation, sympathy, gratitude, patriotism and so on.

BARRIERS TO RECOGNISE BUYING MOTIVES

Following barriers may be recognised as rational and emotional buying motives in the costumes :

1. Unawareness. The customer may be unaware of his own motives which prevent him from communicating to the seller his desires for wanting certain goods and services. Hence, the salesman must play detective, during his talks with the customer, in order to gain necessary knowledge and insight regarding buying motives of the customers.

2. Unwillingness. The customers are sometimes unwilling to disclose their real motives. Hence, it requires a great tact on the part of the marketer to induce them to express their needs.

3. Complexity. The actual motives may be so complex or independent that it is very difficult, if not impossible to recognize them.

4. Barriers to Buying.

(i) Incompatibility of the product with the self-concept. If a product does not coincide with or support a self-concept or how the costumier really thinks of himself, the customer reacts negatively to sales representation.

(ii) Lack of authority to buy or power to make purchase of a particular product.

(iii) The risk of moving away from one's ideal self-image.

(iv) The feeling of guilt.

Buying Motives of Industrial Consumers or Organisational Market

Industrial consumers are business or institutional organisations that buy products and services either to use in making other goods and services or to use in their own business. According to Canfield, following are three types of industrial consumers, *viz.* :

1. Manufacturers. These purchase goods for turning them into finished goes such as cotton, pig iron or steel sheets, and all types of raw materials.

2. Manufacturers and service organisations. These buy goods for consumption in the operation of their business, such as lighting equipments and furniture and fixtures fitting in a cinema hall.

3. Industrial distributors. These buy for resale to industrial consumers. According to R.F. Eider, typical industrial buyers are interested in extractive, processing, construction and transportation industries, public utilities, services and distributive industries, governmental institutions, commercial institutions, specialised service industries (hotels, restaurants, theatres, laundries, dry-cleaners, tailoring and barber shops, etc.).

Items (1)	Ultimate Consumer (2)	Industrial Consumer (3)
1. Product Consideration		
(i) Total volumes of sales market	Smaller than industrial sales market	Larger than ultimate consumer market
(ii) Variety of products offered	Virtually unlimited	Virtually unlimited
(iii) Making of products to buyer's specifications	Uncommon	Very common
(iv) Number of product suppliers	For most products comparatively large.	Comparatively small
(v) Average size of purchase	Small	Very large
(vi) Nature of demand	Sets pace for industrial goods demand	Derived from ultimate consumer demand
2. Promotional Consideration		
(i) Advertising	Extensive use of mass media	More selective — little use of mass media
(ii) Personal selling direct to consumer	Very limited	Very extensive
(iii) Use of trade shows and exhibits	Minor	Major
(iv) Rationality in purchase decision making	Limited	Great
(v) Purchasing skills	Limited	Sophisticated
(vi) Number of people involved in purchasing decision	Two or more	Usually several
(vii) Reason for purchase	Satisfy personal or house hold need	Satisfy business, institutional or governmental need
3. Pricing Consideration		
(i) Price Policy	Usually one price to	Often sell
(ii) Use of discounts	Limited	Very common.

Distinction between Organisational and Consumsers Market

1. Derived demand. The organisational market has a derived demand, *i.e.*, the demand does not exist as an independent force but is dependent upon the demand for consumer goods and services.

2. Fewer buyers. It has fewer buyers, as compared to millions of buyers in case of consumer goods.

3. More concentrated. It is more concentrated than the consumer market, which is usually widely dispersed.

4. More valuable. It is more valuable to fluctuating demand.

5. Greater cash flow. It has a greater cash flow than the consumer market.

Comparison between Ultimate and Industrial Consumer Behaviour

According to Stanon, the industrial buyers have two goals: to improve their position in the firm (personal self-interest) and to further their company's position (in profits, competition, acceptance by society). According to Nystorm, the following motives impel industrial consumers to purchase :

1. Efficiency — Performance, practicability and increased capacity.
2. Economy in money, in use or in time.
3. Good quality materials and workmanship.
4. Simplicity in construction, operation and application.
5. Increased saleability of user's product.
6. Ease of operation such as easier handling, greater convenience, handiness or light touch.
7. Space moving, *i.e.*, compactness, ease of storage and holding.
8. Obsolescence which needs improvement, replacement or additions.
9. Safety to employees, clients and customers.
10. Cleanliness in plant, user's product, of workmen.

Schwartz emphasises, "Since industrial consumption is impersonal and for an economic/business reason, it is understandable that industrial users are motivated chiefly by rational or economic factors, the principal being : (i) production quality; (ii) cost; (iii) post-sales service; (iv) efficiency; (v) seller readability, (vi) the terms of sale, (vii) ease and speed of delivery, and (viii) variety. They generally make a conscious and deliberate attempt to 'think rational' and 'do what is best for the company.' However, they are also influenced to some extent by their emotions.

According to Alexander and others, an analysis of the buying motives, practices, and habits in industrial and organisational markets should produce answer to questions such as the following :

1. What functional activities are affected sufficiently by the purchase so that men responsible for these activities have something to say about it?
2. What part in the purchasing procedure does each of these men play?
3. What language do they understand best?
4. What buying appeals are most likely to influence them favourably?
5. What are the most effective and economic ways of transmitting the selling messages to these men?
   (a) If through salesmen, what should their qualification be?
   (b) If through advertising, what media should be employed?
6. How can buying appeals be used in advertising presented to fit peculiarities of the men and the media?
7. How rapid delivery is required?
8. What are the service needs?
   In connection with sale?
   After sale?
9. What are market customs regarding discount structures and credit terms?
10. How important is reciprocal buying?

WHAT DO INDUSTRIAL CONSUMERS BUY?

According to Vergil Reed, Industrial consumers generally by the following wide variety of goods :

1. Building and sites. Factories, warehouses, piers, cars, casks, store buildings, office buildings, land, mining properties and drilling rights.

2. Installations and/or major equipments. Boilers, generators, rolling mills, conveyers or systems, seamless tube mills, furnaces, kilns, and other items of a stationary or installed nature consisting the major operating equipment and involving usually a high cost per unit.

3. Accessory or secondary equipment. Meters, gauges, hand-drills, time systems, hand trucks, slactiers, jacks, and pinion pulleys; office equipment, typewriters, accounting machines, furniture, etc.

4. Supplies. Finished goods comprising :

(i) *Operating goods* : Lubricating grease and oil, graphite, grinding or polishing compound, welding wire coal,

(ii) *Maintenance* : Paint, nails, night bulbs, cleaning supplies,

Administrative goods : Typewriters, ink, pencil, clips, etc.

5. Fabricated or semi-finished materials. Steel bars, billets, wires; rods, steel sheets, blank stamping, grey cotton piece-goods, wood planks.

6. Process materials. Dyestuffs, acids, waxes, gums, compositions, alloys and other products of chemical processes or combinations.

7. Parts. Finished, or about to be assembled, needed for grinding, polishing, fitting and other finishing operation.

8. Complementary equipments. Finished goods of one manufacturer purchased by another to be supplied with his product at the time of sale and for the purpose of increasing its utility or aiding in its operation, *e.g.*, jacks supplied with coal mining machines and dredges, clam-shell buckets supplied with dredges and careens, tools supplied with trucks and automobiles, tools supplied with milling and grinding machines.

9. Receptacles and packages. Bottles, jars, cars, cartons, cases, drums, barrels and bags, wrappers, labels and stickers, etc.

10. Services. Electric power, telephone and telegraph, insurance, banking, advertising, research, legal, medical and dental assistance, employment, credit transportation, warehousing and business consulting.

SOME COMMON BUYING MOTIVES

1. Freedom from fear and danger. Fear is a negative but very powerful motive. The most basic instinct of a human being is self-preservation. A person can do almost anything to guarantee his safety. Fear is a very powerful and compelling force in human affairs interlinked with the buying motive. The marketing man must ascertain the possible fear of death, fear of loss and fear for the future. Fear can sell anything like hair-oil through fear of getting bald.

2. Economy. Persons desire money to satisfy their other desires. A businessman wants money to make more profits on lower costs.

Saving money is a universal desire. Customers spend money to get more money. Dealers who purchase goods to sell to the customers get more money and profit. The manufacturers make purchase of high priced heavy machinery to lower down their cost of production and thereby increase profits. A housewife will go round the shops to save money for other purchases. This is a motive to which everybody would respond.

3. Vanity. Women spend much time, thought and money on their personal appearance like cosmetics, hair-do and new styles. Both men and women like to be admired. Hence, vanity is a powerful motive in the hands of the marketing man.

4. Appreciation. Everybody desires to be appreciated and complimented and recognised as an important person. He wants to be in a position from where he can issue orders to others. Because of this human trait, it may be useful to follow indirect method in place of direct method that might prove offensive.

5. Fashion. Everyone desires to imitate what others are doing. This is imitation motive. Closely linked with pride or desire for importance, every one is motivated by the desire to show oneself superior and to be in fashion with the elite. This motive can be well exploited by the marketer.

6. Possession. The instinct of possession or a desire to call things as 'mine' leads persons to hoard and collect things. A miser takes delight in possessing money. Some persons collect postage stamps and old coins. Here the hoarding instinct is at work which can be used in selling even unnecessary things.

7. Sex or romance. Fancy clothes, cosmetics, perfumes, etc. are in great demand on account of sex instinct or a desire to attract the opposite sex. Without sex, little interest will remain in styles for men and women. While women spend more on fancy clothes, hair-do and cosmetics to appeal to men, men also do their best to attract women. The sex motive is very powerful; it can sell almost anything. Therefore this instinct is very often used by marketing men.

8. Love of others. This motive plays an important part when parents purchase all kinds of things for their children like toys, fancy garments and other presents. They go in for life insurance to make provision for future of the families. The insurance salesmen use this motive to include the prospect to protect his loved ones by purchasing an insurance policy. The young husband purchases all kinds of labour saving devices for his wife. A bachelor going to marry soon will purchase numerous domestic articles. This particular motive is at times described as that of "home building". It is also related to comfort and convenience motive.

9. Health or physical well-being. Many people purchase health foods, vitamin tablets and patent medicines to maintain their health and physical well-being.

10. Comfort and convenience. Most people like to be easy going and do not exert much. This motive may be well exploited in selling luxury items like motor cars, softest furniture, vacuum cleaners, washing machines, television sets, etc.

USING BUYING MOTIVES IN MARKETING

Human instincts make a person behave differently at different times. The motivation-research is meant to measure the changes of instincts of people. The marketer should plan to make full use of these motives. For the use of low priced, one may suggest approval and quality. If the marketing programme is to be effective and appropriate in terms of product features and advertising strategy, the appropriate motive must be crystallised.

Many people buy their daily requirements from a certain store out of patronage motive. The choice depends on factors such as location, variety of goods stocked, reputation of the store, attitude adopted by the salesmen, the services offered, the general appearance of the store, etc. Advertisement made by the store is to a large extent responsible for the image of the store. Social status plays an important role in the choice of the store and the type of clientele attracted by the store. Some people prefer shopping at glamorous stores while others select economical stores. Thus persons prefer to match with their own values and expectations of the store. The industrial buyer is more objective in purchases on the ground of measurable performance. Thus industrial quality customers are influenced in their patronage motives by factors like product service and price.

QUESTIONS FOR EXERCISE

1. Explain the role of needs, goals and self-image in motivation of consumer behaviour.
2. Distinguish between positive and negative motivation, rational and emotional motives.
3. Discuss the dynamic nature of motivation.
4. Explain different types of arousal of motives.

5. Describe types and systems of needs.
6. Explain and discuss hierarchy of needs.
7. Explain and classify buying motives of the consumer.
8. What are the barrier to recognise buying motives? Explain buying motives of industrial consumers.
9. Describe some common buying motives. How are they used in marketing?

33

Psychology of Advertisement and Selling

WHAT IS ADVERTISEMENT?

If you ask a person as to what is the medicine for headache, he will name Aspro even though he may have never used it, because he has heard the name of this patent medicine so many times that it spontaneously comes to the forefront of the mind as soon as headache is mentioned. Not many persons use Dalda in India but how many are there who do not know it? These days, whenever an educated person goes out to purchase cloth, he checks the mark of 'Sanforised' on it. All this is due to advertisement. Advertisement introduces things to persons. It points out to the special characteristics of commodities. In the words of Husband, "Advertisement may be defined as publicity which calls attention to the existence and merits of certain goods and services."[1]

Importance of Advertisement

One finds a lot of competition in the present day in economic field. The problem of selling is not solved by mere manufacturing. To illustrate, suppose a firm manufactures a particular type of soap. Now, unless the buyers come to know about the existence of this particular brand of soap, how can they buy it? Again, even the knowledge of its existence is not sufficient to boost its sale. They should know its peculiarities and qualities. But the problem does not end, here. Even when the buyer is told of the qualities of soap, it is not necessary that he may come to believe them. And even if he believes it, still he may have no desire to buy it. This shows the importance of advertisement. These days, advertisement has become a science and even an art. In progressive countries, constant researches are being conducted in the field of advertisement. After a thing is advertised, the results of advertisement are checked. This shows the results of special types of advertisement on the

---

1. Husband, R.W., *Applied Psychology*, Harper & Bros., New York.

buyers of particular things. Very interesting facts have been discovered by this research. For example, it has been found that advertisement through moving things, animals and human beings are more impressive than through motionless things and animals respectively. In fact, success in the sale of anything depends on success in its advertisement.

AIMS OF ADVERTISEMENT

The following are the main aims of advertisement :

1. Drawing attention. The first and foremost aim of advertisement is to draw the attention of the persons towards a particular thing or service. In the cities, on big railway junctions and on busy squares, one finds the word USHA in red light, and at another place there is TATA in moving light. Bare names in capital words are written on very sizeable signboards. These advertisements do not describe the qualities of the objects they advertise. They only introduce these names to the public. Electric bulbs are used to draw attention. Big signboards draw more attention than smaller ones. Figures, colours, headings, form, light, etc., all the different items of advertisement aim at drawing the attention.

2. Creating interest. Generally speaking, only that object draws attention which is interesting. Why do you find the pictures of film actresses in the advertisement of Lux toilet soap? Why are pictures of women displayed in posters advertising *bidis*? Have you ever seen the day-by-day of Rexona soap? What is the secret of the success of advertisement? The answer is that it lies in creating interest. The aim of displaying women pictures in the advertisements of things is to create interest in them. Most men take interest in beautiful women. A successful advertiser takes cognigance of the interest of the buyers because interest and attention are closely related.

3. Creating belief. As has been pointed out earlier, mere knowledge of the existence of a thing or mere introduction with its qualities is not sufficient for its being sold. The main problem is to create belief among the buyers that it has these particular types of qualities. This can be done in a variety of ways. One way is to seek recommendations from eminent leaders, film actors and actresses, etc. Certificates from eminent physicians are helpful in the advertisement of medicines. Sometimes, the number of commodities sold is advertised to create faith in their quality, *e.g.*, 50,000 copies of such and such book have been sold.

4. Remembering. Advertisement should influence memory because a person does not need a thing while he reads its advertisement. The advertisement should be able to recall its name and the name of the firm manufacturing it.

5. Creating a desire to buy. In the end, the main purpose of the advertisement is to create a desire among persons to buy it. It is hence, that advertisers check the influence of advertisement on sales. The success of an advertisement is correlated to the success in sales. Though the advertisement is attractive and interesting, this does not constitute its aim. Its main aim is to boost the sales of a commodity. All else is mere means to achieve this end.

Psychological Bases of the Appeal of Advertisement

In the words of Blum, "The core of all advertising is suggestion".[2] Advertisement aims at suggesting buying of a particular thing; advertisement is a science of drawing attention. Some traits attract more attention than others. Much progress has been made in the art of advertisement. In order to understand the importance of attention as the psychological basis of advertisement, it shall be relevant to describe briefly the internal and external determinants of attention.

CONDITIONS OF ATTENTION

As a selective act of the mind, attention depends upon several conditions. These conditions may be of two types — external or objective and internal or subjective. External or objective conditions are related with the environment. In the environment or surroundings of the individual, there are several stimuli, but he does not attend to all of them at the same time, because some stimuli are stronger than others. The factors making these stimuli stronger than others are known as external determinants of attention. Besides, the external conditions, the mental conditions, culture and heredity also influence attention. Owing to these internal conditions some objects attract our attention more than others. These internal factors are internal determinants of attention. The methods of achieving attention are based upon these external and internal determinants of attention.

External Determinants of Attention

The following are the most important external determinants of attention :

---

2. Blum, M.I., *Industrial Psychology and Its Social Foundations*, Harper & Bros., New York.

1. Nature of stimulus. Nature of stimulus means its type, *i.e.*, whether it is visual, gustatory, auditory, olfactory or tactual stimulus. It has been found by experiments that in comparison with other sensations, colour and sound attract more attention. Among the pictures, the pictures of human beings attract more attention than those of animals while among human beings, pictures of beautiful women attract more attention. Besides these, the coloured pictures attract more attention than colourless ones. All these factors are important in advertisement. In the auditory stimulus, the melodious voice attracts more attention than other voices.

2. Intensity of the stimulus. The intensity of the stimulus is a helpful condition in attention. In comparison with the weak stimuli, the intense stimulus attracts more attention of the organism. High sound, excessive pressure and acute pain attract our attention. In the market, there is always some buzzing sound and yet the pedestrians hear the horn of the motor car, since the sound of the horn is louder than other sounds. But it is not always necessary that one should attend to the intensity of the stimulus. Some times while walking on the road, calling of our name attracts so much attention that we fail to hear even the loud sound of the motor horn. As a matter of fact, the attraction of the attention does not depend on any single factor, but on several factors interconnected with one another. Hence, it can be said that other things being the same, the more intense stimulus will attract more attention.

3. Size of the stimulus. In the visual stimuli, the size of the stimulus is also a determinant of attention. As a general rule the bigger size attracts more attention, but a small advertisement on a very wide background also attracts attention. Thus the attraction of an object does not depend upon its size alone, but also on its background. To illustrate, a big black spot on a black face will not attract so much attention as a very small black spot on a white face.

4. Location of the stimulus. The location or the stimulus also affects attention. In the visual stimuli, the most effective location is just in front of the eyes. The role of different pages in the newspaper or the magazine and the different places on the same page, is important advertisement. It has been found by experiments that advertisement given on the front page or on the upper half of any page attracts more attention.

5. Contrast of the stimulus. The contrast of the stimulus is also an important determinant of attention, *e.g.*, the presence of a woman among men and that of a man among women definitely attracts more attention.

6. Change of the stimulus. Attention cannot be concentrated for a long time on some particular object. Hence, the change of the stimulus also affects attention. Attention is sustained by change of the stimulus. The advertisers change their advertisements from time to time lest it may cease to be attractive.

7. Isolation of the stimulus. A man sitting alone in some corner of the park, hotel or club attracts more attention than others. A student sitting alone at the far corner of the class is seen first. Thus, isolation is an important external determinant of attention. This fact is based upon the reason that the isolated individual is not mixed with other individuals and hence, seen separately in his own background. By experiments in advertisement, it has been found that only the fact of isolation attracts 30 per cent more attention. In the British journal of *Educational Psychology* of August 1951, D.E. Berlyne pointed out the following principles based upon latest experiments :

(a) In comparison with the unchanged stimulus, the stimulus changed in the near past has more possibility of attracting attention.
(b) The effect of the change goes on diminishing with the passage of time.
(c) Whenever stimuli are changed together and in which one is left unchanged, the effect on change is not noticeable.
(d) If change goes on in the stimuli, the process of attention is rather permanent and strong.

The modes of change also influence the process of attention. If there is a change absolutely, it attracts more attention. While studying one does not hear the sound of the clock or that of electric fan but if either suddenly stops, one cannot fail to attend to it. Man becomes used to regular changes and does not pay much attention to them. But if some irregular change or any sudden change occurs, it at once draws attention.

8. Duration of the stimulus. As a general rule, the stimulus having more duration attracts more attention. Thus, duration of the stimulus is an important determinant of attention. But sometimes, the smallest flashing of a movement attracts more attention than the bigger stimuli, *e.g.*, a sudden flash of light for several seconds will attract more attention in a dark night than the continuous burning lamp.

9. Repetition of the stimulus. Along with duration, repetition of the stimulus is also an important determinant of attention. It is a commonplace observation that when the teacher has to attract the attention of students towards a particular phenomenon, he repeats it several times. But sometimes, man ceases to attend to a phenomenon simply because it is repeated many times, *e.g.*, if a man says some things about himself, we take interest in it once or twice, but if we find that he always repeats the same thing, we cease to pay attention to it.

10. Movement in the stimulus. In comparison with the static, the moving stimuli attract more attention. The position of a stimulus changes due to movements. An object lying in some corner of the room will not attract our attention, but even if there is some illusion of movement in it, we cannot help attending to it. The influence of movement in stimulus is widely used by the shopkeepers and businessmen, who advertise through moving electric lights.

Internal Determinants of Attention

The conditions of attention as described so far are the external determinants of attention. They can also be called external laws of attention. The presence of these conditions in the environment is helpful for attention. Besides these, internal conditions are also helpful in drawing attention. These conditions are related with motives. As a matter of fact, the influence of external conditions depends on these internal conditions to a very great extent. The hungry man will attend to the form and stimuli of the food A man with full belly will not attend to food, however nice it might appear. In the advertisements, those demonstrating the naked organs of the woman have maximum power of attention. Those interested in cinema look to the advertisements of cinema at first sight. It is difficult to describe all the internal conditions helpful in attention. Hence, only the most important will be ennumerated here :

1. Interest. Innate and acquired interests draw the individual's attention to particular objects. Doctors, engineers, professors, all attend to the objects of their own interest. Even among the professors, an object attracting the attention of a professor of Geology need not attract the attention of a processor of Philosophy as well. Thus, the innumerable differences in interests create innumerable determinants of attention in different men. The stimuli influencing innate tendencies attract more attention than those influencing acquired interest.

2. Basic drives. The basic drives and impulses of the individual are also important in drawing its attention. The animal attends to particular stimulus when driven by the basic drives of hunger, thirst, sex, etc.; a normal man motivated by sex will naturally attend to the individuals of opposite sex. We all know it by experience that when hungry we may not attend to even a distasteful object, but while our belly is full, we may attend to even the most tasteful food. Among the motives, fear has got definite influence upon attention. All men who fear snake will attend to all things resembling the snakes. Like fear, curiosity also influences attention. We attend to even the smallest details of the object towards which we have curiosity.

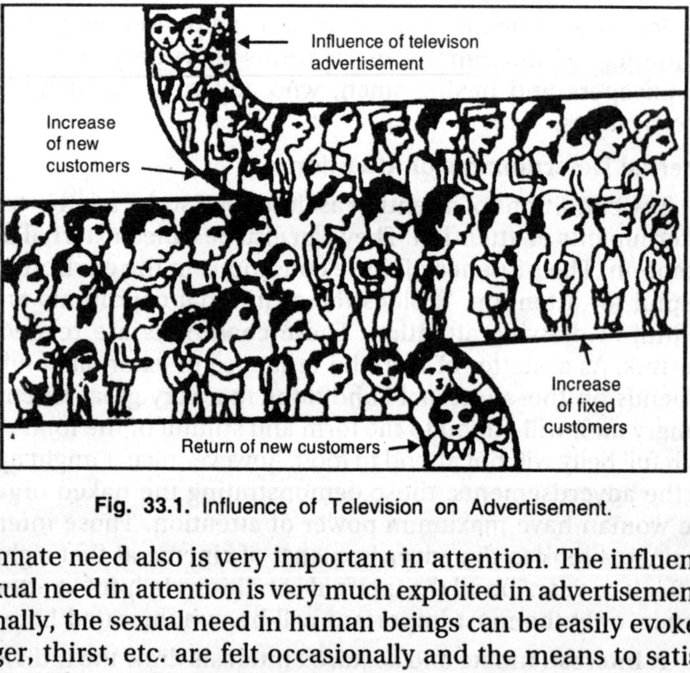

Fig. 33.1. Influence of Television on Advertisement.

Innate need also is very important in attention. The influence of sexual need in attention is very much exploited in advertisements. Normally, the sexual need in human beings can be easily evoked. Hunger, thirst, etc. are felt occasionally and the means to satisfy them are also readily available, but neither the sexual need is ever fully satisfied nor the means of satisfying it, are available to all persons all the time. Hence, most of the advertisements draw attention by stimulating the sexual need in human beings.

3. Mental set. Mental set is one of the most important internal determinants of attention. Mental set means the tendency or bent of the whole mind. A man will attend to those objects towards which his mind is set. In the days of examinations, the mental set of the students is generally towards the examination and hence, even the smallest thing concerning the examination will attract their attention.

4. Aim. Aim also influences attention. Every man has some immediate and some ultimate aims, *e.g.*, the immediate aim of the student is to pass the examination while the ultimate aim may be to get a job, to earn living or anything else. The man whose aim is not to pass the examination will not be concerned with textbooks or notes, etc., but one who has the aim to pass the examination will at once attend to those.

5. Meaning. In comparison with meaningless things, meaningful things and talks attract more attention. A man will not attend to a thing which has no meaning for him. Men do not like to hear meaningless talk. If some persons are talking in Tamil, the Punjabi will not like to hear it since for him it has no meaning.

6. Habit. Habit is also an important determinant of attention. If a man is habituated to rising early and winding his clock early in the morning, he must attend to the clock as soon as he gets up. It has been rightly pointed out that man learns as to which object he should attend and which he should not and thus develops habits of attending and not attending to things. Thus, habit has two aspects in relation to attention. On the one side men develop a habit of attending to necessary and desirable things and on the other side, they develop the habit of not attending to unnecessary and undesirable things. Both these kinds of habit help man in his daily routine.

7. Disposition and temperament. Both disposition and temperament are important internal determinants of attention, *e.g.*, a man having a religious disposition and spiritual temperament will attend to religious matters, while another person having a sexual disposition and criminal temperament will attend to matters concerning sex or crimes, etc. William James has rightly pointed out that it is our tendency to take interest in particular things. Our innate disposition and mental development determine that which, among the crowd of sensations, should attract our attention.

8. Past experience. Past experience also affects attention. If we know it by our past experience that a particular person is sincere to us, we shall pay attention to whatever he advises us. If we know by experience that he is not sincere to us, we shall not attend even to his most serious advice.

9. Emotion. Emotion is also an important determinant of attention. It is a matter of everyday experience that we attend to even the smallest fault of a person whom we hate while we do not attend even to the greatest blunder of a person whom we love. A mother seldom finds faults with her child. The lovers find the whole world singing and dancing and immersed in romance.

10. Social motives. Social motives are important determinants of attention. In advertisements, the human figures attract more attention than figures of animals and things. The reason is that man is guided by his social motives. News about altruism, bravery and saving others' life by putting oneself in danger, attract our attention because we praise these qualities. Men attend to things concerning their duties for social motives.

Besides the conditions described above, many other factors influence attention. Heredity, education and training have a wide influence on attention. The family, school, club, class and society of which an individual is a member, do have some influence on his attention. The physical condition, desire, purpose of the person concerned also affect his attention. Thus, all the factors influencing the personality of a man affect his attention as well. As a matter of fact, it is difficult to describe all direct and indirect determinants of attention. The description given here, however, includes the most important of such factors.

Advertisement and Memory

Memory has got much importance in the psychological basis of advertisement. The advertisement should be such that those who hear, read or see it may remember it. It is then alone that they will buy it when needed. The thing should be named such as also exhibits its function. This leads to the association of name with function, so that it is recalled whenever that particular function is needed. Examples of some such names are Nahan soap, Sina machine, Sulekha ink, etc. There is much difficulty in the advertisement of things which bear difficult names that cannot be remembered easily. Sometimes, the fact of the relation of advertisement with memory is misused. For example, when a particular trademark becomes famous, some unscrupulous persons give a similar name to their products. Names such as Sunlight and Lifebuoy followed after Sunlight and Lifebuoy soaps became well known.

Advertisement and Suggestion

As has been pointed out earlier, the main psychological basis of advertisement is suggestion. The meaning of suggestion is to motivate a person to do a particular kind of work. Some advertisements directly ask for the purchase of a particular thing. Recommendations of film actors and actresses are used as suggestion in some other advertisements. You must have seen recommendations of many beautiful film actresses for the skin care from Lux soap. Such advertisements involve prestige suggestion. Advertisers of vegetable oil often present certificates of its being harmless. Such advertisements suggest for the purchase of particular things.

Advertisement and Attitude

Attitude is also a very important psychological element in the basis of advertisement. It is a permanent organisation of motivational, emotional, perceptual and cognitive processes in a person towards objects surrounding him. Advertisement cannot be effective unless attitude is favourable. For example, in every free country, one finds pro-nation attitude among people. Hence, things can be advertised in the name of Swadeshi.

Elements of Effective Advertisement

While closing our discussion over the psychological basis of advertisement, it will be relevant to analyse different elements of its psychological appeal. In advertisement consists of illustration, colour, headline, text or copy, trademark or trade name and layout or arrangement of the advertisement. All these must have psychological appeal in order to make advertisement effective. Some important points in this connection will be pointed out here :

1. Illustrations. Illustrations in an advertisement should be real and interesting. If they are only real, they will attract less attention. If they are only interesting, they will not motivate purchase.

2. Colour. Colour plays an important role in advertisement, but its success depends on right choice of suitable colours. In different seasons, different colours are agreeable. Distinction of age and sex also have considerable bearing on this issue. As a general rule, while blue colour appeals to men, red appeals to women. Again, while dark colours are favoured by the young, the aged favour light colours. In summer, blue and green colours are more agreeable while in winter, red and black may be more useful for advertisement.

3. Headline. Generally, every advertisement bears a headline. The headline has two aims — on the one hand, it creates interest in the advertisement and on the other hand, it motivates persons to buy a particular thing. Therefore, firstly, the headline should be such as can be easily remembered. Secondly, it should lead to the desire to read the entire text of the advertisement. Thirdly, it should be brief and attractive. Life Insurance Corporation of India have given many such advertisements.

4. Text of copy. An advertisement contains a text or copy to give information regarding the object and its utility. This requires much precaution. Generally, indirect text is more appealing. Sometimes manufacturers of cloth, a rubber and paper advertise the story of cloth, rubber and paper respectively, This is interesting and also advertises the commodity indirectly. Text should be brief. It should tell the truth, create faith and the motive to purchase the things advertised.

5. Trademark or trade name. Generally, every manufacturer has a certain trademark or trade name, *e.g.*, Tata, Bata, Lipton, Brook Bond, Kodak, etc. Gradually, these trademarks become popular and things are bought by trade name. Sometimes, however, a trademark becomes so much popular that; it no more represents a particular manufacturer but becomes a synonym for that particular thing. For example, the word Kodak is used for any camera. Some manufacturers only advertise their trade mark.

6. Layout. In the end, the above, mentioned items in an advertisement should be organised in a proper layout. In a good layout, sufficient space is left bare. The illustration which has to be emphasised should be very clear. If an advertisement is on the whole page, it need not have any border. If it is less than a page, it may have border. The illustration, colour and background should be sufficiently matching. Generally, plain advertisements are better. If many things are huddled up together, the onlooker may not remember any of them.

While advertising, care should be taken to consider sex, age, class, education and economic level of the persons for whom the advertisement is prepared, for all these factors make difference in the interest, disposition, motivation and attention of the persons concerned. For example, persons belonging to lower and middle income group are more attracted to such advertisements as promise to give things in less expenses, whereas such advertisements will not appeal to rich persons because they do not pay so much attention to price as to quality and novelty of a thing. Arguments may be advanced in the text of the advertisements meant for educated buyers whereas they are useless in the case of uneducated persons. Advertisements for young men and women should be interesting and attractive. Women are more influenced by suggestion and less by reasoning. Thus the effectiveness of advertisement depends on the strength of its appeal to the particular class of persons who are supposed to buy that particular thing. Practical success of an advertisement depends upon the psychological insight of the advertiser.

THE PSYCHOLOGY OF SELLING

In the modern context, psychology plays a vital role in the sphere of buying and selling because it has been established that "buying and selling are based more on psychological than on economic factors". Both buying and selling are modes of behaviour and since all forms of behaviour obey certain rules, it is possible to discover the laws applicable in this case and to control buying and selling. Since he is a human being, the individual is influenced by psychological laws. Hence, if the seller knows what he should do to awaken a specific response is the buyer he can do his job much better. The situation of buying and selling consists of the buyer, the seller and the material to be sold. While it is desirable that the seller's behaviour should be psychologically tenable, it must be kept in mind that it is easy to sell goods which the buyer requires and demands. Therefore, it is better to manufacture goods which satisfy the buyer's demands and fulfil his requirements. Human beings have a variety of psychological and physical needs. Physical needs include hunger, thirst, the need to maintain an even body temperature, sleep, sex desire, etc. Among psychological needs are : ambition, sex instinct and other individual requirements, in addition to more social needs such as the desire to win social prestige or to attract the attention of others towards oneself. Nowadays the manufacturer turns his attention to these needs of his prospective customers and tries to make his products conform to the requirements of the customer. If he succeeds in this, he finds little, if any, difficulty in selling them.

VARIOUS STEPS IN SELLING

The manufacturer's task does not end with the manufacture of an article because the customer must be aware of a particular article that he needs and also of the place where he can procure it. In addition to this, conveying this information to the customer, will not suffice because numerous other similar or even identical products are marketed by many other manufacturers and are available in the market. The customer is attracted to one such product but not towards another. The answer to this lies in advertisement. Advertisement is the science of attracting the attention of the people since it informs the customer about the goods available and the distinctive qualities of each. This is the first stage in selling. In the second stage, the manufacturer aims at interesting the customer in his own product. If interest is lacking, the customer does not buy the product, but if it is present, he can at least be induced to inspect and examine it. Once interest is established, the desire to buy it follows. But the act of buying occurs only after the individual has examined the article. The confidence that the customer would get on first hand examination of the article is created by the manufacturer through advertisement, his own credit and through the gift of the gab, the ability to talk and to convince the customer. If the article is dependable, the customer decides to purchase it. The seller convinces him and removes his doubts, and finally the customer's decision to buy is translated into action. After the actual purchase, if the customer is satisfied with the performance of the article, he talks of it to other people and, if need be, returns to buy it a second time. This mental satisfaction is an essential step in the process of selling.

METHODS OF SALES DIALOGUE

The process of going from the first to the six steps outlined above, in the business of selling, is facilitated by psychological laws. People who pay heed to psychological laws and apply them in practice find it easier to sell their product. People who do not, face considerable difficulty in selling. In order to encourage the customer to move over these five steps, the seller has to talk to him. The method and the nature of this sales interview or sales talk changes with any change in the seller, the customer or the product being sold. For this reason, it is not possible to be a successful salesman merely by reading books. Nevertheless, it is possible to formulate a rudimentary pattern for said dialogues in most conditions. The work has been done very successfully recent years by psychologists. Laboratory experiments have been conduct to determine the validity of the various prevalent methods of sales dialogue. The more prevalent methods of sales dialogue include exhibition through use, verbal description, lengthy inducements to buy, brief inducements of a similar nature, serious lecturing or free and informal approach. A brief description of these methods now follow[3] :

1. Practical demonstration. Most people have seen the salesman actually operating a new article in his shop in order to attract the customer. Most manufacturers try to arrange such practical and operational exhibitions of the products in shops, markets and exhibitions. When the customer sees the article in actual use, he is more easily satisfied about its utility and efficiency. But this method cannot be applied to the selling of all objects. For example, it is not possible to display objects of food, medicines, or objects concerned with feelings, in this way. Hence, for such commodities other methods are applied.

2. Verbal description. The shopkeeper or the salesman uses the method of verbal description either when a practical demonstration is not possible or when it does not suit him to arrange such a demonstration. In this method, the salesman describes the article, its qualities and its utility in many ways so that the buyer may be convinced. It is desirable that the description should be psychological. And even if there is an element of deception in this description. It should be mentioned in such a way that the buyer does not suspect it.

3. Entreaty to buy after mentioning facts. In this method, the salesman starts by mentioning facts about the article he wants to sell and then requests, begs or entreats the customer to buy it. This entreaty to buy is made in many ways. Some people talk enthusiastically but seriously about the merits of the article in question. Some salesmen adopt a very rude manner while others assume a friendly manner to win the confidence of the customer. Such salesmen try to convince each customer, that they are concerned only with the customer's welfare and that their aim is not to earn money but to serve the customer by fulfilling his demands. They create the impression that their objective in selling is to provide satisfaction to the customer.

The advantages and disadvantages of each of the above selling methods can be understood by comparing them. One experienced salesman adopted each of these sales techniques so that they

3. Blum, M.L., *Industrial Psychology and Its Social Foundations.*

could be evaluated by forty students. The results obtained were entertaining. It was seen that the method of practical demonstration was better than verbal description. A factual description was found better than a simple entreaty or request to buy. It was felt that a friendly manner during the sales talk was better than the blunt or rude manner. But the enthusiastic and the very serious and grave descriptions were found to be equally effective.

PSYCHOLOGICAL FACTORS IN SALES AND PURCHASE

In the field of marketing, the psychological importance of motivation, research, analysis of concepts, development of the methods of introducing goods, improvement in questions, evaluation of verbal reactions, consumption, effective advertisement of indirect evidence, the evaluation of its effect, group information, etc., has been discovered. Besides, efforts have been made to discover, through research, the effect produced on consumers by particular forms of behaviour. Considerable data have been collected on this subject by circulating questionnaires through post. Although many researches involve the use of questionnaires it has been found that only those consumers care to reply to the questionnaire who are especially interested in a particular product. But in order to encourage the other consumers, some incentives can also be provided. Sometimes, the consumer's opinion has been obtained through interview in a personal meeting or over a telephone. In research of this kind, it is necessary to keep in mind the fact that many consumers do not provide valid information because every individual does not have a uniform capacity to evaluate things. Some people can arrive at a more objective evaluation than others. Then memory also plays an important part in this. Some people can recall facts heard a long time ago while the majority of people forget them rapidly. Generally, a thing seen can be remembered for a longer time than a thing heard. For this reason, in some cases practical demonstration proves more valuable than a verbal description. Suggestion plays an important part in selling and for that reason it is extensively used in marketing.

The power of suggestion works in the case of fashion also. Certain goods sell because they are fashionable. Sometimes fashion is artificially created, and it can be made so powerful that certain goods and articles come to imply status and become status symbols. In such a case, people are willing to pay a very high price for such things. The sex instinct is exploited frequently in advertisement campaigns. In advertising products to be used by men and women, the advertiser often displays nude and semi-nude figures of beautiful women. In addition to the sales talk of the salesmen, the commodity itself should be useful and attractive. If an article is to remain on the market for a long time, it should have some inherent utility but in order to attract attention the first time, it must also be attractive. For this reason, these days considerable attention is paid to the packing of commodities. The packing should be so attractive that the customer's attention should be diverted towards it, as soon as he enters the shop. He should want to pick it up and touch it. This end is achieved by making bottles of various attractive shapes and by making the containers more colourful. The labels and the words on the outside of boxes and bottles also play an important part in attracting the customer. As far as possible, the description should mention all the qualities of the product besides containing some suggestion for the customer which induces him to buy it. Nowadays the customer is induced to buy things because articles of daily use are offered to him in the form of free gifts along with the things he buys. Most of the successful manufacturers conduct research to find out ways and means of advertising their goods in such a way that they should be able to sell more than their competitors.

QUESTIONS FOR EXERCISE

1. What are the psychological factors working in advertisement? Explain.
2. Why do we advertise? Point out some important methods of advertisement and explain their psychological significance.
3. Pointing out the importance of advertisement in modern times, explain the factors affecting advertisement.
4. How far can psychology be an aid to effective advertising? Give some examples of effective advertising with reasons.
5. Discuss with suitable examples how various psychological principles and concepts are applied in advertising and selling?
6. Describe the methods of measuring the effectiveness of advertising and of the means used for the same.

Bibliography

Anastasi, A. *Psychological Testing*, Macmillan.

Bell, J.E. *Projective Testing*, Longmans Green.

Bellak, L. *The T.A.T. and C.A.T. in Clinical Use*, New York : Grune and Stratton.

Bhatia, C.M. *Mental Testing and National Reconstruction*, Hind Kitabs.

Blum, M.L. *Industrial Psychology and its Social Foundations*. New York : Harper and Bros.

Blum and Balansky. *Counselling and Psychology*, Prentice Hall.

Ferguson, L.W. *Personality Measurement*, New York : McGraw Hill, Book Co.,

Gardner, B.B. *Human Relations in Industry*, Richard D. Irwin.

Gray, J.S. *Psychology Applied to Human Affairs*, McGraw Hill.

Ghiselli, E.E. and C.W. Brown. *Personnel and Industrial Psychology*, Tokyo.

Harrell, T.W. *Industrial Psychology*, Calcutta.

Heron, A.A. *Why Men Work*, Stanford University Press.

Humphreys, J.A. *Choosing Your Career*, Chicago : S.R.A. Better Living Booklets.

Jones, A.J. *Principles of Guidance*, McGraw Hill, 1951.

Link, N.C. *Employment Psychology*.

Maier, N.R.F. *Psychology in Industry*, Houghton Mifflin.

Moore, B.V. and Hartmann, G.W. *Readings in Industrial Psychology*.

Myers, C.S. *Industrial Psychology*.

Ministry of Education. *Workshop on Vocational Guidance*, Publication No. 83, India.

Ministry of Education. *Workshop on Vocational Guidance*, Publication No. 300, India.

Mundel, H.F. *Motion and Time Study*, Prentice Hall.

Mursell, J.L. *Psychological Testing*, Longmans Green.

Shafer and Shoben, *The Psychology of Adjustment*, Houghton Mifflin.

Super. D.E. *Appraising Voc. Fitness*, Harper and Bros.

Smith, M. *Introduction to Industrial Psychology*, New York.

Tiffin, J. *Industrial Psychology*, Prentice Hall.

Vernon, H.M. *Industrial Fatigue and Efficiency*, Dutton.

Vernon, P.E. Recent Trends in Mental Measurement and Statistical Analysis. Published in *Studies in Education*, University of London Press.

Viteles, M.S. *Motivation and Morale in Industry*, Staples Press.

Viteles, M.S. *Industrial Psychology*, Norton.

Objective Questions

1. When giving instruction a leader should keep in mind
   (a) that he does so to coordinate the efforts of others with his
   (b) that his authority and prestige are increased
   (c) that he should not disagree with others as far as possible
   (d) that he is helping others when giving instructions.
2. The only real test of leadership is
   (a) getting blind obedience from the workers
   (b) commanding respect and winning cooperation
   (c) satisfying those in higher positions
   (d) trying to satisfy every wish of the workers.
3. Union organisations are more concerned with the workers's feelings and attitudes than in management.

   True False Do not know
4. Many workers like changes in their job.

   True False Do not know
5. Creative thinking attains its highest level under autocratic leadership.

   True False Do not know
6. High turnover can at times led to low morale although the correlation is low between turnover and morale.

   True False Do not know
7. The relationship between and employee and his supervisor is not very important from the point of view of productivity.

   True False Do not know
8. The interviewer's job is to tell the interviewee about what he does not know.

   True False Do not know
9. Application Blank is the only method for selecting a person in industry.

   True False Do not know

10. Industry is least concerned with psychology.

True False Do not know

11. A person who is not accepted by others will scarcely be able to accept himself.

True False Do not know

12. An accurate standard is needed for judging a person's performance.

True False Do not know

13. Positive incentives always accelerate the drive towards a goal directed activity.

True False Do not know

14. Occupational status is related to job-satisfaction.

True False Do not know

15. In Industry people respond to punishment than to praise.

True False Do not know

16. Accidents do not happen to persons on the basis of equal liability.

True False Do not know

17. Time studies have not been widely adopted in the United States.

True False Do not know

18. Non-directive counselling is also known as client-centred counselling.

True False Do not know

19. In mental abilities, men and women are very similar.

True False Do not know

20. Job description is the heart of personal selection.

True False Do not know

21. Mental functions are generally measured by mental tests.

True False Do not know

22. The subject matter of Industrial Psychology is the scientific study of industrial relations.

True False Do not know

23. Job-analysis is the method of obtaining the information that makes up a job.

True False Do not know

24. The atmosphere at an interview should be cordial one.

    True False Do not know

25. The lack of a sense of belongingness is felt by all new employees.

    True False Do not know

26. A result of a good selection procedure is high production.

    True False Do not know

27. Rapport is a very important factor in an interview and should be achieved right in the beginning.

    True False Do not know

28. Job analysis is a characteristic procedure in industrial psychology in which nature of work and method for selection work is found out.

    True False Do not know

29. The employment interview requires prior preparation.

    True False Do not know

30. Good methods of selection reduce the problem of supervision.

    True False Do not know

31. Job-analysis is most frequently done by
    (a) observing the people at work
    (b) having an interview with the employee
    (c) reading the literature available on job-description
    (d) none of the above

32. Job-description is the heart of
    (a) job-satisfaction (b) occupational information
    (c) job-evaluation (d) none of the above

33. Regression means behaviour that is
    (a) childlike (b) mentally depressed
    (c) feeble minded (d) diseased

34. There is a tendency for the bright people to have
    (a) low clerical and mechanical aptitude
    (b) high clerical and mechanical aptitude
    (c) only literary ability
    (d) artistic abilities

35. The strong-vocational interest blank is based on :
    (a) responses of people from various professions and occupations

(b) initiative judgements
(c) intelligence test scores
(d) objectives assessment of the needs of a profession

36. An important reason for the follow-up of a new employee is
(a) to evaluate his feelings
(b) to evaluate the technique he uses
(c) to evaluate the hours of work he puts in
(d) to evaluate the selection techniques

37. The interviewer in an employment interview must be
(a) well placed in society (b) good looking
(c) well trained (d) highly intelligent

38. A condition in which there is diminished productivity, efficiency or ability to carry on work, because of previous expenditure of energy in doing work is
(a) boredom (b) fatigue
(c) tiredness (d) no interest

39. Hawthorne experiment is the famous study, which is often quoted in the books on
(a) experimental psychology (b) social psychology
(c) educational psychology (d) industrial psychology

40. In order to do a good job of selecting and placing workers an understanding of the functions involved in work is necessary. So it is necessary to know
(a) organisation (b) job description
(c) salaries of workers (d) job environment

41. An important role in the industrial production can be due to
(a) punishment (b) more work hours
(c) incentives (d) atmospheric conditions

42. Individual liability to meet with accidents or accident susceptibility is called accident
(a) circumstances (b) errors
(c) factors (d) proneness

43. Making workers feel responsible and personally worthy contributes to making work
(a) a part of living (b) a difficult task
(c) a pleasant past time (d) a boring business

44. Chronic complainers tend to be
   (a) the most intelligent among the employees
   (b) the muscular type
   (c) maladjusted individuals
   (d) the least paid of the employees
45. Supervision in high producing sections tends to be
   (a) self centred (b) production centred
   (c) employee centred
46. The success of an industry requires
   (a) a stress on discipline at all costs
   (b) a stress on cooperation above competition
   (c) a judicious mixture of competition and cooperation
   (d) a stress on competition above cooperation
47. The most basic and important principles in personnel selection and placement is selection and placement
   (a) in terms of least payment of wages
   (b) in terms of the specific requirement of the work to be done
   (c) in terms of attitudes of the worker
   (d) in terms of availability of workers
48. Use of scientific methods in assessing employee attitudes and feelings is
   (a) superfluous if there is personal contact
   (b) a substitute to personal contact
   (c) only a supplement to personal contact
   (d) an unnecessary show
49. Adequate motivation and morale in industry can be achieved only through arranging the industrial environment in such a way that
   (a) employee needs can be satisfied
   (b) no choice be given to employee
   (c) strict discipline can be kept
   (d) higher production is secured
50. One of the important things that should be found out as follow-up of the induction process is
   (a) the amount of socialising
   (b) the degree of understanding of job responsibilities
   (c) the hours of work
   (d) the periods of rest

51. A result of systematic training is
    (a) increase in a friendly attitude to all
    (b) increase in a positive attitude to job
    (c) increase in a positive attitude to self
52. A direct advantage of definite system of rating is
    (a) to know how much an employee can do
    (b) to correct the employee
    (c) to help an employee to produce more
    (d) to evaluate an employee with great consistency or accuracy.
53. The first step in personnel selection is
    (a) interviews (b) application blanks
    (c) trade tests (d) letters of recommendation
54. Sometimes, fatigue is reflected in decreased.
    (a) errors (b) output
    (c) motivation (d) problems
55. If a worried employee comes to you, you will help him best if you
    (a) tell him to stop worrying
    (b) let him solve his own worries. Don't do any thing
    (c) discover the cause of the worry and help him to get rid of it
    (d) help him to forget what is bothering him.
56. To develop a thorough understanding of people you should
    (a) consider every worker alike
    (b) study each worker individually
    (c) be firm with them and observe their reactions
    (d) allow for their weaknesses
57. If an employee's complaint is not unjustified,
    (a) you will carefully explain all the facts to him
    (b) tell him he is wrong and should be more careful next time
    (c) tell other workers about his mistake
    (d) transfer him to another department before he becomes a disturbing influence
58. If an employee has been emotionally hurt, you should
    (a) sympathize with him
    (b) help him to forget his hurt

(c) help him to stay away from people who have hurt him
(d) help him to get an insight into his hurt

59. Supervisors are taught to
(a) advise employees as to how they can overcome their tensions
(b) to talk employees about how others overcome the same tension
(c) to talk employees feelingly
(d) to express the feelings of the employees clearly.

60. You can expect to have others follow you
(a) if you are fond of your men
(b) if you have been a supervisor for a long time
(c) if you are helpful in satisfying their wants
(d) if you fight up for your men, whether rightly or not.

61. A supervisor's relationship with other supervisors improves if he
(a) meets them often informally and gets to like them
(b) cooperates with them fully in conducting the business
(c) is always charming to them
(d) overlooks their actions that conflict with his opinions.

62. If a change in the department is necessary the supervisor should
(a) make the change suddenly so that no one can object
(b) tell the workers about the change that has been planned and why
(c) make the change look an important one so that no one may object
(d) allow time for the workers to get used to the change.

63. A supervisor should make
(a) all the decisions after consulting labourers when necessary
(b) no decision, but leave it to the labourers
(c) important decision without consulting the labourers
(d) decision after consulting the labourers important

64. The success as a superior chiefly depends on
(a) how people react to him
(b) the people he meets in his work
(c) how well he performs his duty
(d) how much he instructs the others.

65. What should be the supervisor's responsibility in respect to company policy?
   (a) to adhere to the policies he approves of
   (b) to ignore the policies that are unpopular with the workers
   (c) to explain all the policies and the reasons for them to the workers so that they all understand
   (d) to carry out, somehow all the policies of the company.

66. Who can be most preferred for the vocational guidance?
   (a) all the primary teachers
   (b) all the secondary teachers
   (c) all the educational institutions
   (d) all the trained persons who have psychological and occupational informations

67. To measure the leadership traits the most useful method is
   (a) application Blank
   (b) interview Blank
   (c) projective technique
   (d) group-discussion techniques

68. The concept of Time-motion study was introduced in industry by
   (a) A.T. Poffenberger (b) Gilbreth
   (c) Tittin (d) Taylor

69. An important cause of accidents relates to
   (a) human errors
   (b) lack of good ventilation
   (c) noise in the factory
   (d) frustration in the worker

70. Motion study is to be conducted for a good advantage
   (a) after time study
   (b) before time study
   (c) not connected with time study
   (d) during time study

71. The most important things in an industry are
   (a) increase of production
   (b) selection of worker
   (c) efficiency of a worker
   (d) working conditions

ANSWERS

1. (a)	2. (b)	3. True	4. True	5. False
6. True	7. False	8. False	9. False	10. False
11. True	12. False	13. True	14. True	15. False
16. False	17. True	18. True	19. True	20. True
21. True	22. True	23. True	24. True	25. True
26. True	27. True	28. True	29. True	30. True
31. (a)	32. (b)	33. (a)	34. (a)	35. (a)
36. (a)	37. (c)	38. (c)	39. (d)	40. (a)
41. (c)	42. (d)	43. (a)	44. (c)	45. (c)
46. (c)	47. (b)	48. (c)	49. (a)	50. (b)
51. (b)	52. (d)	53. (b)	54. (c)	55. (b)
56. (b)	57. (a)	58. (d)	59. (a)	60. (c)
61. (b)	62. (d)	63. (d)	64. (a)	65. (c)
66. (d)	67. (d)	68. (d)	69. (d)	70. (d)
71. (d)				